Phenomenal Justice

Genocide, Political Violence, Human Rights Series

EDITED BY ALEXANDER LABAN HINTON, STEPHEN ERIC BRONNER, AND NELA NAVARRO

Phenomenal Justice

VIOLENCE AND MORALITY IN ARGENTINA

EVA VAN ROEKEL

RUTGERS UNIVERSITY PRESS
New Brunswick, Camden, and Newark, New Jersey, and London

Library of Congress Cataloging-in-Publication Data

Names: Van Roekel, Eva, 1981– author.
Title: Phenomenal justice: violence and morality in Argentina / Eva van Roekel.
Description: New Brunswick, N.J.: Rutgers University Press, 2020. | Series:
 Genocide, Political Violence, Human Rights | Based on author's thesis
 (doctoral - Universiteit Utrecht, 2016) issued under title: Phenomenal justice:
 state violence, emotion, and the law in Argentina. | Includes bibliographical
 references and index.
Identifiers: LCCN 2019012943 | ISBN 9781978800274 (hardback) |
 ISBN 9781978800267 (pbk.)
Subjects: LCSH: Trials (Political crimes and offenses)—Social aspects—Argentina. |
 Trials (Crimes against humanity)—Social aspects—Argentina. | Transitional
 justice—Social aspects—Argentina. | Argentina—History—Dirty War,
 1976-1983—Law and legislation.
Classification: LCC KHA133.P64 V36 2020 | DDC 340/.1150982—dc23
LC record available at https://lccn.loc.gov/2019012943

A British Cataloging-in-Publication record for this book is available
from the British Library.

All photos by the author

♾ The paper used in this publication meets the requirements of the American National
Standard for Information Sciences—Permanence of Paper for Printed Library Materials,
ANSI Z39.48-1992.

www.rutgersuniversitypress.org

Manufactured in the United States of America

For Mariet, my mother, and Gerrit, my father

Map 1. Argentina

Contents

List of Abbreviations

AMIA	Argentinian Israelite Mutual Association (*Asociación Mutual Israelita Argentina*)
AFyAPPA	Association of Relatives and Friends of the Political Prisoners of Argentina (*Asociación de Familiares y Amigos de los Presos Políticos de Argentina*)
CELS	Center for Social and Legal Studies (*Centro de Estudios Legales y Sociales*)
CELTyV	Center for Legal Studies on Terrorism and Its Victims (*Centro de Estudios Legales sobre el Terrorismo y sus Víctimas*)
CIJ	Center of Judicial Information (*Centro de Información Judicial*)
CONADEP	National Commission on the Disappearance of Persons (*Comisión Nacional sobre la Desaparición de Personas*)
EAAF	Argentinian Forensic Anthropology Team (*Equipo Argentino de Antropología Forense*)
ESMA	Higher School of Mechanics of the Navy (*Escuela Superior de Mecánica de la Armada*)
FAMUS	Relatives of the Dead because of Subversion (*Familiares de Muertos por la Subversión*)
H.I.J.O.S.	Sons and Daughters for Identity and Justice against Oblivion and Silence (*Hijos por la Identidad y la Justicia contra el Olvido y el Silencio*)
MTP	Movement Everyone for the Homeland (*Movimiento Todos por la Patria*)
PRT-ERP	Workers' Revolutionary Party—People's Revolutionary Army (*Partido Revolucionario de los Trabajadores—Ejército Revolucionario del Pueblo*)

Phenomenal Justice

Prologue

The Verdict

"Prisión perpetúa," (life imprisonment), Judge Carlos Espinosa spoke in a decisive voice and then paused for a few seconds.[1] Suddenly, a roar jolted the eerie quiet in the courtroom in Buenos Aires: "¡asesinos!" (murderers). Judge Espinosa demanded silence and order. He even threatened to continue in closed session. The gallery downstairs was packed with human rights activists and victims who were yelling in outrage after the first life sentence. In comparative calmness the remaining indicted military officers received verdicts ranging between a life sentence and several years in prison, and one officer was acquitted. Upstairs their family members sat in silence; one woman cried quietly. And that was it. In less than an hour the verdict had been disclosed. After nine long months of testimonies and allegations, the trial for crimes against humanity committed during the military dictatorship against five indicted military officers at the federal court in Buenos Aires had finally reached its closure.

A bit earlier that day, during *las últimas palabras* (the last words), the normally silent general had tried to convince the judges as to the righteousness of their counterinsurgency. For only a few seconds he had lost his temper, slapped his hand, and yelled: "I have lived this period in my own flesh and blood. I do not see these experiences reflected in any book or film. I simply ask for a just sentence!" Despite his hunched back, the old general maintained his rigid military posture after receiving his sentence.

In the hallway, Lucas Davidovich, an Argentinian human rights lawyer yelled that he would start with his appeal the next day. "Three of them are found not entirely guilty; we cannot leave it like this!"

After the judges had left, the family and friends of the convicted military officers also departed the federal court quickly. Outside the federal court stood a group of survivors, children, and other relatives of the disappeared, human rights activists, and the prosecution lawyers. They looked disappointed. Some of them cried and embraced each other and said that they could not believe the outcome of the trial. A young woman was screaming for *true* justice on a makeshift stage on the pavement at the front gate. A victim, whose wife disappeared, said that looking at these old men in court had made him angry: "They don't have the bad faces they had back then. We cannot wipe out thirty years of impunity; it feels as if they are not the ones who did it."

IN SEPTEMBER 2009 I made my first visit to Buenos Aires to determine the course of my ethnography on the trials for crimes against humanity in Argentina. Between 1976 and 1983 a civil-military regime brutally repressed a violent revolutionary struggle that was initiated by the Montoneros and Workers' Revolutionary Party—People's Revolutionary Army during the 1970s. Members of the armed forces committed atrocious crimes that were now finally being prosecuted. Thousands of cases were being tried for the illegal detentions, tortures, killings, disappearances, death flights, and the appropriation of children who were born during detention.

From the books I knew that more than twenty-five years earlier, in 1984, the National Commission on the Disappearance of Persons had published its report *Nunca Más* (Never Again). In 1985 the junta leaders stood trial in *Legal Case 13/84*. Two amnesty laws blocked further prosecutions against middle-rank officers. In 1989 the subsequent government pardoned the convicted generals. For more than two decades the perpetrators had remained at large. But in 2005 the Argentinian Supreme Court resolved that the amnesty laws were unconstitutional. This paved the way for the federal courts to reinitiate the prosecutions (Lichtenfeld 2005).

Against this historical backdrop of transitional justice interventions and setbacks I found myself standing at the federal court in Buenos Aires among a small, deeply disappointed and angry crowd that day of the verdict. As an ethnographer I have come to rely on all my senses to "gather data," including those aspects that we find so difficult to describe, and I could not help but ask: What is transitional justice really about? The observations that day served as my point of departure in rethinking the recent transitional justice developments in Argentina. How do people caught up in these trials experience justice on their terms? How do they judge what is right and what is wrong? How does morality yield feelings that go in different directions and vice versa?

Legal reasoning is one of the most important ways in which people try to make sense of their social worlds (Geertz 1983). Within contemporary cultural anthropology, there has been the tendency to frame social reality in terms of power or to interpret the social world through the dynamics of structure and agency (Ortner 2006). Although power, contestation, structure, and agency may be cogent concepts to seize local transitional justice

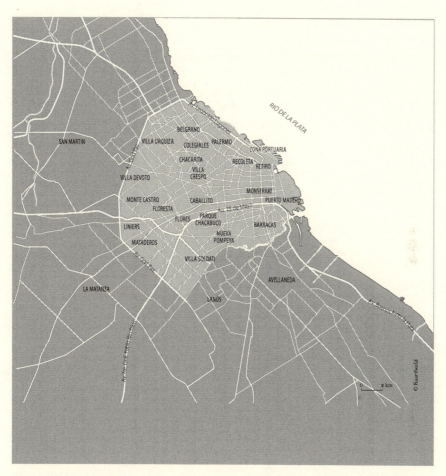

Map 2. Buenos Aires

processes, these factors did not help me come to grips with what seemed to be "at stake" for the Argentinians I met at the courts. The feelings of collective bewilderment and the affective differences in dealing with justice that I noticed among the victims and the military officers pushed me into the only imaginable direction of phenomenological anthropology and the anthropology of emotion that I eventually coined "phenomenal justice."

"Phenomenal" is commonly understood as "remarkable" or "extraordinary." Although the transitional justice trajectory in Argentina has been remarkable, this is not what I mean by phenomenal justice. Despite the extraordinary struggle for truth, justice, and memory by the Argentinian human rights movement for more than thirty-five years, a phenomenal inquiry is an affective study into the immediacy of transitional justice. From a phenomenological perspective, "phenomenal" means what is given and what is explicable in the way we encounter the immediate world (Heidegger 1993, 83). I understand feelings as such phenomenal encounters in the world. A phenomenal inquiry allows one to take an analytical step back and raise fundamental questions about materiality, time, morality, and play that constitute the ways people engage with violence and suffering in their world. Phenomenal justice thus not explores what lawfully counts, but what matters to the people who are (non)voluntarily drawn into truth and justice practices.

CHAPTER 1

Phenomenal Justice

A FEW WEEKS BEFORE the verdict on the five military officers that caused the considerable commotion at the federal court in Buenos Aires, Judge Carlos Espinosa received me in his *despacho* (office).[1] For almost four decades Espinosa had worked for the Argentinian justice system. He began in the lowest rank as a court employee and many years later he became a federal judge. With this career trajectory he knew the Argentinian judicial system very well. Espinosa said that in previous years he had presided at several trials for crimes against humanity, and he considered these trials very different from the earlier cases he had arbitrated. Our conversation that afternoon shifted continually between the technical hazards of being a judge in these large, complex cases of crimes against humanity—such as the lack of statute of limitations, little physical evidence, retroactivity, and direct and indirect offenders of the crimes amid a dense bureaucratic system—and the historical value of the current trials for new jurisprudence on international humanitarian law for Argentinian law but, most of all, for the Argentinian people, victims, offenders, and bystanders alike.

"This part of history is not closed yet," Espinosa reflected, "it is an open wound in our society."

Being a judge in these cases, where an important part of his own personal history was expressed, Espinosa could not be indifferent to such massive forms of suffering and said, "Being indifferent would make me not only a bad judge, but a bad person."

As in many families in Argentina, state repression had affected the Espinosa family in diverse ways. Espinosa's father had been a close friend of a now-indicted military officer, his niece disappeared in 1977, and his mother-in-law had been involved in the appropriation of various babies who were born in illegal detention centers. Judge Espinosa therefore had recused himself from various trials for those accused of crimes against humanity because his impartiality could reasonably have been questioned. Remaining true to his profession, Judge Espinosa hastened to say that he was still able to be objective in this trial, and he stressed that he did not consider all uniformed men in Argentina automatically guilty of the crimes. Later Espinosa reflected again on *indiferencia social* (social indifference) and thought it was instead *culpa* (guilt) people felt about what had happened during the 1970s. Espinosa considered *culpa* the main reason that many people in Argentina did not like to be explicitly confronted with this particularly painful past.

A Detour from Transitional Justice

For twenty months the courtrooms and legal offices at Comodoro Py Avenue in Buenos Aires were my physical point of departure. By openly addressing guilt and indifference and his intertwined professional and personal ethics, Judge Espinosa spelled out that afternoon what lies at the core of this ethnography: the significance of feelings and morality in transitional justice trajectories and their importance as driving forces for the truth, justice, and memory practices of the past four decades in Argentina. The trials for crimes against humanity in Argentina belong to protracted and complex social processes dealing with human rights violations committed during the last dictatorship that ruled from 1976 until 1983.

With two amnesty laws firmly embedded in a society that was largely indifferent regarding impunity and trauma, justice and truth for the victims was blocked for decades, during which accountability for human rights violations has been a major challenge, not only in terms of impunity and denial. Determining who is responsible for state repression remains a moral minefield today. The whole concept of human rights violations is constructed around state involvement, but at the same time human rights organizations also recognize the difficulty of establishing culpability within these blurred boundaries (Wilson 1997c, 140). But the hazardous legal and political practicalities of retributive trials about previous state-led crimes, the dynamic interactions between international humanitarian law, the international human rights movement, and Argentinian domestic law did not seem to matter the most to the people of Argentina. At stake for the Argentinians I had come to know were pain, guilt, fear, indifference, pride, revenge, shame, and remorse. Although more than thirty-five years had passed, these feelings concerning the violent past were still *a flor de piel* (close to the surface). The victims and the indicted military officers had not relegated their feelings to the past. In the courts people shouted and laughed, their cheeks flushed, their hearts pounded, and their eyes shed tears, as they simultaneously experienced and interpreted these reactions within a social and historical context. I therefore decided that the feelings of both the victims and the perpetrators had to be my intellectual point of departure in describing recent retributive practices in Argentina that often are called "transitional justice."

Transitional justice refers to the set of transnational and local judicial and nonjudicial measures that are implemented by different countries worldwide to redress the legacies of massive human rights abuses. Transitional justice aims at the so-called healing of societies after collective violence and state atrocities, by embracing practices of truth, justice, and memory. Transitional justice, as a practice, has grown over the past two decades into a normalized and globalized form of intervention after civil war and political repression (Teitel 2003). Ideologically grounded in a liberal utopia, these practices aim to prevent new violence from breaking out, to establish a rule of law, and to raise respect for human rights and democratic values in these countries.[2]

Trials, memorial sites, truth trials, truth commissions, monuments, financial reparations, and commemorative days all contribute to the way transitional justice looks today. These different truth and justice practices have been largely categorized in restorative, reparative, and retributive justice.[3] Restorative justice focuses on mediation between the victim and the perpetrator. Reparative justice focuses mainly on compensations for victims. Retributive justice generally involves prosecution. Trials have had a central place in discussions of transitional justice. For example, perpetrator-oriented trials ignore victims' needs and subsequently harm them (Nino 1996, 122–123). Trials enable the construction of an unmistakable wall between old and new (Teitel 2000, 29). This definite "before and after" in legal accounting for atrocities has been widely challenged; a trial is just one transitional justice procedure (Arnould 2006, 156). This still growing body of literature contains greatly diverging views on methodology and epistemology, and the myriad practices of truth, memory, and justice have simultaneously been celebrated and discarded either for being too "forward-looking" or too "backward-looking." A sense of justice (or injustice for that matter) is always lived and imagined through memories and in spaces where ideals and desires continue to meet with practical limitations (Brunneger and Faulk 2016). Ethnography of human rights practices in a broader sense also demonstrates that existential problems continue to bedevil human rights as the world continues to be marked by disjuncture and particularity (Goodale 2009, 13–16; see also Wilson 1997b). Analyses of transitional justice therefore require insights into local and alternative perceptions and experiences in the long term.

Disconnections between international legal norms and local priorities and practices frequently mark transitional justice practices, and transitional justice has itself undergone a shift toward the local (Hinton 2010; Shaw and Waldorf 2010, 3–4). Without neglecting the transnational dimension of human rights and international humanitarian law as well as the influence of globalization on local communities and societies, there now seems to be a consensus about the diversity of transitional justice trajectories around the globe; this has favored a culture-sensitive approach in the analysis of truth, memory, and justice practices. Over the past four decades, experiences and practices in Argentina have been key to localizing this debate on transitional justice.[4] In

Argentina new norms and practices have been continually invented and implemented to provide more accountability for human rights violations. Despite structural impediments that have blocked accountability for crimes, the creative and innovative force of the truth, memory, and justice practices of the human rights movement for the disappeared and their relatives has even identified Argentina as both "an instigator of the justice cascade" (Sikkink 2010), and an important contributor to global trends in transitional justice practices (Sikkink and Booth Walling 2006, 301).

Within transitional justice debates and practices not only "revenge" but also "remorse," "forgiveness," "trauma," and "guilt" are often used to address the feelings of people whose lives have been affected. But how and why people experience and interpret these feelings are mostly absent in this body of literature.[5] To my knowledge this is the first ethnography addressing the feelings of both the victims and the perpetrators of state repression in Argentina. A universal approach to feelings in transitional justice literature and reports tends to formulate a set of norms that would apply to all cultures equally. My phenomenal detour mainly aims to denaturalize these taken-for-granted ideas about feelings in transitional justice. With firm grounding in the anthropology of emotion and social phenomenology, I show instead how the nature, scope, and meaning of the feelings that underlie transitional justice practices and the lived experiences of the structural impediments and setbacks vary greatly among the victims and the now-convicted military officers in Argentina.

The pages that follow therefore contribute to the interdisciplinary debate of transitional justice and human rights violations by focusing on the recent "retributive turn" in Argentina (Skaar 2011; Varsky 2011), but the affective stories definitely go beyond that. They build further on the recent debate on post-transitional justice that allows us to study the underlying social processes of retribution and restoration in post-conflict societies (Collins 2010; Davis 2013; Laplante and Theidon 2007). Post-transitional justice mainly looks at the ways in which transitional justice and long-term injustice are felt, experienced, interpreted, and shaped by multiple actors. This allows discussions on the underlying causes of structural injustices and inequalities that belong to long-term processes of social, economic, and political configurations and relationships and the ways they shape local transitional justice trajectories. This emerging debate is a welcome move away from limited analyses of political transitions from authoritarian regimes and toward more democratic societies to understand how people live with large-scale violence and protracted suffering.

It has been tempting to label the current trials for crimes against humanity and the ongoing truth, memory, and justice practices among established and emerging groups in Argentina as "post-transitional justice." But post-transitional justice still implies that the recent developments of retribution and memorialization in the courts of Argentina are transitory. This is not the way transitional justice is felt in Argentina. Many Argentinians involved in trial proceedings had never heard of transitional justice or were skeptical about it and linked it to concepts of impunity (Figari Layús 2015, 13). By looking at feelings from "within" and "in-between," we become aware that transitional justice in Argentina does not mean closure or a movement away from violence and suffering (Van Roekel 2018a).

The logic of transition is deeply embedded in contemporary theorizing about violence and suffering, including transitional justice. Transition implies the act of passing from one state or place to the next and comes from the Latin word *transire*, which means crossing over or passing away (Oxford English Dictionary 2015). I noticed that many Argentinians experienced truth and justice practices in contrasting ways: their truth and justice acts were to keep the violence and suffering in the ongoing present, because both have not been achieved and never will be achieved. The legacies of impunity and denial will always remain and are entangled with an existential incompleteness of truth and justice creating logics aimed at continuance of memorialization, compensation, and retribution. Truth and justice are instead ongoing moral practices aimed at keeping the violence and suffering in the here and now. Obtaining justice for crimes that were committed during the civil-military regime in Argentina, for that matter, is not intended to close the past; it is an enduring practice for "justice to come" (Vaisman 2017). In other words, truth and justice have been unachieved for decades not only because of underlying structural impediments causing widespread impunity and denial but also because, existentially, truth and justice are ongoing processes of becoming.

The significance people attach to feelings should never be taken for granted in such high-stakes environments. How and why people experience feelings like remorse, anger, pain, and guilt (or not) should always be looked at from an integrated view of social mores and personal feelings both within oneself and in one's relations with others (Jackson 2017, 7). Exploring the feelings of conflicting individuals who are drawn into truth and justice practices confirms this intersubjectivity of engaging with and in the world. The way one feels always belongs to ambiguous affective spaces within oneself and in between others and objects.

Feelings

This ethnography on feelings complements growing academic interest in emotions. This intellectual interest belongs to a renewed Western inclination that is highly appreciative of the affective dimensions of human life and prefers a romantic, self-reflexive, and emotional person, to a cold, calculating, and rational figure.[6] No longer dangerous and irrational, feelings are now often valued as indisputable and as communicating one's true self (Davies 2010, 1). From this perspective "feelings never lie" (Lupton 1998, 89). This is not a natural fact of life though. The universality of this contemporary notion of affective authenticity is rather a bourgeois invention (Jackson 1995, 130). Feelings, like any aspect of human behavior, are subject to appraisals people attach to them.

Notions such as "emotion work," "display rules," "constitutive rules," and "cultural scripts" have been introduced to analyze affective life in practice, and still greatly influence the way we think and theorize about feelings in much social science research.[7] But feelings in everyday life do not easily adhere to rules.[8] Such conceptualizations leave too little room for variation and contestation, and they explain even less the ways people experience feelings on their own terms. The significance and locus of feelings in social life vary widely—some feelings are more significant than others, depending on context. In response, the anthropology of emotion looks at the inconsistencies, ambiguities, and transformations of historical, social, political, economic, and moral determinants of people's feelings in everyday lives.[9] For example, Nora Ortega de Sánchez, whose son is "disappeared," often felt that she was not doing enough to actively "work through" her pain and guilt (see chapter 4). She definitely had trouble sticking to the "emotion work" done by many mothers whose children disappeared in Argentina.

The choice of an affective lens through which to study transitional justice was not only academically fashionable. The field itself pulled me toward feelings, which I noticed were very important to the social glue in Argentina as well as highly appreciated and socialized. In 2010, as I began my second stint of fieldwork, an Argentinian acquaintance said, "Feelings are the only truth." His statement did not surprise anyone that night, except me. I also observed that "subjectivity" and "interiority"—notions that obstinately circle in social scientific views about feelings—were much more social and exterior in Argentina.

My Argentinian interlocutors and friends do not consider feelings individual or inward; instead feelings are vibrant social matters. From an early age many Argentinians are socialized so that feelings are easily expressed, highly valued, socially shared, and carefully analyzed on a daily basis. Despite variations in the ways Argentinians experience feelings as a result of the widespread presence of psychoanalysis, military education and training, gender ideals, migration, Catholicism, urban and rural backgrounds, and Mediterranean ancestors, there is an overall tendency to accept shared analysis about one's feelings as an important social practice in Argentina. This sociality of feelings configures an important aspect of the ways Argentinians experience and interpret their social world.

Even though Argentinians most often used the word *emoción* (emotion), I have opted to write about "feelings" for two reasons. First, feelings focus on the long-term conscious aspects in understanding how people feel, without ignoring the physiological aspects (Damasio 2003, 256).[10] Second, and more important, because I believe that "feeling" comes closer to the way Argentinians make sense of affective life as a social experience in which self and other, the physical and the psychological, and the conscious and unconscious smoothly meet. But to be honest, I have not yet found a concept that does justice to the full range of Nora's feelings and all the other people I met. We should therefore never reduce people's experiences to mere abstractions. Listening and carefully describing what was at stake for people like Nora made more sense (Beatty 2010). Therefore, a return to a descriptive philosophy is necessary to faithfully investigate the affective tone of social life.

PHENOMENOLOGY IN PRACTICE

The importance of the philosophical schools of phenomenology and existentialism in the anthropology of emotion has been quite underestimated in recent years. But phenomenological concepts and methods, like the lifeworld and direct description, have been (tacitly) very important in many anthropological representations of the diverse, dynamic, and ambiguous character of lived experiences (Desjarlais and Throop 2011, 88). In brief, phenomenological anthropology describes human consciousness in its fully lived immediacy, before it is subjected to theoretical elaboration or conceptual systematizing (Jackson 1996a, 1–2). Phenomenology has also become important in new fields of study, such as neuroscience, which looks at how our conscious experiences and mental representations can be grounded in brain activity (Laughlin, MacManus, and D'Aquili 1992). With expanding technological possibilities, neuroscientists today observe structures of experience through MRIs and PET and CAT scans of the human brain.[11] But reducing experience to brain activity is an unfortunate act of reductionism. Not the brain, but the living body should be considered our null point through which we experience the world. We should also not impose analytical categories or computational structures based on theoretical frameworks, instead focusing on people's own articulations and representations of their experiences and using *their* stories as units of investigation (Turner and Bruner 1986, 9–10; emphasis added).

I therefore believe that phenomenological anthropology better facilitates the exploration of the full range of human experiences that can be encountered among different cultures and improves our understanding of the diversity of human experience (Laughlin 1996, 924). The way in which a person experiences is always constituted by different constellations of speaking, moving, sensing, feeling, and remembering (Al-Mohammad 2011, 127). This phenomenal process always takes shape in a particular cultural and historical setting. We must therefore examine epistemology first and explore the tensions between the noticeable and the unnoticeable in every field site anew (Al-Mohammed 2011, 134). For example, one's experience of hardships such as illness and violence is always subject to positioned physical and mental constellations. Phenomenological anthropology thus allows us to rethink consciousness and the way experiences are constituted and simultaneously affect and are affected by the meanings that things of the world have in our experience.

I am aware of critiques against phenomenology that claim it is only good for understanding people's subjective experiences of life on the surface and it fails to analyze structural processes that create experience. Others claim it is too descriptive of subjective details, pays too little attention to power struggles, and therefore dismisses important underlying socioeconomic and political determinants of life (Desjarlais and Throop 2011, 95). But shifting the focus to the microcosm of the personal, the sensible, and the moral does not mean a denial of impersonal powers beyond our control that govern our lives (Jackson and Piette 2015, 5; Kleinman 2014, 134–135). Larger structural processes of inequality and interdependence were always part of the microcosm of my Argentinian friends and interlocutors. But these impersonal processes and larger structures are not the main focus here.

Another critique states that it is simply an impossible project to investigate consciousness through direct experience. I find this critique redundant, as many aspects of social life pose challenges to inquiry. The claim that researching consciousness is impossible belongs to a philosophical tradition that sees consciousness as an inherently individual realm. There is, however, an important shared component in our experience of the world (Schutz and Luckmann 1974, 4). Despite various challenges, I believe that this sharedness allows the practice of phenomenology. To sustain this claim I now turn briefly to four main dilemmas in the study of experience and how to (partially) resolve them in terms of epistemology and methodology.

First and foremost, examinations (of any kind) are always partial. As the phenomenologist Alfred Schutz (1967, 169) argued five decades ago, we might be much more aware of our own past lives than those of others, but we never catch ourselves in the act of actually living through an experience. For that matter, my own experiences and those of others are both partial. This impossibility of fully knowing intrinsically belongs to social life. All-encompassing knowledge is utopian. Only through the interchangeability of standpoints and bodily accordance can we recognize this partiality of perception (Merleau-Ponty in Bakker 1969, 42; Schutz 1970, 183). Intersubjective engagement thus allows for a partial understanding of the way structures of experiences constitute the various ways of engaging with and in the world. Partiality and incompleteness are thus foundational to human life. It is through the partial recognition of mutual differences that we can understand more of the other (Bakker 1969, 191–192). The social is therefore more than a fundamental structure of being alive. Intersubjectivity becomes the very method by which we achieve knowledge (Jackson 2005, 31–32).[12]

Second, the imperceptible also shapes the contours of the ways in which we live with and in the world. But the tangible and intangible are not separate spheres. They both create one "meaningful totality" (Bakker 1969, 72). People experience these meaningful totalities in various ways. What is imperceptible for one person can be tangible for somebody else. Feelings for my Argentinian friends and interlocutors were not intangibly separated in their individual inner minds. They were very palpable and social matters. These objectifications of the boundaries of self and other and mind and body are always culturally constituted, and not only biologically given (Csordas 1993, 149). However, the way we experience feelings normally does not enter into this "grip of consciousness." It is often in new social situations that the boundaries between self and other can be uncovered (Schutz and Luckmann 1974, 174–175). New situations often cause misunderstandings that evoke self-estrangement and confront us with otherwise unrecognized aspects of our assumptive worlds (Desjarlais and Throop 2011, 89). Ethnographic practice is mainly about making the unfamiliar familiar. And eventually (hopefully), we learn through these "problematic situations" (Schutz and Luckmann 1974, 124).

Third, the way we engage with and in the world is not random, but intentional. This means that our experiences are always directed toward the world through varying concepts, thoughts, and ideas that provide content to the given experience (Husserl in Mohanty 1977). In other words, we are all "geared into the world" differently (Desjarlais and Throop 2011, 91–92). By scientifically "bracketing" everyday assumptions that derive from cultural and theoretical heritages, we can try to understand the diversities of experiencing the world (Desjarlais and Throop 2011, 88–89). Our experience of the phenomenal world is thus not accidental and always takes different directions. This may sound like a passive approach to human life. But everyday experiences are always open and developing. This "stock of knowledge" derives from ongoing and accumulative processes of experiences (Schutz and Luckmann 1974, 123).

Finally, intentionality also makes it impossible to experience the world in its totality. The experiential world is an open project. As the lifeworld never closes, knowledge is also open and infinite. Openness and infinity are part of human life. Therefore, we cannot, in principle, develop definite conclusions about experience as it is lived (Merleau-Ponty in Bakker 1969, 85–128; Schutz and Luckmann 1974, 163–171). I therefore do not approach knowledge as an intrinsic or static property of a belief system or as a scientific theory. It is more valuable to observe what happens to a belief or a theory when it is put to work in the lifeworld (Jackson 1996a, 11). This pragmatic approach proved very valuable. Argentinians' feelings about violence and justice disclosed opposite but entangled truths about how the world works.

LIFEWORLDS IN CONFLICT

Self and other are never existentially given. They are an outcome of intersubjective engagement (Jackson 1995, 163). New challenges for the production of knowledge about how people experience feelings in their daily lives rest in the fluidity between coexisting affective attitudes. I believe that a focus on conflicting lifeworlds further helps to describe the way intersubjectivity creates feelings in myriad directions. Conflict not only sharpens social divisions and categories between affective attitudes but also illuminates the intersubjective character of being. Both otherness and sameness are always at play in modes of engaging with and in a world. The exploration of feelings in a conflict-ridden environment thus facilitates the rendering of the intersubjectivity of being. Otherness, difference, and estrangement among victims, human rights activists, and military officers and their kin were mutually necessary. This desire for difference is common in conflict situations (Kakar 1996, 12–16). Yet intersubjectivity also governs affective lives in conflict. To put conflict at the center of an investigation of feelings allows an exploration of the dialectic relationship between opposing subjectivities.

At the courts in Argentina this was very palpable. ¿Querella o defensa? (plaintiff or defense?), the judiciary employee always asked us before we could enter the courtroom. To avoid clashes, the courtrooms that mediated in the trials for crimes against humanity in Argentina often had divided public galleries. In the public gallery for defendants, there were often few people who dwelled in a quiet atmosphere. On the other hand, the victims' gallery was often packed with survivors and relatives who brought along friends and paraphernalia that visibly commemorated the disappeared. All these people and objects were enveloped in shared suffering. Experiencing justice then, becomes something dissimilar: shared actions of solidarity or solitary acts of support.

In the field I noticed that the desire for difference in everyday life also materialized in other social realms. Often living in the same city, the victims and the indicted military officers shared the same streets and squares. Yet traditionally there are neighborhoods in Buenos Aires where many military officers and their families live. In other residential areas, coffee bars, and squares, victims and human rights activists commonly dwell. The most famous square is Plaza de Mayo, the main square where the mothers of the disappeared have marched since 1977. Military men and their kin gather mainly at Plaza San Martin, have coffee and lunch at the neighboring military social club, and they read different newspapers. Political opinions among victims and military officers often belong to opposite ends of the ideological continuum. There were also aesthetic differences. Some people belonging to the human rights groups openly disliked the neat and conservative appearances of those in the military. For some young relatives of the disappeared, wild hair and unconventional clothes are thus not only fashionable but also a political statement. In return, military officers and their wives expressed similar dislike and dismay about the alternative looks of the human rights activists and victims. Differences could be seen even in entertainment and the arts.[13] Everyday materializations of otherness, difference, and estrangement indicate that living together in the same city produce important boundaries.

Dwelling in these social worlds not only defines geographical, aesthetic, and ideological otherness but also constitutes differences in the ways Argentinians affectively engage with and in the world. By analytically making space for contrast and analogy, phenomenal justice seeks to understand how feelings emerge and are experienced differently in people's everyday lives. Both sameness and otherness are foundational to the ways in which we engage with and in the world. I believe that this entanglement of affective difference and affective similarity define what it means to be alive.

METHODOLOGY

Ethnographic fieldwork examines social life by exploring people's daily life activities and behavior in a particular context, by employing field methodologies, such as participant observation as its central method, but also socializing, informal conversation, semistructured and informal interviews, and life history to learn about other people's lives. From these concrete and intimate engagements with everyday concerns and experiences of social actors living in particular places at particular times, ethnographers try to articulate often-unrecognized historical, political, social, economic, and cultural forces that define what it means to be human (Desjarlais and Throop 2011, 96). This view from "within" enables us to look beyond monolithic assumptions such as "victim," "truth," "forgiveness," "perpetrator," "justice," and "revenge."

Grappling with people's various feelings about violence and justice may seem methodologically challenging. My fieldwork experiences in Argentina proved otherwise. People's feelings were much more social and tangible than I had expected. Writing about these experiences in a conventional academic fashion turned out to be much more problematic though. The feelings people experienced and shared in the field were difficult, if not impossible, to capture in numbers and charts, neat models of behavior, or one grand narrative. Feelings reside much better in first-person ethnographies.[14] Therefore, I kept writing person-centered stories and small narratives. My choice of words to address the violence, such as "appropriation" or "adoption," "genocidas" (genociders) or "political prisoners," "war on subversion" or "state terrorism," alternate throughout the book. Not only did these words help me to be more faithful in representing the ways people experienced these life episodes and social categories, but I believed that this alternating form of storytelling also counteracted wrong assumptions regarding cultural homogeneity, coherence, and timelessness (Abu-Lughod 1993, 13; Price 1996). By using thick description and multiple small narratives, ethnography can do justice to the complexities and ambiguities of how and why people experience feelings (or not).

Phenomena such as feelings that are difficult to measure, probe, or represent do not make them less important. But grounding an entire study on stories and fleeting moments about feelings can be tricky in an interdisciplinary field of transitional justice. By explaining some of the choices I made and the reasons for them during my ethnographic fieldwork among the victims and the indicted military officers and also among the court professionals, I hope to avoid possible criticisms based on validity and representation. A phenomenal approach simply requires an ontological and epistemological outlook grounded in intersubjectivity and pragmatism and field methodologies that combine the conventional with the unconventional.

Between 2009 and 2012, I conducted almost twenty months of ethnographic fieldwork, mostly in Buenos Aires and Córdoba but also in La Plata and San Martin. I primarily attended court hearings and talked with the head judges in federal court in Buenos Aires and Córdoba. I met with colleagues and human rights activists working on the trials and I joined human rights rallies and meetings with families of the indicted military officers. Over the years I have talked with more than 160 people who were directly or indirectly involved in the trials in Buenos Aires, La Plata, San Martin, and Córdoba. I had numerous fleeting contacts with many people at the federal courts, memorial sites, public and private offices, and street rallies. Obviously not all of these contacts made it into to my field notes. In 2014 and 2016, I returned for two brief field visits of about two months each, during which I stayed in Buenos Aires only. My last visit to Buenos Aires was in November 2018. During these visits I met interlocutors and friends with whom I maintained contact via email and other social media. I return to these recent findings in chapter 7.

The indicted military officers and the judges were almost exclusively men, but overall men and women were almost equally represented. Two generations of Argentinians, those who lived through the period of state violence and those who were born afterward were included in the field research. I use victims to address the survivors of detention and the relatives of the disappeared. Some victims considered themselves instead to be human rights activists; therefore, I use the two terms equally and interchangeably. Within the enormous heterogeneity of interlocutors, I established close relations with eleven survivors and relatives of the disappeared, nine military officers including their kin, and six professionals working on trials for crimes against humanity. These twenty-six Argentinian men and women of different generations form the principal research population.

My engagement with both groups was organized loosely, mostly depending on their agendas and the legal and social activities that evolved throughout the week. My main concern was to balance the time I spent engaging with the victims and the perpetrators. Practically, this meant that if I had spent several days with the indicted officers and their families, I would telephone one of the victims and plan a meeting. This may sound forced and even contradictory to ethnographic practice, as anthropologists tend to follow their interlocutors in the field. But doing fieldwork in a post-conflict setting among victims and perpetrators simultaneously requires these interventions, otherwise I would easily have stayed with one group.

I also interviewed and talked several times casually with three federal judges who arbitrated in the trials for crimes against humanity. I conversed almost weekly with seven prosecution lawyers, defense lawyers, and other legal staff, three psychologists, one forensic anthropologist of the Argentinian Forensic Anthropology Team, and various journalists, scholars, and local experts on transitional justice who were involved in the trial proceedings. Some of them were also victims of the last dictatorship, with whom I conducted extended semistructured interviews. I taped only thirty-two interviews because, due to prison regulations and the ongoing trials, there was often no opportunity to record, or because sensitive topics were more easily addressed in a less formal setting. Therefore, the bulk of the empirical data comes from these weekly informal conversations and weekly participatory observation at home, in and outside the courtrooms, at the tribunals' offices, in two prisons, during exhumations, during street rallies and demonstrations, during official meetings with ministers and court judges, and at memorial sites and museums. The ethnographic method of jot notes allowed me to describe these encounters in detailed field notes later.

I followed the court proceedings of four trials for crimes against humanity that took place between 2009 and 2012 at the federal courts in Buenos Aires and Córdoba.[15] In total I have spent more than two hundred days at

the various tribunals, mainly the federal courts of Buenos Aires and Córdoba, but I also visited the federal courts in San Martin, Tucumán, and La
Plata. Besides visiting multiple small family memorials and memorial stones
in these cities, I also visited five large memorial sites (the Higher School of
Mechanics of the Navy, Parque de la Memoria, Automotores Orletti,
Olimpo, and La Perla), some of which I frequented more often when my
interlocutors invited me to social events. I participated in several large
human rights events in Buenos Aires, such as the annual National Day of
Memory for Truth and Justice on March 24, but also smaller ones, such as
the commemoration of a group of disappeared at the local church of Santa
Cruz in a Buenos Aires neighborhood. I also participated in human rights
seminars and debates with academics, psychologists, and legal professionals
about the trials, and I attended premieres of theater plays, films, and documentaries concerning the violence and the trials. Besides the monthly visits
to military prison in the province of Buenos Aires and a civilian prison in
Córdoba, I also took part in the social events of family and friends of the
indicted military officers, such as book presentations, annual commemorative practices of soldiers and civilians who died during the left-wing bombings in the 1970s, and street protests.

By "being there" (Sluka and Robben 2007, 24–26) at all these different
sites during all these different activities, I was able to grasp what social life
meant for these Argentinians, which allowed me to see that categories of
"truth" and "justice," and "victim" and "perpetrator" are utterly positioned
and vary greatly in meaning. All these unstructured conversations and participatory observations were valuable for understanding the legal, political,
social, and historical context of the trials for crimes against humanity.

Document and archival analysis account for only a small amount of the
stories presented in this book. Several Argentinian victims have published
their testimonies, and these detailed narratives offer an understanding of
their experiences of the violent past and subsequent suffering. The tribunals'
offices provided print and digital copies of accusations and verdicts, footage
of previous trials, and other legal documents, which facilitated an on-the-
ground understanding of the trials' proceedings. Likewise, I collected more
than three hundred news articles about the trials from local newspapers
(primarily the popular daily *Clarín*, the conservative daily *La Nación*, and
the progressive daily *Página12*), which provided an understanding of contemporary public opinion about the trials and the last dictatorship. Moreover, to obtain a knowledge of military codes and military education, I
visited the libraries of the San Martin National Institute and the Military
Circle in Buenos Aires to examine local military handbooks and previous
military justice codes. The official program for psychological assistance and
witness protection of the secretary of human rights of the Ministry of

Justice, Security and Human Rights provided documentation about working procedures. Lastly, besides the annual reports of the human rights organization Center for Social and Legal Studies, the online database of the Judicial Information Center also provided valuable data about the verdicts and statistical information about the trials for crimes against humanity. But understanding of the feelings that lie at the core of this ethnography also emerged from various other investigative methods.

AFFECTIVE FIELDWORK

When I asked Argentinians to explain how to define and clarify feelings, they often spoke in figurative terms such as *herida abierta* (open wound), *el circo* (the circus), *poner el cuerpo* (to put one's body on the line), or *tragar el sapo* (to swallow the frog).[16] These everyday tropes, metaphors, and metonyms provided valuable insights about feelings beyond literal speech. Metaphors, although still partial and incomplete, yield a sense of integrity (Fernandez 1974, 129). In a sense, a metaphor is where bodily being and representation meet (Csordas 1994, 11–12). Tracing the transfer of meaning from one literal domain to another can be helpful in grappling with local understandings (Durham and Fernandez 1991, 191–196), such as in understanding the "open wound" that traveled from an individual and physical domain to a shared psychological domain. But I examined mainly the ways in which local metaphors appeared in everyday life and how and why people employed them (Jackson 2005, 37).

Feelings also materialized in "culturally specific" ways (Solomon 2007, 199). The famous white scarf of the Mothers of Plaza de Mayo, the black-and-white pictures, and the silhouettes of the disappeared were powerful objects that embraced "knots of feelings" and were continuously re-created by means of words, enactments, and shared experiences in particular places (Carrithers 2005, 443). My understanding of how people were emotionally attached to these objects and places emerged gradually. I also mapped people's endless ways of expressing themselves in the courts beyond speech, for example, in smothered voices, repressed applause, judgmental gazes, or aggressive gestures. The body is an "active expressive forum" (Lock 1993, 141). I believe that by openly discussing these physical expressions, bodies can become important sources for understanding feelings. I therefore discussed what the gestures, sounds, gazes, and movements meant to various Argentinians. This not only gave me an understanding of bodily practices from different viewpoints, but also provided a stepping-stone for insight into different modes of being. Silence was another source used to tackle the "conflicting feelings" that many military officers considered immoral and uncomfortable (Sheriff 2000, 117). These spaces in-between words are often undertheorized, because of a Western epistemic perspective on life that draws our intellectual attention mainly toward speech (Crapanzano 2004, 52–53). Silence in whatever form should also be included in our theorizing. As with bodily gestures and sounds, in contextualizing and discussing each silence anew, silence becomes hermeneutically important to the art of interpretation.

Looking at figurative speech, bodies, spaces, artifacts, and silences are standardized procedures in ethnographic fieldwork. But in the field meaningful data on feelings can sometimes also be grasped through "empathic processes" or "acts of resonance" (Throop 2010, 772–773; Wikan 1990, 269). Empathy is the act of understanding, being aware of, being sensitive to, and experiencing the feelings and thoughts of somebody else. Empathy involves several methodological and epistemological dilemmas. First, empathy is not a linear process and the experience between empathizer and the one being empathized is not homologous (Throop 2010, 772). This makes it a very uncertain practice for research and not something one can simply implement. Empathy (or not) emerges beyond the intentions of an ethnographer. It was, for instance, often easier to empathize with victims than with military officers. Gender, age, professional background, and ideological stances certainly influenced these "empathic variations." More important, trying to be empathic with perpetrators is not without consequences, as I have argued elsewhere. For many friends and interlocutors, empathy meant more than a temporal collapse of the boundaries between self and other. Empathy "sticks" and is transformative, and this can be dangerous in post-conflict settings (Van Roekel, forthcoming).

Reflexivity has also been recognized as an important field procedure for learning about feelings (Hollan 2008, 477–480). This awareness of the ethnographer's relationship to the field of study and hence conscious self-examination of the interpretative presuppositions shape the actual processes through which knowledge is acquired, shared, and transmitted (Robben 2007, 443). In other words, through critical self-awareness, knowledge about others arises from an intersubjective space in-between (Finlay 2009, 12–13). Reflexivity thus plays a significant role in understanding feelings.[17]

This way of understanding the other has been criticized. For example, some believe that ethnographers' feelings lose their explanatory power away from home as they belong to narratives that are too different, and the fundamental differences between interlocutors' and fieldworkers' feelings thus delegitimize an inquiry into ethnographers' feelings in the field (Beatty 2010, 433; Hage 2010, 144–149). Yet I believe that it is exactly within these differences that knowledge can be found.[18] The ways in which ethnographers and interlocutors position and interpret feelings open up a whole new space for understanding. These criticisms also underestimate the—at least temporary—transformative field processes whereby cultural logics regarding feelings can be acquired, shared, and internalized. Renato Rosaldo's (1989) work on headhunters' rage and grief and the tragic loss of his wife Shelly is therefore still significant. The challenge remains in learning how feelings are positioned, interpreted, and experienced differently. Therefore, I suggest a shared form of reflexivity. This means explicitly mirroring and discussing ethnographers' feelings with others in the field and trying to interpret them by their cultural logic (Van Roekel 2014). This turns reflexivity into a more social and collaborative enterprise and further problematizes a modern epistemic perspective toward feelings. A quick detour into dreams and laughter shows how shared reflexivity works.

DREAMS AND HUMOR

Argentinian survivors of torture and detention rarely testified about rape or spoke about it in other testimony. The few women I witnessed at court who did speak about it only addressed a few apologetic words to these disturbing memories. I do not claim the ability to fully comprehend rape and other forms of forced intimacy, but I believe that enhanced understanding can partially rise out of triangulation between conventional field methodologies and shared reflexivity that can be labeled as affective fieldwork.

Besides listening to the testimonies in court, over the period of a few weeks I interviewed and spoke informally to female survivors who talked about guilt and shame, I read female survivors' testimonies, and I had private conversations with the indicted military officers. While listening to a female survivor at court who, surprisingly, testified about her guilt and shame regarding rape and other forced intimacies with her torturer, I suddenly remembered a dream I had the night before about a forced intimate encounter with an indicted officer of a trial I had been attending for quite some time. It felt wrong, and I immediately interpreted it as shame and guilt. Somehow, I had transgressed an important moral boundary, although on an imaginary level. My first impulse was to silence the dream. But I did the opposite. Relatives of the disappeared and survivors interpreted the dream and the shame and guilt—which they phrased as anxieties—as normal and even a good thing. For them it clearly showed caring and commitment about the enduring traumas survivors had to cope with. The testimonies tapped into our unconscious and were finding their way through these dreams. They admitted they were also having disturbing nightmares, and agreed that going to court too often was dreadful. At the same time our dreams and anxieties were important moral resources. Even in their dreams, survivors and relatives made subconscious efforts to live a good life (Van Roekel 2018b). Sharing anxious dreams and "becoming moral" again was comforting. Disturbing dreams thus represented a reflexive (and comforting) source in the field.

We also tend to forget that, even in rough times, people, including ourselves, laugh and play. Phenomenal justice discloses the often-ignored role laughter plays in transitional justice practice and debate, a role that allows the exploration of the way justice concerning past crimes is ambiguously imagined, bodily enacted, and advocated for in the present and by future generations. My own laughter and play were important fleeting moments in making sense of an affective world involving state violence and suffering. Joking with an important indicted general in his cell, chuckling at the cover of a well-known local satirical magazine, or having fun with various indicted military officers and witnesses momentarily eased the ambiguous research position I had placed myself in. In discussing this laughter, many Argentinians considered these amusing reactions as sound responses to hypocrisy and disgrace; others thought it was distasteful and unethical (see chapter 6).

PHENOMENAL JUSTICE

In conducting this research and writing about Argentinians' experiences of justice, I realized that the trials for crimes against humanity were never aimed at closure and had little to do with transition. A different justice was at play. For many Argentinians justice means keeping the violence and the suffering in the ongoing present, because truth and justice have not been achieved on multiple concrete and existential spheres. The legacies of impunity and denial and lifeworlds that embrace incompleteness of being equally constitute this local conception of justice. Instead of explaining away this ontological defiance, by embracing it, a new approach to transitional justice was conceived: phenomenal justice. Phenomenal justice explores the local meanings of materiality, time, morality, and play and how these constitute everyday engagements with violence, suffering, and injustice. Phenomenal justice therefore does not explore what is officially recognized, but what matters to the people who are (non)voluntarily drawn into truth and justice practices.

In so doing, chapter 2 looks at the materiality of justice in the federal courts. The things that mattered in court formed the existential ground for justice and were my first entry points to culture and self in Argentina. Chapter 3 tells conflicting stories of state violence and transitional justice that are both entangled and reactive. Chapters 4 and 5 disclose opposing webs of everyday morality that enable victims and the indicted officers to live good lives. These everyday moralities never follow one regime of truth, but rather arise out of moral messiness. Chapter 6 explores laughter and play regarding state violence and transitional justice, and ties together the material, temporal, and moral aspects of experience. Chapter 7 further investigates where transitional justice belongs in Argentina.

I believe that the future of an anthropology of justice involves bringing into productive relations the ways that structural impediments and inequalities *and* feelings shape people's lives in the aftermath of atrocities. We must therefore consider the ways in which these projects are mutually constitutive. The current debate on post-transitional justice looks at underlying social processes and structural inequalities, such as discrimination, postcolonialism, and new forms of global interdependency. Phenomenal justice also looks beyond limited analyses of political transitions from authoritarian regimes to more democratic societies, but on a different level. Phenomenal justice combines the urgent themes of dark anthropology with the ways in which people try to live a moral life in a world at risk (Ortner 2016). Phenomenal justice basically tries to bring home the way justice about violence feels for various people.

CHAPTER 2

Things That Matter

THE OPENING DAYS of trials for crimes against humanity and the days of verdicts were often jam-packed at the federal courts in Argentina. But many people also attended courts during the ongoing proceedings— mostly relatives, survivors, and activists. They sat in court for entire days and listened to the testimonies as well as the opening and closing statements of the lawyers and the defendants. In September 2009, I went for the first time to the federal court in Buenos Aires. That morning, the prosecutor read for more than three hours in a very monotonous voice. With a small group we sat in a closed-off air-conditioned space with a dim fluorescent light and we listened, case after case, to the detailed information concerning what was known about the conditions in which the illegal detention took place (often in broad daylight), the names of the relatives of the detainee and their addresses, and the illegal detention centers where the disappeared person was last seen. I jotted down my impression that *Nunca Más* (Never Again), the truth commission report, came eerily alive in this monotonous repetition.

That day I also met Oscar Watzlavik. His wife Mónica disappeared in 1978. Mónica was a twenty-seven-year-old sociology teacher at the University of Buenos Aires. The disappearance of Oscar's wife was one of 240 cases grouped together in one trial for crimes against humanity at the federal court in Buenos Aires. He believed that each case had its own unique story of disappearance and loss.

Although Oscar and Mónica were not officially divorced, but separated at that time, Oscar still seemed confused about his identity. "What am I? She is not dead under the law. So, am I widower, or am I still married?" he asked. I was not used to the social mores of sharing terrible stories of the disappeared yet. Oscar's concerned question about his identity caused me to ask him whether it was too troubling to talk about the disappearance of his wife and if he preferred that I keep quiet. Oscar replied the opposite: it was good that I was interested in his story and all the other stories of the disappeared. He always eagerly shared his story with people from abroad and with the next generations. Everyone should be informed about what had happened in Argentina during the 1970s, he said.

Oscar had given his testimony months ago; he was only at court the day we met to show his solidarity with other relatives and survivors. It had been quite difficult to relive the moment of his wife's disappearance. "And for what?" Oscar asked rhetorically. "These old men will eventually get house arrest." For Oscar it all seemed a political act. "What should be *justo* [fair]?" I asked. Oscar smiled and was silent for a moment. "Thirty years ago, I would have asked for a firing squad, but now . . . it is so long ago." "What does justice look like for you?" I probed again.

Again Oscar smiled, a bit sadly, and replied: "[The trial] is necessary, as it is necessary to eat, to sleep, and to have fun." Thinking back to Oscar's sad smile about his expectations of the trial's outcome, I feel that all-encompassing statements about accountability and closure in Argentina are pointless. Other things seem to matter more.

JUSTICE HAS BEEN an important moral incentive in contemporary Argentinian history. The current trials for crimes against humanity follow a long-lasting trajectory of transitional justice measures and setbacks, starting with the National Commission on the Disappearance of Persons well-known report *Nunca Más* (Never Again) published in 1984 during the Alfonsín administration. The subsequent junta trial in 1985 was exceptional in terms of time. Only two years after the authoritarian regime fell apart, its most important generals were convicted. But military uprisings against the prosecution of rank-and-file officers in the mid-1980s were brought to a halt by two amnesty laws. The Full Stop Law set a sixty-day deadline for the initiation of new prosecutions. The Due Obedience Law granted immunity to army personnel ranked colonel or lower on the grounds that they had been following orders and could not be held responsible for the crimes. Four years later the succeeding government of Carlos Menem pardoned the convicted generals.

The myriad groups of Argentinian survivors, relatives, and human rights activists, however, found a legal loophole that made it possible to prosecute for the appropriation of babies born in captivity. The amnesty laws did not protect cases of appropriated children because the kidnapping and concealment of identity met the legal qualification for a continuing crime—meaning crimes that persist over time. Besides the invention of *juicios por la verdad* (truth trials) in the courts of La Plata, and subsequently in Bahía Blanca, Mar del Plata, and Mendoza where perpetrators were subpoenaed to speak about the crimes without facing penalty, the struggle for justice, truth, and memory for the disappeared also continued outside the courts. The so-called years of official impunity (1989–2005) show that human rights groups in Argentina have worked endlessly for justice and truth in various social and legal realms. Their struggle gained momentum in the first years of the twenty-first century.

When Néstor Kirchner assumed power in 2003, a political shift toward "human rights" as national policy was implemented. Truth and justice for the disappeared and the survivors of state repression became major items on the political agenda. Besides formal arrangements to make prosecutions of human rights violations possible, symbolic interventions to punish the armed forces were also implemented, such as naming them publicly *asesinos* (assassins) (Faulk 2013, 126–130) or the removal of paintings of General Videla and General Bignone from the Patio of Honor at the National Military School. Both generals were notorious members of the military junta. The idea behind this intervention was that these men should no longer serve as examples for future army cadets (Badaró 2009; Frederic 2012). Actively supporting the National Day of Memory for Truth and Justice, the annual commemorative celebration of March 24 (the day of the coup), together with the expropriations of former illegal detention centers that turned detention centers into memorial sites or commemorative museums were also part of the human rights policies (Van Drunen 2010).

But the main focus of *el kirchnerismo*—at least in the early years—was to try those responsible for the human rights violations of the last dictatorship, following the argument of human rights organizations that legal justice was essential for overcoming the legacies of authoritarianism (Faulk 2013, 21). The Kirchner government made important reforms in the judicial system that enabled the prosecutions. First, it officially ratified the United Nations Convention on the Non-Applicability of Statutory Limitations to War Crimes and Crimes against Humanity, which prohibits statutes of limitations for crimes against humanity. Second, it asked Congress to give the treaty provisions precedence over national law. The possibility to reopen the trials also heavily depended on the Supreme Court ruling on the constitutionality of amnesty laws (Lichtenfeld 2005, 5–6).

Argentina has a long history of a politicized, opaque process for appointing Supreme Court judges, which involves the selection of judges primarily based on loyalty to the executive power (Bill Chávez 2007). With the Kirchner government new judges were appointed, but by a new, more democratic system. Despite these positive steps toward transparency and autonomy from the executive, the historical intertwinement of politics and the law remained. Not surprisingly, Supreme Court judges in favor of the human rights policies were assigned in 2003.

Based on new international jurisprudence and international humanitarian law, on June 14, 2005, the Argentinian Supreme Court annulled the two amnesty laws that since the mid-1980s had protected members of the police and armed forces from prosecution for crimes against humanity that were committed during the years of the dictatorship. The annulments set in motion hundreds of indictments. This was a clear triumph for human rights organizations after so many years of impunity and endless struggle for justice. Not only were legal structures that had blocked accountability finally uplifted, but new spaces for commemoration were also created. Between 2006 and 2017, 174 trials for crimes against humanity were held in more than a dozen federal courts throughout the country. In total, 742 people were convicted and 75 people were acquitted, 65 prosecutions were dismissed, and 197 prosecutions were dismissed before reaching trial due to lack of prosecutorial merit or insufficient evidence. Almost 3,000 people are still awaiting trial (CELS 2017, 159). These enormous legal proceedings have occupied a dozen federal courts throughout Argentina.

Despite graphic media output, the official reporting on the trials has been largely legalistic and reductionist. Documents of *mega causas* (a conglomerate of legal cases of multiple victims against various accused) often consisted of hundreds, and even thousands of pages of legal language. As an ethnographer I was not so much interested in how justice was spelled out on paper. Justice is also a tangible experience. The materiality of justice immediately attracted my attention in the courts, and played a fundamental role in my engagement with and in this legal world.

The full range of study of law should therefore always look beyond textuality and into the ways law affects and is affected by the larger social surroundings. This pragmatic empiricism is not an argument against legal abstraction and interpretation, but rather seeks a combination of text-in-context or law-in-action (Richland 2013, 210–211). The courts in Argentina were fraught with multiple, seemingly meaningless, physical interactions, such as violent encounters, torn-down banners, heavy panting, angry whispers, cold and artificial lighting, and hostile glares. These behaviors were undocumented not only in the legal reports but also in our theorizing on transitional justice. The sensory and material have been largely ignored in both. Retribution, then, easily turns into a discursive world detached from the tangible. By not taking the tangible for granted, phenomenal justice engages with words in intimate relation to bodies, objects, and spaces that mutually make up the existential ground for justice. Tracing the histories and meanings of the things that mattered became vital for understanding justice beyond the four walls of the courtroom.

DOCUMENTING MATTER

After my first encounter at court with Oscar Watzlavik and after witnessing several testimonies and a verdict, I returned to the Netherlands. Four months later, on arrival in Argentina for my second fieldwork, I ran into Mercedes Martínez, the wife of an indicted military officer, and another elegant-looking lady in her late fifties. They were both extremely out of breath and looked quite agitated, which seemed a bit out of place. Still panting, Mercedes said that they had just gotten out of a fight at the entrance gate. Only a few minutes earlier they were hanging some posters on the fence, when "human rights people" passed by and tore down their posters for reconciliation, justice, and harmony. Minutes later, during registration at the tribunal's office that allowed entrance to the public gallery, Mercedes whispered in my ear: "*They* just tore down our banners." Disturbed by the sound behind her, a woman turned her head. Both women looked angry, but respected the court rules and remained in line as if nothing had happened just outside on the pavement.

This second woman was Carla Ávila. She had survived detention and was now working for an important local human rights organization that documented the legal testimonies as expressions of memory. Carla was often at the court for personal and professional reasons. When we met at her office, she vividly remembered the fight with Mercedes.[1] These encounters with the women supporters of the repressors made Carla feel deeply uncomfortable. Carla immediately began using the pronoun "we" to refer to other victims and activists. Physical contact with defendants and their kin was quite disconcerting; nevertheless, both sides always tried to respect the tribunal's rules. Everyone prioritized the court proceedings, Carla said. They would not dare to do anything that would jeopardize the trial's outcome. The street fight with Mercedes also reminded Carla of her illegal detention thirty-five years earlier. The clash with the two military wives triggered Carla's memory of her torturer saying that he had to leave to pick up his daughter from school. During her detainment, Carla had thought it impossible that these cruel men had real children and real wives. Her clash with a military wife outside the court revived that memory quite literally.

Inside the courtroom, more things mattered, such as wedding photographs of a disappeared couple, intimidating glares and gestures between defendants and witnesses, small notes written by a disappeared father, weeping inside the courtroom and the public galleries, the white scarves of the Mothers of Plaza de Mayo, supportive applause and embraces, print and digital images of Che Guevara, sleeping indicted officers, absent bodies, the black-and-white pictures of the disappeared, jokes and laughter, indistinct disapproving whispers and moaning, the Argentinian flag, *The Apology* by Plato, and a doll that a woman made out of fabric during her illegal detention thirty years earlier. Justice materialized through all these bodies and objects, disclosing experiences and interpretations of suffering, fairness, and justice from various perspectives that solidified the legal world of words.[2] This materiality of justice in the courts made me rethink what justice is and does for people who live every day with the atrocities of state violence.[3] As the body can be considered the null point through which we experience the world, the materiality of justice became a productive starting point for the analysis of culture and self (Csordas 1990, 39). The social importance of the largely undocumented matter starkly contrasted with its designated legal insignificance. The materiality of justice in the courts thoroughly shaped this legal world, producing moments of care and provocation, outside the official books.[4] Each thing that mattered caused the experience of justice to materialize in different directions that need to be thought through anew every time.

THE SAME DAY of the clash between Mercedes and Carla, just before the official opening of the court hearing, a prosecution lawyer casually ticked the keyboard of his laptop. The screensaver depicting Che Guevara immediately vanished. When the judges opened the session with a quick strive of the gavel an indicted officer walked to the stand with *The Apology* by Plato under his arm. A victim among the human rights public whispered something, while cautiously tying her white scarf around her head.

The captain's declaration was an extensive description of the political violence during the 1970s aimed to justify the military counterattack. After an hour people in the public gallery had dozed off. The defendant's voice was sometimes provocative, and he sounded like a military officer shouting orders, but the judges let him talk. Despite his fierce voice, his body, situated below the judges' desk, looked small and powerless. This noticeable contradiction in voice and body provoked suppressed laughter among the human rights public who were still awake. The indicted officer continued by condemning the replacement of judges of the Argentinian Supreme Court in 2003 by calling it a coup d'état. The human rights public groaned in return, behaving according to the rules that restricted applause and uproar. But after a few seconds, all of them left the public gallery. The defendant and the judges looked slightly baffled, but the court session continued as if nothing had happened. Outside in the hallway, a victim-survivor shouted joyfully that leaving the courtroom was their only tool for acting against the defendant's declaration. By abruptly leaving the public gallery they had expressed their disapproval of the officer's interpretations.

That day I learned that presence and absence in the public gallery were embodied acts of solidarity and dissent among the victims. Attending court sessions on the one hand involved reciprocal exchanges between victims, and on the other hand embodied expressions of dissent against the military officers. Victims' bodies carry the histories of torture, injury, and disappearance *en carne propia* (in the flesh) that transfer gendered sacrifice and resistance to others. The silent body then becomes an "active expressive forum" (Lock 1993, 141).

Other things also mattered that morning at court. The indicted military officers often brought books with them to the stand with titles like *Fuimos todos* (Yofre 2007) and *Volver a matar* (Yofre 2009), translated roughly to "We did it all" and "Return to killing." These works discuss the political violence of the armed guerrillas in the 1970s in calling for "complete memory" about the 1970s and early 1980s among military officers and the conservative right in Argentina (Salvi 2012). Although the tribunals often did not allow excessive ideological historical interpretations during testimonies and declarations, these well-known books were tolerated, or simply not noticed.

The book *The Apology* that afternoon communicated something other than "complete memory." *The Apology* is Plato's version of Socrates's unsuccessful self-defense against charges of corrupting the young and not believing in the gods in whom the city believed. Here apology does not mean confession or regret, but speaking in defense of a cause and one's beliefs and actions. The ancient story of *The Apology* narrated how the defendant interpreted the crimes as part of a "just war" for which he did not feel guilty. The absence of guilt among the indicted officers became an important point of entry for disclosing the military logics of due obedience and esprit de corps that co-constituted their experience of justice.

There were more things that mattered to the military at court. For the indicted military officers and their kin, the white scarf worn in the courts was offensive. For them the white scarf was an object of revolutionary principles the military had viciously tried to annihilate. The tribunals should prohibit such ideological symbols during the proceedings. In response, they brought the national flag or dressed in national colors: light blue and white. The flag reenacted their loyalty, patriotism, and pride. For example, Victoria Hererra de Quiroga, the widow of a military officer, often brought the national flag to the court sessions.[5] Once when a security guard prohibited her entrance with the flag, Victoria became very angry: "It is the flag of our fatherland; it has no inscriptions on it! When these ladies with their white scarves are [barred from entry], well then, I might put my flag down!"

The white scarf is typical clothing among the Mothers of Plaza de Mayo. From the first organized walks at Plaza de Mayo, the white scarf symbolized the diapers of their disappeared children (Robben 2000, 81–82). Like many Mothers of Plaza de Mayo, Ana Luis Campos, whose brother disappeared, wore the scarf during the court sessions.[6] Her mother, formerly an active member of the Mothers of Plaza de Mayo, had died a few years earlier, and Ana Luisa had inherited her scarf. Not being a mother, Ana Luisa normally wore the scarf on her shoulders, but when the trials began, she asked permission from the Mothers of Plaza de Mayo to start wearing the scarf around her head to make it more noticeable in the court-room. The Mothers gave Ana Luisa permission.

Ana Luisa's entitlement to and use of the white scarf in court belongs to a changing hierarchy of suffering in which the mother of the disappeared is crucial (Filc 1997; Jelin 2010). For Ana Luisa, the scarf belonged first to her mother and the other Mothers of Plaza de Mayo. As a sister of the disappeared, she was less entitled to wear it, but after her mother died, she inherited it. Now she had to fulfill the responsibility for wearing the scarf during public events. The scarf embodied her brother, and during the public hearing her scarf represented a direct accusation concerning his disappearance. Ana Luisa once told me she had the impression that the judges always waited until she had tightened her scarf before formally opening the court hearing. She was convinced that wearing the scarf fundamentally comforted the witnesses during the retraumatizing experiences of the testimony.

Testimonies

The testimonies of relatives and survivors at various tribunals often lasted for hours. Remembering the disapproving whispers of a foreign lawyer at court about the validity of the ongoing stream of upsetting testimonies on survival and disappearance, I asked Judge Bernardo Martínez for his opinion about the witnesses' testimonies.[7] Martínez replied that he always purposefully asked the *testigo-víctima* (witness–victim) if they had something else to say. Their testimony functioned mainly as a form of catharsis, he said. Although it was not always legally relevant, Martínez said that he always let the witnesses talk freely, sometimes for hours, because the act of testifying was an important part of their justice experience.

The Argentinian witness approach at the trials for crimes against humanity fits well in the global tendency toward greater participation of victims in retributive trials.[8] Victims were key and cared for as much as possible in the federal courts. Handbooks and manuals to support the *testigo-víctima* were widely distributed among legal professionals. Many tribunals gave them extensive time to testify and allowed them to be accompanied by therapists if desired. *Testigo-víctimas* had a leading role mainly because of their memories. Their long testimonies were not problematic or insignificant, but incorporated into the way in which justice was being carried out during the trials for crimes against humanity.

The importance of the testimony in the courts was built on rich legacies of social practices of memory and truth in Argentina. These practices not only consisted of words but also materialized through various objects and bodies constituting a shared story of suffering that challenged dominant legal and psychological notions of individuality and interiority. The sharing of memories, pictures, songs, jokes, crying, dolls, and small drawings belonging to the disappeared was part of an ongoing process of retraumatization and an open project for justice among relatives of the disappeared, therapists, and close friends. Each testimony in court was part of a larger ongoing project for truth and justice, and against impunity, indifference, and denial of the crimes.

For the psychologist and daughter of a disappeared father, Laura Figueroa, the trials were therefore not about the verdicts, but about this process of justice.[9] It was always difficult to predict how witnesses and the public would respond to the testimonies. Unforeseen events occurring during the court hearings could be very retraumatizing, she said. This was one of the reasons that Laura Figueroa became involved in a program initiated by the Ministry of Justice, Security and Human Rights in 2007 to accompany witnesses in the trials for crimes against humanity. Another reason was that after the new disappearance of *testigo-víctima* Julio López in 2006 many witnesses were afraid to testify (chapter 6 further explains the new disappearance). Besides police protection, this special program for witnesses was set up mainly to provide guidance and assistance during the trial. It consisted of several therapeutic sessions and the supportive presence of a therapist during the court testimony. According to Laura, many witnesses coped with fear and stress in remembering, and in dealing with anxieties caused by physically confronting the defendants. I think the testimonies of Guadalupe Pereyra and Ludmila Godoy are cogent examples of the way this process of justice looks in Argentina's courts.

Both Guadalupe Pereyra and Ludmila Godoy were children of disappeared parents. Guadalupe, a young woman in her late twenties, was three years old when her parents were kidnapped and disappeared. The morning of her testimony, as she sat next to the judges, Guadalupe looked terrified. Before she began, she apologized for being nervous and feared that it would negatively affect her memory. In her testimony she recollected vague memories of the person who took care of her during the first days after the disappearance of her parents. She remembered how one of the indicted officers accompanied her parents during a controlled visitation at home. With a trembling voice Guadalupe also read some words her father wrote on a small piece of paper to comfort her during his illegal detention and to explain to her why he was not at home. In the remainder of her testimony, Guadalupe spoke mostly about her experiences as she grew up not knowing where her parents were. The testimony was distressing not only for Guadalupe but also for members of the public who were noticeably moved by her account. But her testimony did not provide much evidence about the culpability of the accused officers. Before she was dismissed, with her arms crossed and almost crying, Guadalupe confronted the tribunal: "When I was waiting for this court hearing to begin, I passed, within only fifteen centimeters [of] two of the repressors present here in the courtroom. . . . This made me feel unwell and generated tremendous fear, which was unnecessary."

As the physical encounter had happened just before her testimony, Guadalupe considered it unfair. She asked the tribunal to take measures to prevent it from happening in the future. The public applauded in support, but ceased immediately when the presiding judge demanded silence. The next witness, Ludmila Godoy, had already come to the stand.

Ludmila was a bit younger, and was only one year old when her parents disappeared. She entered the courtroom with confidence, smiling and waving at the public with her arms high in the air. Despite the similar experiences of having disappeared parents, the differences between the two women's testimonies and appearances were remarkable. Ludmila's memories of the day her parents were kidnapped were accurate and detailed: two blocks away from her grandmother's home a *grupo de tarea* (task group) of eight civilian cars and people dressed in civilian clothes kidnapped her father and mother in broad daylight. The driver was short with lots of hair. From the car in which she was being kidnapped, her mother shouted the address of Ludmila's grandmother so that neighbors could take Ludmila and her sister there. A slender woman with straight hair took the sisters to their grandmother. Ludmila said that she never knew who that woman was.

Ludmila reconstructed her memories of her parents' kidnapping from what relatives had told her when she was young. Her family also told Ludmila that her mother had visited them once at home with the same officer who had taken Guadalupe's parents. During the controlled visitation, Ludmila's sister pulled off the bandages that covered her mother's injuries from being tortured. To minimize the harshness of the story, friends often joked about these bandages when Ludmila was a young girl.

Ludmila's hand clutched a piece of fabric. She showed it to all of us. It was a doll her mother had made during illegal detention. After her last visit home, they received one more phone call from her mother. That was their last contact. Soon after, Ludmila's mother dropped off the face of the earth. The remainder of the testimony was based on what other survivors had told Ludmila over the years. They told her that both her parents were put on a death flight and most probably pushed out of an airplane above the South Atlantic. Ludmila also read aloud the lyrics of a song her father had written during detention, she projected a drawing of the genealogy of the militant group her parents belonged to, and showed a yellowed black-and-white photo of her parents' wedding. Despite all her confidence and the accurate details she gave about the kidnapping of her parents, it had been very difficult for Ludmila to testify: "We are afraid. We think that justice perhaps is not justice at all."

Ludmila, like Oscar whom I met on my first day at court, did not really believe that justice would come from the trial for crimes against humanity. The potential for retraumatization and the absence of truth about what happened to the disappeared made justice fragile and uncertain, and rather an unreachable yet desired project for the future. Retribution did not mean closure of any kind. After Ludmila's testimony, the judge asked her if she wanted to say anything else. Ludmila replied no. She no longer wished to be alone in the courtroom, she said. She wanted to be with her family and friends who were present in the gallery. There was a short recess as Ludmila left the stand. In the hallway Guadalupe was crying, and Ludmila embraced, one by one, both families as well as other victims and activists who had accompanied them during their testimonies. Finally, they received long and heartening applause.

I was not always granted the opportunity to speak with witnesses after their testimonies, and I thus did not talk to Guadalupe. I did meet Ludmila a few months later when she participated in the film production of a documentary on the trials for crimes against humanity. At an earlier time, Ludmila had been summoned to testify at a trial in Spain. She had been very afraid and had hesitated, uncertain whether to testify or not, she said in front of the camera. She had been very young when her parents disappeared and only had a few memories of that day. But friends of her father had time and again convinced her that she had an obligation to testify. Although she was an experienced witness, the testimony always made her very anxious. Ludmila had spoken with many people, including Laura Figueroa, her therapist, about what it would be like this time in a domestic court. How would it be similar to and different from her previous experience in Spain? Ludmila was convinced that every testimony was a new experience resulting in unexpected outcomes. It was particularly difficult to physically confront one defendant during her testimony, but "the toughest part was to remember everything."

The testimonies of both young women were powerful stories that circulated among the human rights public. Everyone was noticeably distressed by the women's statements. When I met Laura Figueroa a few weeks later, Guadalupe's and Ludmila's testimonies also cropped up in our conversation.[10] Laura thought that Guadalupe had been unable to testify that day, but the fact of bumping into the murderers of her parents turned out to be an empowering moment for Guadalupe. Laura's interpretation was that the shocking experience, instead of breaking Guadalupe, had fortified her in the ongoing confrontation of her traumatic past: "It is always unforeseen how people react [to the testimonies]. . . . I almost broke down emotionally when Ludmila appeared with her doll. . . . Taking the doll with her during the testimony had been the best way to address her *dolor* [pain]."

Ludmila's testimony had also reminded Laura of a little drawing Ludmila had made for her mother. Laura had seen the doll and the drawing before. The first time she saw it, she had cried for two days. Indirectly, Laura was telling me that not only Ludmila and Guadalupe but she too had done much mental work in reliving and reorganizing the traumatic memories. The retraumatization of witnesses in the courts was a social and shared experience. I began to recognize an underlying working logic and interpretation of self and trauma in the witness protection program and in the role of testimony grounded in local adaptations of psychoanalytical theories that challenged stubborn modern ideas of individuality, human plenitude, closure, and cure.

CONSUBJECTIVE SUFFERING

The witness protection program Laura belonged to, aimed at instructing legal personnel, lawyers, and psychologists regarding the transformative process involved for *testigo-víctimas* in giving testimonies, and for the public in experiencing the testimonies at the trials for crimes against humanity. Laura had given me copies of the handbook and the first evaluation reports. The handbook stated that the testimony was simultaneously retraumatizing and healing for everyone. According to the underlying rational of the program, the witnesses' testimonies affected entire families and the public. The witness program was principally about facilitating and accompanying the witnesses and their relatives and friends during the difficult, but reparative process of the legal testimony.[11] The handbook explained that traumatic experiences often impede precise verbalization of the crimes. Therefore, to enhance the accuracy of memory during testimony, the program aimed at creating a trustworthy environment for the witness. The program understood the act of testimony as an intimate and unfinished intervention made in public: "To give testimony . . . is to talk about what we have lived through, not by saying everything, but by making an intimate intervention in a public space; an intimacy that is nothing more than the unknown remains of the person."[12] Two things struck me while reading the handbook: the importance of the unspoken in the testimony and the conflation of intimacy and alienation at court. The conflation of interior life and public life engendered a bodily being that went well beyond the boundaries of individual skin. The body has often mistakenly been considered as the unit of individuality, which is a skin-bound, rights bearing, communicating, experience-collecting, and biomechanical entity (Farquhar and Lock 2007, 1–2).

What it means to be in a body and how we bodily engage with and in the world is always intentional and varies widely. Experiences of trauma and justice in Argentina's courts were closely tied to units of corporality that were not individual. I believe that the notion of consubjectivity is helpful here.

Consubjectivity points to a flexible understanding of bodily content in the transmission of individual memories (Kidron 2011, 454–457).[13] It is the copresence of sensory bodies interacting intersubjectively that allows empathic consubjectivity.[14] This constitutes a shared bodily being through which memory is experienced collectively and *en carne propia*. Consubjectivity helps to unmake notions of individuality when thinking about memory, trauma, and other psychological activities.

There was no clear divide between individual suffering bodies in the courts in Argentina. Sometimes *dolor* had physically bound everyone among the public and the human rights lawyers to their chairs. People were so disturbed that they literally could not raise their bodies.[15] I first reasoned that it was just a matter of speech, but I came to understand that this was the conflation of multiple bodies and minds. Beyond family lines and the confines of home, continuously being with survivors and relatives whose bodies carry "the truth of suffering" and being surrounded by cherished objects that belonged to the disappeared engender a consubjective being that transcends the body proper.

Consubjectivity emerges from culturally elaborated ways of attending to and being present with one's body in surroundings that include the embodied presence of others, which Csordas (1993) has described as "somatic modes of attention." Somatic modes of attention are grounded in Maurice Merleau-Ponty's understanding of the unity of subject-object. Our experience of bodily being is biologically determined, but it is also culturally constituted and not universally given. The relation (or absence of relation) between body and mind and between object and subject can therefore vary widely. What is object and what is subject in the world (thus what is considered bodily being and belonging to one's body) clearly depend on how the body is objectified in consciousness (Csordas 1993, 140). Consubjective suffering in the courts was thus more than the sum of multiple suffering individuals. Continuous sharing of intimate and embodied testimonies allows consubjective suffering to come into being, which erases the boundaries defining who is a direct victim and who is not. Attending a testimony was therefore retraumatizing not because victims and activists in the public listened to it, but because they were part of it.

TO PUT ONE'S BODY ON THE LINE

One late afternoon in May 2010 at the federal court in Buenos Aires, an older man sat on a chair in the dark hallway outside the public gallery. He stared for quite a while in silence before saying that he was a future witness. His name was Laureano Menotti, but everyone called him Lalo. He did not have a fixed date for his testimony, but the waiting and preparation were already very stressful for him. Lalo was also anxious for his family; they feared that his testimony might cause a new disappearance as had happened in an earlier trial for crimes against humanity. During the past months Lalo had thought a lot about what to say during his testimony. He decided to focus on the economic motivations of the military junta. The junta ransacked and appropriated the houses of the people they had made disappear. These financial crimes had not yet been addressed adequately during the trial proceedings. According to Lalo, it was time to reveal the dishonest moneymaking business behind the disappearances in Argentina.

As he talked about his future testimony, a woman rushed out of the gallery and started briefing Lalo about what the current defendant was declaring inside the courtroom. I was a bit surprised, and asked him why he did not enter the courtroom himself. The tribunal had informed Lalo that while he was waiting to testify, he was not allowed to enter the courtroom. Article 384 of the Argentinian penal code indeed states that before giving testimony witnesses are not permitted to communicate with each other or with others, and are not allowed to see, hear, or be informed about what happens inside the courtroom.[16] Lalo came to the courthouse anyway to show his solidarity. He simply sat for hours in the hallway. The legal rule for isolating a witness from evidence did not make much sense in trials for crimes against humanity and it was almost impossible in the context of state violence and collective suffering. For decades, survivors and relatives have continually shared their experiences so as to reach a better understanding and momentary alleviation of their traumatic loss. Due to the collectivity of crimes committed during the last dictatorship, there have been more than thirty years of social reconstruction of past crimes between victims and relatives (Varsky 2011, 54).

Elena Brodowski, a survivor of illegal detention, had ambiguous experiences concerning her bodily being in the court.[17] Like Lalo, before her testimony, Elena had waited for days outside the public gallery. By being there, she wanted to support her *compañeras* and *compañeros* (comrades) that were testifying. The public gallery was located in a dark basement, and during these long waiting sessions Elena started to feel *mal* (bad). She often wanted to get up and run away. The sensation of walking down the little stairs, time and again, transported Elena back to the months when she had been detained in the dark basement of an illegal detention center. After days of waiting as she showed solidarity with her friends, Elena finally testified for four and half hours. Sharing the same physical space with the indicted officers was a torture for her, she said. Elena had been afraid that she would forget to mention each disappeared *compañera* and *compañero* and survivors like her whom she had seen during her detention. But testifying felt as if she only had to open her mouth and simply vomit all kinds of images of the past. It had felt uncontrollable, but Elena was almost sure that she had not forgotten to mention anyone. I knew by then that amnesia was a terrible thing, not only in legal terms. For the victims, forgetting equaled a crime of consciousness in a context of pervasive impunity and denial. Remembrance of the disappeared was both a moral issue and a political act and it was central to their lifeworld.

After her testimony, Elena did not go to court anymore. This had been a hard decision for Elena. "I can't, I can't, the first image I have . . . is that I feel that I cannot walk down these stairs anymore." Elena wrote long emails to her *compañeras* who still had to testify that she would not be joining them during their testimonies. She felt really sorry. Elena was well aware that, by no longer attending the trial after her testimony, she had broken the rules.

Although Lalo and Elena were not inside the courtroom before testifying, their presence in the hallway during court sessions was not without meaning.[18] Being at court, whether inside or outside the actual courtroom, meant being *for* and being *with* the disappeared and fellow victims. This bodily being at the courts was imbued with moral obligations aimed at resistance and sacrifice. In the Argentinian idiom, this bodily presence was called *poner el cuerpo*, which enacts a dynamic and plural notion of the body. It means "to put one's body on the line" or "to give one's body" and marks bodily being during human rights protests, demonstrations, and memorial activities. "*Poner el cuerpo* means not just to talk, think, or desire but to be really present and involved; to put the whole (embodied) being into action, to be committed to a social cause, and to assume the bodily risks, works, and demands of such commitment" (Sutton 2007, 129–130). *Poner el cuerpo* therefore emphasizes the importance of material bodies in social relations and history and practically involves bodily presence in protests and the daily work of activism. *Poner el cuerpo* during the long court sessions lay somewhere in between, as protest and daily work blended.

Poner el cuerpo is understood mainly as embodied practices of resistance and sacrifice, but it also constitutes being-in-the-world where there must be coherence between words and actions.[19] Words alone are not enough. Putting one's body at risk shows greater commitment and care. *Poner el cuerpo* in reference to the act of giving testimony therefore points mainly to the physical act of being there, speaking up, and withstanding painful feelings associated with memories of torture (Sutton 2007, 143–146). Putting one's body on the line is therefore an ongoing sacrificial gift for a specific cause that brings political resistance into everyday modes of engaging with and in the world. Words and actions, or text and embodiment, should always be one.

The famous practice of drawing silhouettes of the disappeared (*siluetazo*) in Argentina is also a way to give one's body. Since the last days of the authoritarian regime, the human rights movement and the organizations of relatives of the disappeared have used silhouettes during their protests (Druli- olle 2009, 78). Through these practices the disappeared become existent and receive corporeality and life again, and they are fundamental in making sense of the way activists and victims identify (and live) with the disappeared (Druli- olle 2009, 82). Drawing the silhouettes is therefore a way for the living to identify with the disappeared and the dead, and fill the void of their absence with corporeality and life (Buntinx 2008, 260–261). Nowadays, at many memorial sites, during protests, and also outside the courts, one finds either hanging or standing (on poles) human-sized silhouettes made of cardboard, newspapers, or thin wood, entirely painted in black, or simply drawn contours of the silhouettes (see figure 1).[20] The act of *poner el cuerpo* during *siluetazos*, whereby people use their bodies as templates, carries an intrinsic ambiguity, because using one's physical body as a template signifies accepting that anyone could have disappeared (Longini and Bruzzoni 2008, 30–31). *Poner el cuerpo* and *siluetazos* are more than embodied acts of identification, representation, or resistance. The commitments to sacrificing one's body everyday shows a way of engaging in and with the world that defies stubborn (and impractical) defi- nitional boundaries of self and other, life and death, body and mind, suffering and resistance, and words and actions.

Figure 1. Silhouettes of the disappeared, Buenos Aires

GOOD SOLDIERS GO DOWN FIGHTING

Aldo Domínguez had been an active military officer between 1976 and 1983, but he was not held responsible for crimes against humanity. The first time I met Aldo and his friend and colleague Victoria Herrera de Quiroga was in 2009. They were at a coffee bar in Buenos Aires holding a meeting for their nonprofit organization, which struggled on behalf of the "political prisoners in Argentina," referring to military officers who had been indicted and convicted for crimes against humanity. Aldo's brother Ignacio was one of them. He was a retired lieutenant colonel who had recently been indicted for assassination and torture. Their friend Cesar Torrates, a retired major, was also prosecuted and held in pretrial custody at a military prison near Buenos Aires. Victoria and Aldo had been advocating for their cause on social media and at international conferences for some time. For three hours they spoke ardently about their interpretations of the current trials, contemporary Latin American history, and *la teoría de los dos demonios* (theory of two demons), which emphasized that the violence had been perpetrated by two armed actors—the state and the guerrilla. They also discussed the regional conspiracy theory of the Forum of São Paulo that envisioned the trials as part of a larger plot to overthrow the conservative elites in Latin America.[21] Victoria's husband, a member of the same generational cohort as Ignacio Domínguez, was killed in combat during one of the last left-wing assaults in the 1980s. Victoria was loyal to the "political prisoners," because she was sure that if her husband had still been alive, he would have been in jail too. At the end of our conversation, Aldo called his brother Ignacio to ask if he could bring a Dutch anthropologist to the prison tomorrow. For all Aldo understood I was studying "political prisoners" in Argentina, and going to a prison would be a great opportunity. Instead of dealing with months of bureaucratic procedures to get in, in a few minutes my entry was arranged: Ignacio had put me on the list of acquaintances and I started to visit them frequently during the weekends together with their families and friends.

Ignacio Domínguez and Cesar Torrates were both in their late fifties. Ignacio was a lean man with carefully cut gray hair. Cesar's hair was still thick and dark brown. Both looked vital for their age. There were widespread accusations that Cesar had tortured a detainee for more than twelve hours, which had made him one of the cruelest torturers of the regime in the local media. When I confronted him with this accusation Cesar reasoned that it had all been complete nonsense: "There have been so many contradictions in the witnesses' testimonies about my involvement in this torture. The doctors did not mention anything about torture in the medical chart of the autopsy. The man simply died of a respiratory arrest."

During our conversations at the prison, the prisoners always questioned the legitimacy of witnesses' memories and the applicability of civilian law for crimes committed under military jurisdiction. They thought that military warfare and war crimes followed a different logic of liability. Ignacio often supported his judgment with the Argentinian military justice code. Article 514, for instance, states that if a military offense is committed as the result of obeying an order, the superior who issued the order will be the only one held responsible; the subordinate will be considered an accomplice only if he has exceeded in the fulfillment of the order. According to Ignacio, civilian law was unable to fully understand these workings of the military chain of command and the retributive consequences of military accountability. Their argument for military exceptionality clearly fell on deaf ears, as both men faced trial for the crimes they committed in a civilian tribunal.

As my relationship with Ignacio and his family grew stronger, I asked him to write about his court experiences. In general he expressed his anxieties about his first day in court. He questioned the legitimacy of the judges and had been extremely bothered by the overwhelming presence of cameras that had fired flashes like a machine gun. Ever since his experience, each court hearing had begun with photographers taking pictures of the defendants. Despite these daily "firing squads," Ignacio wrote that he was finally able to make his official statement about the violence that had been perpetrated. He had really enjoyed this moment of action after having been sick of passively waiting. "Now, with anxiety and eagerness, and no fear at all, I wait for the next opportunity to take my only available weapon, the microphone, to return to the arena."[22] Ignacio's words read like a combat story, and his war metaphors triggered my thoughts about what the trial looked like to the indicted officers. It somehow seemed as if their "war against subversion" was still raging.

Ignacio's warlike impression of cameras firing flashes and the microphone as his "only weapon," well illustrated his experience of the legal procedure, as if the battlefield of the 1970s had now moved to the courtroom. Combat had clearly not ended. Like Ignacio, many indicted officers who fought during the last dictatorship now continued their war in the courts. They constantly challenged the authority and credibility of the courts, the judges and the witness–victims.

Time passed and I started to visit Ignacio and Cesar in their new home. A few weeks before the oral phase of the trial had begun, they were transported from military prison to a civilian prison near Córdoba. The prison was located in a deserted and arid area with high wire fences. The conditions were harsher than those in the military prison. After passing through several long corridors and five heavy doors, Ignacio and Cesar shared the canteen with two dozen inmates. I was surprised to see that both men looked much more animated than they had a few months back, when they were confined in a rather comfortable military prison. Now that the trial had begun at last, they felt they could finally do something, they said. They were in combat; now they had to fight with a microphone. "I really gave an accurate lecture about the guerrilla structure and functioning in the 1970s," Ignacio said. I could see that he had been proud when one general congratulated him afterward for his comprehensive statement about military warfare and geopolitical history.

The next day at court I could see Ignacio's story of combat with my own eyes. Wearing a smart dark-brown suit, Ignacio radiated confidence in the courtroom. He openly smiled and casually waved to Victoria, the widow of the befriended officer who had died during the conflict. The judges arrived and eight photographers were allowed access to the courtroom. They took dozens of pictures of all the defendants. The cameras zoomed in and out. Ignacio did not react visibly. All the indicted officers stared fixedly to the front and did not move an inch. A middle-aged woman entered the courtroom. The judges invited her to walk toward the defendants, whom she was asked to identify. She recognized the two generals and Ignacio Domínguez and Cesar Torrates as the main torturers of the detention center. I confronted Ignacio with this identification during a recess. Ignacio reasoned with a cynical smile that the identification had no real legal value. "It is just another formality of this circus!" He continued that the judge had denied permission for house arrest that some of the indicted officers had applied for instead of prison. Ignacio thought that house arrest was for sissies. He would only ask permission to exchange his prison time for a firing squad, he said. Carlos in turn had greatly disapproved of the fact that the indicted generals had not challenged the legitimacy of the civilian tribunal or given declarations as to why the violence they had perpetrated had been necessary and just. He was nevertheless still expecting their superiors to come forward.

These shows of masculinity, strength, and fearlessness in the courts, such as those of Ignacio and Cesar, often alternated with images of illness, weakness, and dysfunctional militaries, real or not. At various times I saw indicted officers who could hardly walk to the stand, who looked absentminded during their statements, or were even brought in on a stretcher due to illnesses. It mostly produced outrage among the victims and pity among the relatives of the military. For Ignacio and Cesar these dysfunctional military bodies in the courts were primarily signs of the internal breakdown of the chain of command and the absence of good working esprit de corps. When discussing these shows of weakness, Cesar was convinced that the generals did not want to jeopardize their right to house arrest and were thus deliberately being docile, absent-minded, and weak in court. I was aware that in 2008, new regulations had been implemented stating that people over the age of seventy who were prosecuted or convicted were no longer automatically entitled to house arrest; it now depended on their physical and mental health.[23] Ignacio and Cesar condemned such weak behavior. Their generals lacked military honor.

Among the lower rank and file, dysfunctional military bodies at the courts, such as sleepy captains and lieutenants and untidy military appearance, represented acts of military rebellion against superiors for not protecting their subordinates or against the civilian tribunal for its unacceptable jurisprudence. Some officers put on deliberately casual jeans with a T-shirt and did not shave. Wearing casual clothing was a way to express disapproval to the tribunal, but mostly to defy one's superiors. Cesar, however, was always impeccably groomed and ready to fight: "We have our codes, but they do not fulfill them. At least I will die fighting. You know, the trial is a like Roman arena, where we are thrown to the lions. But I will not break down, and at least I will die in dignity!"

Although defendants were allowed to remain in the adjoining room behind the courtroom, and physical presence in the courtroom was not mandatory, Cesar and Ignacio always remained seated in the courtroom. This was not as an act of solidarity, but a method to catch witnesses' inconsistencies and to take notes for their lawyers and wives. Then they could further investigate the matter by searching documents in local archives or comparing the testimony with previous testimonies of witnesses that might delegitimize accusations against them. Although they had little faith that they could change the outcome of the trial, insofar as many indicted officers and their relatives believed that the sentences were determined beforehand, many indicted officers were prepared and ready for court sessions. Their note taking represented acts of counterintelligence. But all this was mostly without any result. The inconsistencies in victims' testimonies did not often nullify the accusations against them. But despite any positive results, being prepared and attuned to combat made them good soldiers. Their bodily presence had less to do with solidarity than with readiness for combat. The losing battles were not entirely without accomplishment. Their bodily readiness and impeccable grooming made me understand that Ignacio and Cesar wanted to be good soldiers who go down fighting. Losing the fight against a life sentence in the courtroom equaled death on the battlefield. At least then their families and friends would be less ashamed of their relatives' life imprisonments.

Military Bodies

Soldiers' bodies in training take on new meanings, like "weapon," "vehicle," or "armor," and new values, like "physical endurance" and "human sacrifice."

At the Argentinian Military School a corporeal pedagogy about bodily characteristics among military cadets is an important part of the transformation of *blandos* (weak civilian bodies) into *duros* (hard or tough military bodies) (Badaró 2009, 144–151). Argentinian cadets are taught that immaculate physical appearance and clothing are expressions of duty and respect. Restrained bodily gestures, fixed staring, and stern voices further constitute appropriate military bodily being. Being a good officer means respect for authority, loyalty to one's comrades, and combat readiness, which is first of all expressed through these physical capacities and body images. A *blando* has not internalized an embodied military morality that differentiates the civilian body from the military body. These shared corporeal movements of physically strong soldiers express first and foremost the moral health of the institution (Badaró 2009, 120). Clear, harsh voices, upright postures, immaculate clothing, and synchronized movement are all manifestations of moral strength. Competent military actions are attuned to this shared sense of movement, behavior, and performance. When this is lost, the group falls into confusion, its members fall out of formation, and the group's integrity and security is lost (Lande 2007, 100). Changing corporeal schemas such as military training implies new dispositions and kinetic and sensory powers that alter the very foundations of social interaction and conduct (Lande 2007, 96). Physical readiness, technical competence, strenuous movement, and calm breathing become fundamental moral categories that constitute a particular mode of bodily being (Lande 2007, 97–99).

Such bodily notions of the modern soldier as an interchangeable, uniform bodily subject who, thanks to drill, training, and relentless routine and sanction, and despite physical hardship, will always perform his or her duties, are clearly a myth (MacLeish 2012, 55–56).[24] The armored, galvanized body is a fantasy that suggests the illusion of military invulnerability, and this form of cultural anesthesia does not imply military bodily insensitivity, but instead means that others (civilians) are sealed off from military experiences (MacLeish 2012, 63). Rejecting military anesthesia is not to say that members of the military never experience bodily being in these terms or envision it as their ideal. The tough and armored body is an ambiguous ideal perpetuated in the way military embodiment comes into being and is central to the military lifeworld. The courtroom as a battlefield (*campo de batalla*), the prison as a barrack (*cuartel*), the microphone as a weapon (*arma*), cameras as enemy rifles (*fusiles*), camera flashes as bullets (*balas*), were not only figures of speech. These words epitomized what a military world feels like. I agree that this is by no means insensitive—it shows how soldiers engage with and in the world in manners that we still find difficult to understand. I believe we need to further delineate what it means to be in a military body without framing the military in dichotomies of vulnerability and invulnerability or sensitivity and insensitivity, but exploring how both co-constitute military lifeworlds.

IGNACIO SHOWED ME time and again that their tough military bodily characteristics, capacities, and images were not always in place in the courtroom. Despite his having been filled with pride that he had spoken for more than two and half hours and that "truth" had finally been stated in the court, the battlefield was often a site of failure and disappointment. Being "at war" under entirely different circumstances sometimes made the indicted officers awkwardly powerless. Although some officers displayed physical readiness and technical competence, group cohesion was lost in the judicial structure. Ignacio often said that he did not understand why *he*, a subordinate, had to explain the revolutionary violence and the counterinsurgency to the tribunal. Superiors were no longer in charge, the chain of command was broken, and a proper esprit de corps was absent. Aging did not help either. The mature military bodies did not function properly during the long court sessions: officers, mostly the older ones higher in rank, accidentally fell asleep. Ignacio was often irritated because the generals were not fulfilling their duty to explain the warfare. They had given the orders and therefore had to defend their actions in court. Instead the generals were sleeping. Ignacio once shared his criticism with his superiors. One general had become very angry and stopped greeting him. In speaking up against his superior, Ignacio reversed the military hierarchy. In officers' eyes, military structures and logic did no longer work in a civilian system, and instead made them look ridiculous. Since the first day of oral proceedings, many officers had felt like *payasos del circo* (circus clowns). Besides the abundant number of war metaphors and embodied struggles, the trope of *el circo* (the circus) was widely used among indicted military officers and their relatives, sometimes also among more critical victims who shunned the public character of the trials.

Being described as the circus clown referred to the public disclosure of this shameful disintegration and dysfunction of the military apparatus. The inversions of hierarchies and the uncontrolled movements in the courts were manifestations of institutional disintegration and meant that military personnel were under threat. *El circo* conveyed a criticism not only of the way the trial proceedings were dealt with on a daily basis—for example, the flashing cameras—but also of the lengthy testimonies of the *testigo-víctima*. Tropes tend to have multiple meanings. *El circo* also showed strong disapproval of the intertwining of politics and the judiciary in Argentina. According to many indicted officers, it made the trial a mockery. The trials for crimes against humanity existed only for economic reasons, and therefore they were utterly illegitimate and immoral. *El circo* also meant that the civilian criminal justice system was inappropriate for judging the crimes committed. These crimes should have been filed in military tribunals.[25] Only military jurisdictions could prosecute the military for crimes they committed during their service, because the civilian judiciary was unable to fully understand how military logics of warfare functioned.[26] They believed that civilians knew nothing of the military. The idea that civilians are unable to understand military values came up in almost all my conversations with the indicted and loyal officers. Only the military can really understand what due obedience, *espíritu de cuerpo* (esprit de corps), the duty to kill, and the employment of torture really means.

This "real" understanding of combat and counterinsurgency was significantly related to bodily experiences of hardship, endurance, readiness, loyalty, and respect. Although the battlefield had shifted to the courtroom, I noticed that the same ideals of bodily characteristics and capacities still manifested, or were contested. Ignacio's physical fitness had been a result of working out in prison to keep in shape with his fellow inmates. Many officers appeared at court impeccably groomed, thus maintaining a military respect and readiness. This was more than performance. Military life co-constitutes the ways in which officers assess bodily characteristics and capacities, project their body image to the world, and ultimately engage with and in the world.

MATERIALITY OF JUSTICE

Theories and reports on transitional justice have largely ignored the materiality and the sensory nature of retribution. However, the materiality of justice (or the things that matter) in the courts in Argentina was an important entry point to cultures and selves. Consubjective suffering among many of the victims and activists, for instance, clearly challenged the definitional boundaries of self and other, suffering and resistance, and words and actions that have indirectly influenced much of our thinking and theorizing about the causes, expectations, and outcomes of transitional justice. By looking into the tangible at the courts we can start to see underlying structures of being that constitute experiences of justice.

The bodies, objects, and spaces at the courts were more than physical coding systems for underlying human structures. Too often, culture has been passively "inscribed" onto people's bodies and objects. Instead materiality is the null point through which experiences of justice come into being. Bodily being in the courts showed that the trials were not movements away from conflict and suffering, but instead the reenactment of both. If war is the continuation of politics by other means, as Carl von Clausewitz argued regarding the Napoleonic Wars, then at the courts in Argentina the trials were both the continuation of war by other means and another realm of mourning. The courtroom was a place where the battlefield and the consultancy room paradoxically coincided. These tropes are more than figures of speech. They co-constitute what transitional justice is about in Argentina.

Neither space—the warlike or the psychoanalytical—was extraordinary or liminal. The immediate encounters in the courts revealed that retributive justice for people who are confronted with the atrocities of state violence day after day were a paradoxical mixture of ritual, resistance, and daily life. The sentences produced neither a significant "before" nor "after." Recent Argentinian history, with its various reversals of sentences and amnesties, has shown that there is no such fixed understanding of legal justice. Although they were remarkable, the trials for crimes against humanity in Argentina somehow descended into the ordinary. Perhaps shifting the focus to the mundane and the undocumented aspects of the trial makes retribution a less stimulating transitional justice practice for thinking and theorizing about coming to terms with collective violence and human right violations. One might argue that the trial has lost its power, but that would be unfaithful to the lived experience of justice, as Laura Figueroa has stated: "Justice is not about the outcome; it is about the process."[27]

CHAPTER 3

Time

IN 2009 A TAXI DRIVER, a man around his fifties, drove me to federal court. He was quite forthright in his criticism of the trials that were prosecuting the crimes against humanity committed by the regime between 1976 and 1983. I had not asked how he judged the trials, but the *porteño* (inhabitant of Buenos Aires) spontaneously reasoned that the Argentinian officers on trial had simply been doing their jobs. "Why is no one prosecuting the *Montoneros*? They killed too you know!" he said angrily. I knew that he was referring to the armed guerrilla groups in the early 1970s that had planted bombs, carried out assassinations, or taken key figures of the Argentinian elite (e.g., political, business, and military) hostage. He indirectly voiced *la teoría de los dos demonios* (the theory of two demons) that equates revolutionary violence with illegal state repression. The taxi driver's fierce reaction disturbed me. It was not so much unsettling, because he was being critical of the current trials, but I realized that violent histories are hard to document in an impersonal manner. How was I to write about this history as if there were only one official story to tell?

Contemporary Argentinian history has experienced various cycles of political violence and authoritarian regimes in the twentieth century. The fragile political climate worsened in the early 1970s and a systematic process began that was directed by the state apparatus to annihilate and disappear its own people.[1]

The military appropriated the children born in captivity by using false birth certificates and without informing the families of the disappeared and, furthermore, their houses were raided. During this last and most infamous period of state terrorism in Argentina, tens of thousands of political dissidents were kidnapped, tortured, killed, and disappeared, among them guerrillas, intellectuals, journalists, priests, union leaders, and schoolteachers.[2] Anyone could be *chupado* (sucked up) by the regime never to be seen again.

This last political confrontation in recent Argentinian history was particularly violent. Both the regime and the armed revolutionary groups widely justified the violence they had committed to protect their way of life

(Robben 2005, 172). Although any form of protest was repressed, a group of mothers of the *desaparecidos* (disappeared) started to gather at Plaza de Mayo in 1977 demanding to know the whereabouts of their children and grandchildren. This was the beginning of the ongoing struggles of human rights groups in Argentina for truth, justice, and memory. In 1982 the regime handed over power to an interim government after the military defeat by the British in the Malvinas/Falklands War. As discussed in chapter 2, with the democratic government of Alfonsín in 1983, an unstable transitional justice trajectory began during which the executive objectives aimed at retribution and impunity alternated for more than two decades. Although opinions have softened to some extent, contrasting justifications for the violent past are still dominant in Argentina. The recent history of political violence and transitional justice has become an important field of social contestation, both on the streets and in books. This is not only because many of the "violent facts" remain concealed but also because the memories, documents, and physical evidence of revolutionary violence and state repression are inherently partial and disputed.

There is a timely debate on history, memory, and the dictatorship in Argentina (Brennan 2018; Crenzel 2010; Jelin 2014; Van Drunen 2010). The historical facts of the violence (and its lack) and their meanings do not exist separately. The violent past is a field of contradictory stories and truths. We hardly ever experience history in a neutral sense, even less when this past is violent. Meaning, fact, and conflict all constitute the pasts, presents, and futures in the lifeworlds of victims and perpetrators. Disagreements in people's memories of violence powerfully confirm the intersubjectivity of the ways we engage with and in the world.

There is always an unbreakable link between history and what it means to be a person (Geertz 1973, 389–404). Providing one single, detached history of violence would depend on outdated notions of history that cannot do justice to ongoing remembrance on the ground. The anthropologist, for that matter, is on some sort of fault line between the large and the small, which requires anecdotes, tales, and mini-narratives along with their narrators (Geertz 1995, 65). The writing of a single, comprehensive, and detached history of state violence and truth and justice practices in Argentina is thus an almost impossible task and, furthermore, I think it is incongruous if you seek to tell various competing stories of justice. A more practical option is to eliminate the objective of establishing a single account of what actually happened. History, then, becomes a set of multiple, changing memories that eternally recycle its heritage (Nora 1989, 7–8), always reinventing and tied to identity and consciousness (Price 1998, 184), and continuously in competition with other ways of making sense of the past, present, and the future.

Following in these footsteps, in this chapter, I have therefore opted to write a contested, partial, and flexible story about the memories of various Argentinians whose lives have been directly or indirectly affected by the revolution and repression of the 1970s and 1980s. Instead of framing the violent past and transitional justice in Argentina in terms of history, phenomenal justice investigates the multiple entangled stories and various temporalities through which the past and future intersect differently in the present. A focus on entangled temporalities can further help us to make sense of the way the violence of the past is lived.

How we experience time is never one-dimensional. "Lifeworldly time" is co-constituted by "subjective time" and intersects with the rhythm of the body as "biological time," with the passing of the seasons as "world time," and with organized calendars as "social time"; we live in all these different temporal dimensions simultaneously (Schutz and Luckmann 1974, 47). Temporalities thus coexist at different, or even intersecting, moments in people's lives (Das 2007, 99). The point is to do justice to the indeterminate relationship of cultural representations of temporality and the variety of experience of being-in-time (Jackson 2018, xv). How we live in and with time is messy and interconnected: we coexist with other people who dwell in different (conflicting) temporalities. This plural and intersubjective examination of time is a valuable start in disclosing different coexisting (and sometimes competing) social realities (Jackson 1996a, 38).

The way we imagine and experience time differently can also be an important source of otherness. In studying transitional justice, this analytical step back to the existential meanings of time is fundamental and has often been ignored (Mueller-Hirth and Rios Oyola 2018). Various competing and overlapping temporalities tell us that violence and justice can have multiple meanings and concerns simultaneously. Conceptual awareness of the ways in which subjects are actually immersed in various entangled temporalities that shape the contours of their lived events is often lacking in our understanding of transitional justice.

Most important, I came to realize that theories of transitional justice often engage incorrectly with the atrocities and the human rights abuses as transitory aspects and experiences that belong to a linear past. This linear and progressive focus has often generated the illusion that transitional justice is a temporal process with a starting point in the past and an end point in the (near) future. Yet political transitions from violence to nonviolence do not per se imply that the atrocities become "historical" or "something of the past." The violence and the suffering because of the disappearances and assaults I encountered in Argentina followed temporalities that resisted this transitory and linear nature. In the lifeworlds of the victims and the perpetrators, the past was an urgent and present matter. The atrocities were never distant histories. For the victims, for instance, experiencing disappearance and torture continually in the present took place mainly because justice had not been done for decades. The structural inequalities and setbacks did not magically evaporate after a sentence was handed down at a trial for crimes against humanity. I believe that in accepting the existence of "temporal messiness," this chapter about entangled temporalities allows us to rethink the underlying meanings, expectations, and experiences of violence and transitional justice to people who have directly or indirectly lived through violent episodes.

HISTORY AS MEMORY

The ways in which societies and communities remember following state repression has also been an important field of study in recent years in the Southern Cone of Latin America.[3] The violent past is constantly redefined through contestation, conflict, and negotiation. These pasts are thus not fixed histories, but rather ongoing social processes of memory making. History can then be conceived as memory. This notion of "history as memory" was also dominant in the trials for crimes against humanity. Each intimate testimony contributed to the reconstruction of a social truth that exceeded the individual memory, and therefore contributed to the historical reconstruction of the past.[4] The legal testimonies were just another little piece of an ongoing process of mnemonic reconstruction without an end. All these memories were an eclectic and dynamic conglomerate of personal and official stories with no definite closure.

Argentinian readers would not be surprised by this conception of "history as memory" (Visacovsky 2007a, 54). Since 1983, commemoration has been a dominant practice in Argentina; it is based on human rights organizations' claims and actions for justice, truth, and memory of the dictatorship. Victims' memories were set against the military pact of silence. Remembrance of the disappeared became both a moral duty and a political act against impunity. Memory then becomes not only the antidote to amnesia but also a fundamental social critique of impunity. In tandem, a critical view of historiography as a universal perception of history emerged that was based on the organization of evidence according to the principle of linear classification and a progressive temporality. Instead, a new view of history appeared in which each man was considered a historian, and the past became an eclectic and contentious repertoire of voices (Visacovsky 2007a, 57–63).[5] It was not possible to crystallize or inscribe each commemorative meaning permanently. The subjective work of memory in Argentina has been full of ambiguities, and acts as stimuli for new rituals, cultural productions, and interpretations of the past (Jelin 2014, 227).

Among the victims in Argentina, at the center of their subjective and changing memories were the "irreparable ethical holes" that needed to be filled with references to moral values of justice and solidarity that must honor the disappeared (Vezzetti 2010, 112–113). Consequently, besides the secrecy of the crimes, the military pact of silence, and the lack of a credible official history, these ethical performances of the past were vital components for understanding how the victims in Argentina made sense of their pasts. Something irreparable may seem distressing, but these ethical holes were not uncanny. They were valuable and exemplary and converted remembrance into objects of obligation, locally phrased in terms of *el deber de la memoria* (the duty to remember) with reference to Primo Levi's work on the Holocaust (Jelin 2014, 226; Vezzetti 2009, 23; Visacovsky 2007b, 285–286). The nature of constructions of the past completely changes then: remembering an incomplete past becomes a lifelong and ongoing commitment. The principle of not being able to fully know the past was meaningful for many victims, and even intrinsic to being alive. I will discuss this further in chapter 4.

The psychologist Laura Figueroa defines the chaotic and ongoing processes of remembering the last dictatorship as logical, but not chronological. Rather than a chronological order of events, critical personal moments continue to establish momentary *antes y después* (before and after) in a victim's life. For many victims the last dictatorship and its aftermath was thus not one chronological narrative, but a collective jumble of significant personal episodes that did not follow an established sequential thread of events. This is not to say that the whole was not greater than the sum of its parts. Personal memory always involves something more than individual's psychological processes and is bound up in a reciprocal relation with social representations of the past (Dawson 2007, 13). In Argentina, both were partial representations. There was a continuous oscillation between partial personal episodes and a larger, yet inherently contested, historical account that never reached narrative closure. The personal character of the memories fueled ongoing contestation and constituted temporalities that are inherently unstable and incomplete.

Within this social world of "history as memory," the *testimonio* (testimony) has become the legitimate approach to (inherently partial) represent violence among victims of state repression. The testimony's subjective stance gave authority to the reconstruction of the violence.[6] The secrecy of the crimes committed, a lifetime of impunity, feelings of pain and guilt, and questions of individual and social responsibility regarding the violence were all enveloped in this subjective enactment of the past. For some victims the option of going beyond personalized affective responses even stopped being a possibility (Achugar 2008, 201–202). Thus not a fixed, single, and official history, but numerous subjective and open-ended memories became the historical norm among victims of state repression. This temporality with an intrinsic subjectivity, changeability, and uncertainty was entangled with competing military temporalities of stability, detachment, and certainty.

The work of time operated indeed differently for various indicted military officers. I noticed that their memories were infused with fixed institutional chronicles of combat, and their temporalities were rather inspired by the glory of war and a chronological arrangement of detached facts that worked against the uncertain and subjective memories of the victims. The way one experiences time can then equally become a form of othering. The indicted officers regularly expressed their disapproval of the unstable conceptualization of the past by the victims. This is not to say that there was a single monolithic military narrative of the dictatorial past, but that military officers' recollections of the past, in their professional discourses of war and multiple stories of bloody combat and fallen soldiers, greatly depended on steadiness, chronology, solidity, homogeneity, and coherence. Their commemorative resources of detachment, such as chronological references and institutional events, were manifestations of entangled temporalities between the personal and the institutional, and the stories of the fallen soldiers were not retentions of the past, but reenactments of their loyalty to the military and *la patria* (the homeland).

The ways that victims in Argentina experience time is therefore another method of distancing themselves from temporality among the military and vice versa (see also Vezzetti 2009, 17). This dialectic intersubjectivity is key for understanding how multiple entangled temporalities are at play in the experience of violence. The way we engage with and in the world in terms of time is always imbued with this intersubjectivity. Time and intersubjectivity are inseparable in understanding the living present.

The way we experience time is thus crucial to understanding the way we engage with and in the world. The way time shapes people's daily life depends on competing relations between natural and social rhythms, cyclical and linear time, and repetition and irreversibility (Gell 1992). Social worlds, for instance, do not always consist in the "common" Aristotelian temporal order of experience that involves a cumulative and chronological layering of events that builds a whole greater than its parts (Desjarlais 1996, 86–87). One temporal mode is thus not the accurate or the only mode for how to experience time. Temporality for that matter differs from time-as-lived (Van Roekel 2018a). I noticed among the victims and the indicted military officers that their experiences of time were entangled, and they competed between uncertainty and certainty, spirals and chronology, and the personal and the institutional. Among the life stories of all the Argentinians I met, I believe that of Nora Ortega de Sánchez is the most illustrative of the entanglement of multiple competing temporalities and how it affected and was affected by her way of engaging with the world. Nora's son disappeared, but she was not a prominent figure in the endless struggle for truth, justice, and memory in Argentina. Rather the opposite.

NORA'S MEMORIES

Emilio Váldez had already related bits and pieces about how his uncle David Sánchez disappeared in 1977. Nora used to walk at Plaza de Mayo with the other mothers, but since the late 1980s she had not been actively involved in the memory, truth, and justice struggles of the human rights groups. When Emilio introduced me to his grandmother Nora Ortega de Sánchez, he had been worried about her and her growing solitude. Since her husband Salvador Sánchez had died, Nora hardly got out of the house anymore. The first time we met, Nora showed me the small family shrine in her house. The portraits of David and Salvador stood in the middle, always surrounded by fresh flowers and candles. Nora had preserved Salvador's ashes in a safe place. David's pictures were the only things she had left. I remember how apologetic Nora's words sounded. She repeatedly said that she did not care much about a trial. She just wanted the forensic anthropologists to call and tell her that they found David's remains so she could lay him to rest.

At home, we drank *mate* (herbal tea) and often spoke of David's disappearance, a topic that easily intertwined in everyday talk. In discussing new events at the courts and political scandals, Emilio brought documents that they had archived. Often spread out on the table were books and papers that revealed small details of David's disappearance, about which there were few official documents. But Nora had written dozens of personal letters and communiqués asking for the whereabouts of her son. Our ongoing table conversations visibly illustrated how David still existed in their home. The disappearance intersected not only with contemporary political events and current family issues but also in our silence and laughter. He was always present in larger family dramas and more insignificant episodes of everyday life.

Nora once recalled the day before the famous verdict of the junta trial in 1985; she had gone to court to see the prosecutors Julio Cesar Strassera and Luis Moreno Ocampo. Strassera and Ocampo told Nora that the people who had committed the crime had acted in such a way that Nora would never know what had happened to her son. The crime would never be exposed. Nora vividly remembered sitting in their office as they cried together.[7] The next day Nora listened to the testimonies of the victims and the persistent denial of the crimes by the generals. There was no grand narrative of violence and injustice in Nora's story. Her past was a jumble of personal events related to David's disappearance and her actions to find him. Once an ordinary housewife and mother, Nora had changed into a politically conscious woman.

Many mothers emphasized a similar awakening of political consciousness after the disappearance of their children (Robben 2005, 300–306). These processes of emerging political awareness were often stories of incredible personal depth, subjective reflections, and present urgency. In her book *Memoria de una madre* (Memory of a mother), Nora reifies this depth, reflection, and urgency. It contains all the letters, diaries, and poems that Nora wrote after David's disappearance (see figure 2).

The preface starts with:

> Notes of a mother, her pain and her martyrdom in search of her son David and his fiancée Belén during the years 1977–1979 (years of lead), black pages in the history of Argentina, of state terrorism by the military dictatorship (Videla, Massera, Agosti).

> The idea [of this book] is to leave a testimony of everything that has happened, to give it back to David and Belén when they reappear, that was my innocence . . . and I released my anxieties on paper when I arrived home "crazy" from Plaza de Mayo.

The book is an intimate personal reflection and includes a great deal about what Nora and Salvador did to find David. The diary began in August 1977 with a brief factual description of how six people entered their home at four o'clock in the morning and pointed a weapon at Nora and Salvador's faces. The intruders threatened them and asked for their son and his girlfriend. David was not home that night, but the armed men took Belén. The next day David did not come home either. Nora wrote that her martyrdom began on that day. The last pages contain a letter of David's sister, Emilio's mother, addressed to General Balza dated April 1995. General Balza had participated during the last dictatorship and became commander in chief. It was no coincidence that Emilio's mother wrote the letter in 1995; a few weeks earlier Balza had publicly apologized for the atrocities that were committed by the armed forces during the last dictatorship.[8] After eighteen years of searching, Emilio's mother did not ask for her brother's remains or about what had happened to him. She only wanted them "to clean the memory of a boy with ideals whose life was taken by a group of criminals in military disguise." The brief official note in reply stated that they had received the letter and would look into the matter.

After more than thirty-five years the Ortega de Sánchez family still did not know what had happened to their son. Survivors never saw him at a detention center. David had simply vanished. The politeness of the official reply note represents the working methods of bureaucratic institutions during civil-military regimes and democracies. Notes of reply and meetings with officials, politicians, and clergymen used bureaucratic words that communicated

Figure 2. Nora's book *Memoria de una madre*

practically nothing. Structural blocking of information about what had happened to David persisted. As a result, the disappearance lacked any solid and coherent narrative. Nora depended on the repetitive sharing of memories, pictures, and personal notes, combined with the scarce official information on David's disappearance. Scarcity, uncertainty, and repetition were key to Nora's temporality, which was set against an infamous military pact of silence.

I noticed that besides the personal, the proximate was always dominant in Nora's lifeworld. David and his disappearance were never distant memories; they were both intrinsically part of the here and now. For example, Emilio's presence at home and their political discussions caused Nora to vividly remember the agitated conversations with David at the kitchen table. Nora had not changed anything amid these mounting family conflicts. We still sat at the same table in the same chairs, and they slept in the same beds. Nora and Salvador had tried everything to stop David from getting involved in politics and the revolutionary struggle. Now Emilio, having become politically involved in a local human rights organization, had moved in with his grandmother just after Salvador had died. These recent changes in work and residence cogently intersected with David's previous political activities. Nora did not really like that Emilio had become politically active.

Once the financial compensation Nora received for David's disappearance came up in our conversations.[9] Emilio overheard us and teased his grandmother saying that she had received "blood money" for David. His sudden grin referred to other mothers who had publicly declined the reparations during the 1990s. The reparations were often an uneasy topic of conversation with relatives and survivors who received the money. Nora mumbled that they were humble people and they had only bought the small apartment that enabled her to write and read easily and to go to a theater play downtown once in a while. She did not make a statement about the immorality of reparations after systematic state violence, like more politically active survivors and relatives often did. Again Nora kept her justification entirely personal.

Emilio left and the uneasiness about the financial reparation dissolved and was replaced by nice memories of David and recent events with Emilio, who was now living with Nora. Then Nora apologized again, this time for gossiping. She was worried about Emilio. Past anxieties became very proximate again. He had not moved in with his grandmother without reason. Emilio had already reluctantly said that he was having troubles with his mother and sister, and his mother wanted him out of the house. The idea of Emilio wandering around in the streets of Buenos Aires was unbearable for Nora. The idea of losing another relative was dreadful. But Nora was not very confident about her protective actions and doubted whether she was doing the right thing. Her daughter had become quite angry when Emilio moved in with her. Emilio needed to become independent and look for a job and a house, instead of wasting his life in political activism and living for free at his grandmother's house. Besides Nora's current indulgence toward her only grandson, the ongoing name confusion between Emilio and David was really harming him, according to his mother.

Nora was feeling very *mal* (bad) about the whole situation. She wanted my opinion and help, but I was not able to be of any real aid, and uneasiness was again palpable. We openly reflected on that feeling of being unable to do anything. I asked her if she also felt *mal* about David's disappearance. Nora waited before starting a sentence: "Well, if we had listened more carefully to my family-in-law, perhaps . . ." and she asked me in turn: "How do you handle a boy in his twenties?" Knowing that we were unable to answer that question she quickly began talking about her little book *Memoria de una madre*. Not only writing but also reading the book gave her solace, she said. Besides mentioning the book, Nora also justified Emilio's presence. He was helping her. She was too old to live alone and she could also use some companionship. She admitted that she enjoyed looking after Emilio. Some friends even told her that she had lost her son, but was given a grandson like him. Yielding a smile, Nora said that Emilio was David in her home.

BECAUSE OF THE TIME I often spent with Nora and Emilio, I started to realize that theories of trauma often focus too much on the violent event. The effect of a traumatic experience, such as the disappearance of a child, would radically destroy the link between the past and the present. Temporality, then, would be discontinued because the traumatic event is an experience beyond narration that blocks the ability to consciously incorporate the past in the here and now (Caruth 1996; Felman 2002). These theories focus too much on the idea that trauma destroys temporality. The past would be frozen in time and temporal normality would cease to exist. But all this made little sense in regard to the way Nora lived with the disappearance of David. Her past and present were hyperconnected. Theories of trauma often ignore that we live simultaneously in entangled temporalities and that one temporal mode is not the only mode in which to experience time. Nora's temporalities were not all broken. David's disappearance had rearranged her way of living in time that had more to do with what it means to be a moral person than with a discontinuation between the past and the present. Suffering, scarcity of truth, and a lifetime of injustice were not things of a frozen past but of the ongoing present that was closely tied to the past.

OPEN WOUNDS

Up to this point, only in the confines of her home had Nora shared printed and spoken words, silences, photos, worries, and laughter concerning David. Nora never felt very comfortable during street events. She often apologized for not attending. I was therefore surprised one day when I received a phone call from Emilio asking if I wanted to join Nora and him in the scattering of Floreal Avellaneda's ashes at the Parque de la Memoria (Remembrance park).[10] Floreal was a well-known figure among the Argentinian human rights groups.[11] Nora shared similar experiences of loss and injustice with him and his wife Iris. Their son Floreal Edgardo, better known as Negrito, disappeared when he was fourteen years old. A verdict had been reached in 2010 in Negrito's legal case in a trial for crimes against humanity. A few weeks after the verdict the doctors detected Floreal's cancer.

Rio de la Plata normally sparkled as its name implied, but the scattering of Floreal's ashes took place on a cloudy, chilly winter morning, and the water was opaque and gray. Emilio and Nora were waiting at the entrance to the park. In front of the riverbanks people were holding banners depicting typical slogans of truth and justice, and black-and-white pictures of Negrito and other disappeared Argentinians. Looking simultaneously strong and sad, Iris stood in the middle of the group. After some words of solace to Iris, Nora started to walk along the dark stonewall to look for her son's name. The walls bore the engraved names of the thousands of Argentinians who disappeared during the last dictatorship. The names were arranged by the year of disappearance and alphabetically. Every now and then Nora looked up to see whether she had reached David's name. It all felt a bit obligatory.

After fifteen minutes Nora finally found "David" on the wall. Standing there out of breath, Nora was tired from the long walk and had just found a white carnation on the pavement: she stuck it in the wall's seam (see figure 3). It was a difficult day for Nora, she murmured. David was supposed to be married in 1977 on this very same day. David and Belén had disappeared just three days before their wedding. "They were such a lovely couple," Nora whispered, "David was such a handsome young man with gorgeous dark eyes." With a slight giggle she continued, saying that Emilio looked a bit like him. But David was more attractive. A few meters away people were caressing the engraved names. A young woman was crying. As she stared at all these names and the crying couple, Nora suddenly said she did not really like Parque de la Memoria—it had too many dark stones and too little green.

Figure 3. Flower at Parque de la Memoria, Buenos Aires

Nora and Emilio joined the crowd that had gathered for the Avellaneda family, and indirectly for all the disappeared. Various digital cameras were recording the solemn parade. We only stopped at the spot where Negrito's name was engraved. At the riverbank, Iris had trouble holding on to the wooden urn because of some sudden squalls. She was about to scatter his ashes. A man raised his voice to dedicate some words honoring Floreal, his son Negrito, and Iris; the tears from a young woman's tear-stained eyes caused her black mascara to run and smudged her cheeks. Everyone shouted: "¡30,000 desaparecidos, ahora y siempre!" (30,000 disappeared, now and forever!). With one firm motion, Iris scattered Floreal's ashes into the wind. People near Iris hugged her and a girl started singing the *International*.

People stayed with Iris, but Nora immediately left the crowd. She walked fast for her age, as if her tiredness of that morning had evaporated. I did not really understand the sudden rush. The white carnation next to David's name had fallen, but Nora did not care. On his way past, Emilio tried to put back the flower; Nora did want to stay any longer than neces-sary. She wanted to return to her small apartment. It was Emilio who had pressured his grandmother to come to the commemoration for Floreal. Emilio thought it would help Nora to be around other relatives and survi-vors. Emilio's actions to reunite his grandmother with other mothers and relatives were not out of place. At many places in Buenos Aires and in other urban areas, victims of the last dictatorship gather daily to commemorate and share their violent past.

Instead Nora wrote about the things that troubled her, such as why she did not like public commemorations. Writing comforted her, she said. She wrote about why she abandoned the Thursday walks at the Plaza de Mayo in 1984. Her daughter had given birth to her first granddaughter and her mother was also very ill. Nora had to take care of both. Despite her political aware-ness, Nora was first a mother and housewife. After so many years she still seemed worried that her maternal duties had obstructed her search for David. Other women had also been mothers and housewives in the 1970s, but some of them, such as Hebe de Bonafini, one of the leaders of the Mothers of Plaza de Mayo, had stronger leadership instincts. Thinking about everything she could have done, such as demonstrations and commemorations, and did not do, the old notebook with personal writings about David again offered her solace. Nora often read about the day he was born, about his carefree child-hood, and about how and why David became politically active. She always finished with apologies and a description of her prolonged search right after the disappearance. As the book seemed to be an important symbol of her way of dealing with David's disappearance, I made the mistake of asking if she wanted to share the book with a larger public by publishing her testimony, as many relatives and survivors did. Nora shook her head resolutely. She had only written it for herself. Just as she suddenly walked away from the memo-rial site, Nora said she was tired of talking about the same things all the time. Talking about David's disappearance confused her too much.

Nora's recollections of the past depended on the entanglement of the personal and political, which made her memories urgent matters in the present. Experiencing trauma similar to that of the Mothers of Plaza de Mayo, Nora continually compared her remembrance to theirs. She often felt she had failed in her maternal duty to demand to know David's whereabouts and to speak up about his disappearance. I noticed a similar urgency in the way Nora compared Emilio, almost forcibly, with David all the time. In fact, since Emilio had been a small boy Nora often mistook him for David. These analogies were often comforting and disturbing at the same time. It was not so much the content of Nora's memories as her relationship with the past that made me understand how the violence was never bygone. Nora constantly made direct links between her past and present life. This imbrication of suffering with a lifetime of impunity is vital to understanding why the disappearances continue to spiral in the present.

Dwelling in a social world where the disappeared were center stage, other victims made these temporal entanglements of past and present all the time. This temporal analogy was crucial to their world and it challenges the idea that trauma splits the past and the present. Although unstructured and not chronological, the past and present were not disconnected, to the contrary: the past and present were hyperconnected. I believe that the widespread notion of *herida abierta* (open wound) exemplifies what time is and does for victims in Argentina.[12] The common medical understanding of an open wound is an injury that causes either an internal or external break in body tissue. Many victims as well as local media use this metaphor often to express ideas about suffering based on unpunished violence.[13] The wound perpetuates eternally because justice has not been done. Impunity, then, forcefully ties the past to the present (Sanford 2012, 367).

In Argentina, the expression *herida abierta* is used to connect past experiences of disappearances and illegal adoptions to ongoing suffering and notions of impunity.[14] In other words, the past continues into the present because it is not past: the suffering and the injustice are not over (Ignatieff 1996, 119–121). People's lack of knowledge about what had happened to the disappeared and the appropriated children, and because burials and trials had been impossible, they had not mourned properly and accountability was repeatedly negated. Suffering constantly intersected in the present. The disappearances were thus ubiquitous in the everyday social lives of many victims of state repression. One might argue that the experience of people disappearing does not interrupt, but reconfigures the "normal" linear process of time, in which life has a natural end—death (Crenzel 2008, 34). Time can indeed differ from modern linear time that follows a progressive thread of clear events.

Linearity was not the way victims made sense of time and they did not perceive a suspension (or freezing) of time concerning the disappeared because they had vanished. The trauma of having a disappeared relative neither made them live in a fixed present. Time worked differently with *herida abierta*. The past and present were instead continuously being revised in new directions. The victims' traumatic pasts were not fixed or frozen, but fluid and dependent on instability and uncertainty. Victims did not move away from a past event, but spiraled in time without repeating the past. The memories of violence spiraled, because they followed a different temporal logic that was connected with a lifetime of impunity and denial and an inherent incomplete notion of what it means to be human, as will be further discussed in chapter 4. Time then progresses not in a linear way or a series of identical cycles, but it evolves in spiral fashion, rotating without repetition. Being alive embraces this inherent unfamiliarity and uncertainty.

Within this chaos of temporal existence, Cheryl Mattingly (1998, 33) argues that moments of timely coherence help us better understand the inconsistencies of time as lived. In the case of many Argentinian victims it was instead the opposite: they incorporated the incoherent, the unfamiliar, the indeterminate, and the impossible to fully know. There was no need for timely coherence. By continuously redefining personal memories, a coherent narrative of the violence was not only impossible because the facts were structurally blocked, but also unnecessary. As an ongoing open wound, history was forever changing and without closure. Expectations of justice, then, take different directions, not in terms of an accessible result, but as an ongoing process that requires constant adjustments of these changes of the past and present. This is not to say that the past, present, and future were always incoherent and incomplete in Argentinian lifeworlds. Other temporalities were mutually at play as people found ways to contest temporal incoherence, uncertainty, and scarcity.

THEORY OF THE FORUM OF SÃO PAULO

During the hot summer of 2010, although Christmas shopping sprees had not even begun, many ATMs were already empty. The local media reported violent evictions from several occupied houses in Buenos Aires and ongoing power cuts, mainly at night, became the rule rather than the exception in various residential areas of Buenos Aires, which had high rates of air-conditioning. A few weeks earlier Néstor Kirchner had died suddenly of heart failure. Still personally involved in the management of Cristina Kirchner's government, his death forced a complete and hectic rearrangement of the administration. The darkness, the heat, the shortage of cash, and an inadequate administration at the *Casa Rosada* (Pink House, office of the president of Argentina) caused an atmosphere of heightened anxiety among many *porteños*. It seemed to me to be unconnected, unfortunate events, but many of my Argentinian friends and interlocutors interpreted these critical factors as not being accidental, and they believed that something bad was about to happen.

It took me some time to realize that we used different temporal logics to make sense of these events.

In the midst of these daily uncertainties, the retired lieutenant colonel Ignacio Domínguez was about to receive a verdict for killing and torture during the last dictatorship. I remember that his wife Valeria had lost all hope. She was convinced that Ignacio would be sentenced to life imprisonment. The recent severe punishments handed down at other trials for crimes against humanity, together with the troubles in Buenos Aires, could not have been a coincidence. The federal courts had forged an evil plan to sentence her husband and his fellow accused officers just before the Christmas holidays. She was certain that as good Catholics they would be doubly punished. The trials were one large conspiracy against the military in which the judges were a minor cog in the wheel. The effects of conspiracy also sent expectations of justice in different directions. Ignacio's brother, ex-major Aldo Domínguez, was instead convinced that the ongoing troubles would definitely generate a positive change for his brother. Aldo predicted that the Kirchner government would collapse before February. This would finally end the trials for crimes against humanity.

Conspiracy theories tend to create stable temporalities and certainty in times of chaos. Although Valeria had it right this time, both she and Aldo shared a temporal logic that connected recent unforeseen episodes and predicted a radical political turn or a new economic meltdown. Against the backdrop of recent political and economic history in Argentina, such as at the beginning of the twenty-first century, these prospects for the future were not paranoid or completely irrational. Unforeseen change is always present in Argentinian everyday life. Conspiracy can help to elaborate a stable temporality that significantly illustrates important elements of the ways in which the indicted officers and their kin made sense of time. Conspiracy provided an important interpretative frame of complex sociopolitical operations in the past and present, and this created moments of timely coherence.[15] Entanglements of seemingly competing temporalities then fit perfectly in lived reality. Some of my friends and those who had been victims understood the sudden changes as the uncertainty of life, others saw these as the inscrutable will of God, or as hidden, deliberate human orchestrations.

Conspiracy theories and thinking about plots as exemplified by Valeria and Aldo have existed since the late nineteenth century in Argentina, particularly among right-wing groups, which have mainly cultivated nationalistic ideologies about the relationships between nation, territory, and culture and have persisted far into the twentieth century (Bohoslavsky 2009, 18).[16] I noticed that among the indicted military officers, but also former *guerrilleros* (guerrillas) who had either survived or gone into exile, daily troubles like

power cuts and empty ATMs stirred conspiracy–driven theories in the interpretation of these present events. Besides the omnipresence of unforeseen and
abrupt political and economic change, we must also not underestimate their
active engagements with (covert) military and guerrilla actions. Covering up
objectives and concealing larger political agendas had been part of their
everyday craft for years. I am aware that these previous experiences may well
have played a role in this, and that these direct engagements clearly influenced
the way these men and women experienced and interpreted past and present
political developments. The past, present, and future are then meaningfully
connected and point to a larger scheme or plot for social change, for better or
worse. Coincidence, then, does not exist, and conspiracy can make seemingly
random everyday events extremely meaningful.

Conspiracy-driven models of historical storytelling allow narrative
assemblages of details from the past to be comprehensible and to appear real
and true, and ultimately reveal to a great extent how people understand the
world in which they live (Bock-Luna 2007, 183–184; Fenster 2008, 123).
Some conspiracy-driven narratives transcend the individual and become
widely shared. The theory of the Forum of São Paulo was just such a revealing conspiracy theory among military officers, and it illustrates how past,
present, and future were often dangerously connected. Events, actions, and
episodes are then never accidental: everything is connected and has a purpose. This regional conspiracy theory promulgates the idea that the armed
left-wing groups in Latin America gathered in 1992 at a forum in São Paulo.
There the revolutionaries agreed that the armed struggle of the 1970s and
1980s had failed, and they decided to opt for political trajectories by dis-
guising themselves as democrats to reach their communist objectives.[17]

In April 2010, while driving to military prison just outside Buenos
Aires, a casual conversation with the retired colonel Alfonso Palacios almost
routinely slipped into talk about the forum. The forum often made everyday incomprehensibility comprehensible. That week it was rumored that
Congress was trying to facilitate future prosecutions of relatives of deceased
military officers who had committed crimes against humanity during the
last dictatorship. Like trauma, blame and accountability would be passed on
to the next generations. The crime was not having shared childhood memories about fragments of conversations of fathers who had perpetrated the
violence. Alfonso and I both knew that it was legally problematic to prosecute perpetrators' kin for crimes they did not personally commit. But
Alfonso was nevertheless infuriated that his government was attacking the
armed forces on all fronts now; even their wives and children were no longer safe. This form of retribution was so unusual to Alfonso, and it seemed
to make no sense. Such levels of uncertainty about the future of their families had to be circumvented.

When Alfonso's anger cooled down a bit, he began analyzing the current retributive events with the theory of the Forum of São Paulo. For military officers, the emergence of the political left in Latin America in the past twenty years, including President Chávez, President Lula da Silva, and President Rousseff in Brazil, President Morales in Bolivia, and President Néstor Kirchner and his successor President Cristina Fernández de Kirchner in Argentina, could only be explained through a regional antidemocratic left-wing conspiracy. Without the forum it would have been impossible that these presidents and their radical left-wing policies could have gained sufficient support in Latin America. The trials for crimes against humanity that were initiated, partially due to interventions of the Supreme Court in the Kirchner governments, fit logically into this conspiracy against right-wing and conservative sectors and the armed forces in Argentina. Grounding his arguments in the Forum of São Paulo, for Alfonso and many military officers the trials in Argentina were part of a much greater, regional scheme that aimed to destroy the armed forces in Latin America. The retribution of their families had to be part of this cultural destruction of the military.

That day the forum and the Latin American conspiracy against the conservative right became even more tangible in prison. A right-wing opponent of President Chávez would give a talk to the inmates. He was considered an expert on the theory of the Forum of São Paulo. Ignacio and Aldo had already arranged seats for his talk. His analysis would definitely broaden my knowledge about the trials in Argentina and put it in regional perspective, they said.

About thirty indicted officers and their wives sat under a *quincho* (thatched-roof area) in the prison garden and listened to an analysis of the current sociopolitical situation in Venezuela, using terms like "communism," "insecurity," "military takeover," and "revolution." The speaker made direct connections between the political situation in Venezuela and Argentina and the crimes against humanity with which these men were charged: they were the "political prisoners" of an evil regional left-wing human rights ideology.

For more than two hours we listened to how a new media law in Venezuela, the Argentinian trials, and the expropriations of land in Argentinian provinces were merged into one large plot against the conservative right and the armed forces in Latin America. Everything was put in perspective. Although to my ears it was not a directly comforting moment, for Ignacio and Aldo it clearly was. The forum cultivated their desire to ward off accountability and deny the humiliations of being stripped of power. Their sentences were part of an ongoing ideological war. They expressed their gratitude to the speaker for sharing his analysis and information about the political conditions they were confronted with. They were not meaning-lessly put behind bars. It was all part of larger plot in which they were an important part. To me the forum made little sense. When I told a friend in Buenos Aires about the Venezuelan guest at the military prison, she directly assumed a plot to overthrow the Chávez government. Left-wing and right-wing conspiracies followed similar logics to grapple with uncertain futures, incoherent presents, and undetermined pasts.

Conspiracy-driven understandings of the recent and more distant past make interpretations of contemporary political events less uncertain and provide (good or bad) expectations for times to come. Although this future can be dystopian, these expectations create stability and coherence and, above all, meaning. Uncertainties become fleeting certainties, and confu-sion turns into clarity. This temporality discloses how the past and the pre-sent are connected with a meaningful future. By threading together these apparently arbitrary events, strategic narratives emerged that clarified why certain events could not have happened at random and created fleeting moments of timely coherence (Mattingly 1998). This tendency toward (or desire for) coherence entangled with other temporalities of certainty and stability in military lifeworlds.

CHRONICLES OF WAR

In September 2009 I met the retired lieutenant colonel Leopoldo Car-doso who had fought in the "war on subversion." Leopoldo was confined to a wheelchair, a consequence of combat, he said. Looking for printed evi-dence concerning the military actions he was to discuss, Leopoldo wheeled himself easily through the apartment. After reading some military journals from the 1970s, I asked him how he got injured. Leopoldo gave me an accu-rate and detached chronicle of his military career and the unfortunate event of his injury.

In 1974 he had just started his military training when the guerrilla movement Workers' Revolutionary Party—People's Revolutionary Army (PRT-ERP) entered the mountains of Tucumán. In early 1975 his com-mando unit was sent out to the edge of the Andean highland in the north-west corner of Argentina for a counterinsurgency campaign. The area was full of PRT-ERP partisans. A few days after their arrival, a violent confron-tation took place between sixty military men and seventy *guerrilleros*. "And [there] I became how I am right now." A special helicopter unit transported him back to Buenos Aires and after nine months, in December 1975, he was rehabilitated. "Nobody lives in the past!"

These generic assessments of time were common in Leopoldo's story: first there is the future, then there is present, and finally there is the past. People should always look forward first. His preference contested the temporalities of scarcity and uncertainty that many victims shared, in which the past and pre-sent were hyperconnected. Not only Leopoldo had a preference for the future. Military recollections of the past were often fixed and focused on the future. Spiraling in time, for that matter, was not their preferred temporality, nor did they appreciate the widespread practice of changing interpretations of the past. Leopoldo had been very angry about the ongoing reinterpretations of past violence by the current government and the local human rights organ-izations. He believed that these revisions were vindicative and immoral. They deliberately omitted from history the political violence of the guer-rillas during the 1970s, he said. I noticed that Leopoldo was bitter about the latest modifications of the past, not only because the armed forces had largely become the culprit for the state crimes that were committed. His actions in war had been in vain: "There may come a time [when it is said] that I have ended up in a wheelchair because I slipped on a banana, as if I had never been in combat in Tucumán. I do not like that they change the history that I have lived!"

Leopoldo admitted that he could not wipe out the state crimes, as other military officers had done in their stubborn silence about their illegitimate actions. But the ongoing revisions of the past reflected in the contemporary trials for crimes against humanity and the new official educational programs and commemorative practices about what had happened during the last dic-tatorship were equally wrong in his opinion. Leopoldo's temporality of detachment, linearity, and fixity seemed a desperate response in a social landscape that favored chaos, plurality, and uncertainty. Although new mil-itary attitudes have emerged, which are more democratic, flexible, and indi-vidual, leadership and the persistence of a "traditional cosmology" continue to shape a shared military identity (Badaró 2009, 217). Reluctance to accept an ever-changing plurality of historical truths remained.[18]

Not only Leopoldo was bitter about revisions of the past. Other retired military officers were equally upset and angry about ongoing transforma-tions and personifications of the violence. In this sense, ex-general Jorge Rafael Videla's historical account was an example. Corresponding to his rank, his narrative was confident, determinate, and clear, and presented little opportunity to discuss alternative historical interpretations.

In pretrial detention at a military prison outside Buenos Aires, I asked Videla how and why *he* as an individual had ended up in prison. Instead, he gave an institutional analysis about the legitimate transfer of power from a democratically elected government to the armed forces. His brief words: "They knew it would be war," communicated little doubt about his assess-ment of the coup. He was convinced that the regime had won the war in a military sense, but they had lost it politically. In 1985 the regime stood trial for kidnapping, torture, and murder. Videla confirmed that they had not been prosecuted for a systematic plan to kidnap babies back then. In the way he pronounced the phrase "systematic plan," I noted his strong disapproval of having stood trial in the 1990s for a systematic plan to steal the children of the disappeared. I had expected Videla's unwillingness to acknowledge accountability for specific crimes, but I was surprised about his disapproval of historical reinterpretations.

Military recollections of the past often depended on chronological events with strong and coherent narratives about their military actions. In the courts, officers' statements often concerned troop movements and military analyses of the emergence of the different guerrilla groups in Argentina and Latin America. Although never entirely omitted, feelings were less relevant in their stories. Detached historical narratives have been a preferred genre among various armed forces that participated in state repression in Latin America (Achugar 2008, 122–123; Huggins 2000, 68–69). It would help the armed forces to construct chronological explanations that favor causality and circumvent accountability. This focus on strategic behavior is plausible, but it overlooks what such narratives do in terms of temporality and the military lifeworld. Detached historical narratives became entangled with military memories that followed a temporal spin that was physical. The personal was manifested in bloody memories of combat. In other words, detached institutional temporalities were entangled with a particular focus on career moves, combat facts, and the bodily wounded. For example, retired colonel Alfonso Palacios remembered the junta years as follows:

> In 1972, I graduated from the military academy.[19] Afterwards I was assigned to an artillery group located in the province of Buenos Aires. Then in January 1974 I got my baptism of fire, when the guerrilla movement PRT-ERP attacked the military barracks. That night more than 120 men entered the barracks, while 120 others blocked the entrance. We had returned fire and apprehended several *guerrilleros*. After fighting the entire night, the battle had ended with three casualties.

His chronicle had no references to the experiential depth I was used to hearing in victims' stories, so I asked him about it. "How did *I* experience that night?" Alfonso repeated to me a bit surprised and gave the following account: "We heard a gunshot, which at first we thought was an accident. Then we heard two gunshots, followed by machinegun fire and several explosions. Then we knew that something serious was happening."

"But how did these events mark *your* experiences of the past?" I probed again, very much seeking answers that seemed irrelevant to Alfonso. He replied that they had already been living with the war against terrorism for some time. At that moment the armed forces had received political instructions not to intervene. After another detailed account of how a federal chamber with national jurisdiction to combat terrorism came into being during the military government of General Lanusse in 1971, he repeated my question: "How did it mark *me*?" His memories went back to the battle-field. Alfonso had lifted the bodies of a dead soldier and a dead commander in chief, and he had held the dying wife of the commander in chief in his arms. Apologizing for his physical descriptions, Alfonso narrated how his own large hand entered the exit wound in the woman's back. His hand was full of bloody pieces of human flesh. His feelings were strangely mixed—satisfied that they had successfully managed to overpower the guerrilla attack, but pained that human lives had been lost. But then Alfonso changed his position and said determinately: "No . . . to be completely honest, the main sensation was that we had accomplished our mission."

LOYALTY

Stories about fallen soldiers were equally important to military tempo-ralities. This is not extraordinary in the assembly of military memories. Primarily based on the principles of a national security doctrine, the mili-tary narrative of having saved the nation from internal aggression may have evolved over time; essential messages of sacrifice and glory have not changed in the armed forces of the Southern Cone (Hershberg and Agüero 2005, 32–33). Military formation in the Argentinian army still celebrates the glory of the nation and military loyalty. Soldiers' ultimate sacrifice (death in combat) has often converted military remembrance into objects of loyalty and duty. Institutional rituals, such as daily chanting of the national anthem, reproduce ideas of military transcendence and mythical times of the father-land whereby the glorified past should always be revivified in the present and projected into the future (Badaró 2009, 185–222). This is often done through commemorating fallen soldiers. These military rituals generate the internalization of loyalty and aim to project long into the future. No inno-cent life has been lost. Violence, then, becomes meaningful in a military lifeworld and is justified for this (imaginary) glorious future.

The stories of fallen soldiers and combat were powerful narratives in the officers' daily lives and were repeated over and over again in public commemorations and private conversations about the past. The kidnapping and subsequent death of Colonel Argentino del Valle Larrabure was one such recurring event. Or the bombing of the apartment of Vice Admiral Armando Lambruschini, in which his fifteen-year-old daughter Paula died. Since 1983, different social groups loyal to the armed forces have remem-bered these acts of political violence perpetrated by the guerrillas during the 1970s. Like victims' memories, these "complete memories" also emerged from a personalized approach to the violence, in which certain symbolic cases such as that of Del Valle Larrabure were placed center stage. The officers' roles as fathers and husbands were particularly emphasized, thus better fitting the cultural image of a victim than the image of a courageous military officer who had died in combat (Salvi 2012, 270–275).

These stories provided the missing part of the recent history of Argentina and were a form of countermemory within the military. Because of the continuous human rights struggle, and particularly since the "human rights politics" of the Kirchner governments, according to many military officers, there existed a too selective remembrance of the violence perpetrated by the state. Several civilian organizations, such as the Center for Legal Studies on Terrorism and Its Victims (CELTyV) and Relatives of the Dead for Subversion (FAMUS), have also worked on the transmission of these "complete memories" or "complete histories" and struggle for the recognition of military and civilian victims of terrorism.[20]

The cultural image of the military victim was not only a public commemorative strategy or enactment of victimization. The repetitions of stories of fallen soldiers were continuous military enactments of loyalty that meaningfully tied the past to the future. Repeatedly telling stories about figures like Del Valle Larrabure answered the need for honoring those who have fallen in combat, and it indirectly expressed deep loyalty to the military institution and the nation. Loyalty and tribute were also always present in Aldo's life. His memories of the past were an entanglement of fallen soldiers, rebellious actions, the military hierarchy, and a declining capacity to save the nation. These three realms (self, institution, and nation) were not separate domains, but were tied together by Aldo's loyalty and service to his fellow men, the armed forces, and fatherland.

Ex-major Aldo Dominguez participated in the *Carapintadas* (painted faces). The *Carapintadas*, a group of dissident military officers of the Argentinian army, took part in the uprising during the presidency of Raúl Alfonsín in the mid-1980s. Despite (or rather because of) his rebellion, tribute to the fallen soldiers and loyalty to the fatherland and the military institution were always important to Aldo's understanding of the past, present, and future. Aldo had lost his commission during the last military uprising Operation Dignity. He seemed to enjoy remembering how they rebelled against the legal accusations of murder and torture of fellow officers.[21] He had revolted against his superiors who did not press the government to block the ongoing prosecutions of fellow officers.

The military uprisings in which he had participated also marked the definite end point in military history. For Aldo it had been the beginning of the end: "[After our last rebellion], the armed forces soon stopped being a real threat to the executive power. From then on the enduring destruction of the armed forces really consolidated." Although Aldo and the other insurgent officers had been in military prison for their part in the rebellion, he still thought they had done the right thing. It had been harder to accept that in the past two decades the authority of the armed forces had crumbled and political decisions to implement financial cuts and legal restrictions for military intervention had destroyed the military capacity to defend the fatherland. Temporalities based on these "essential" military messages, military rituals, and professional discourses of war became entangled with multiple stories of bloody combat and fallen soldiers, together with conspiracy theories that provided moments of timely coherence in the midst of social and political uncertainties. These entangled military temporalities do not only exist as detached historical narratives.

ENTANGLED TEMPORALITIES

How we experience time is first and foremost a social enterprise. Dialectic intersubjectivity underlies the coexisting and sometimes overlapping temporalities of victims and military officers in Argentina. For many Argentinian victims, time evolved in a spiral by rotating without repetition. Being alive embraces this inherent unfamiliarity, instability, uncertainty, and change. This temporality coexists with but also counters more confident and stable temporalities based on chronological causalities of events that emerge from conspiracy theories, tributes to fallen soldiers, and other bloody narratives. Argentinians whose lives have been affected by the violence imagined and experienced time differently, and they became important perceptual resources for othering. I cannot say more often that one temporality is not more accurate or more dominant than another; they all intersect and co-constitute the way people engage with and in the world in terms of time. We become entangled in all these multiple temporalities. This is not without friction. Contestation of temporalities is another form of othering in times of violence and peace. I believe that temporal entanglement and temporal contestation, or time-as-lived, is often ignored in discussions about transitional justice. Meanings of time are closely connected with what is just and what is wrong, or even impossible, when dealing with violence, like closure and cure.

The temporal mode of spiraling uncertainty and openness that prevails in the lifeworlds of many victims in Argentina is essential to the understanding of the production and experience of transitional justice practices, such as the trials for crimes against humanity. Victims' personalized memories of the violence are manifestations of a lifetime of impunity and a form of being alive that is intrinsically incomplete. Silences about the affective part of memories of the violence on behalf of the military officers in Argentina, as perhaps in other Latin American countries, are not only a strategy to circumvent accountability but also a temporal mode in how the past intersects in the present lives of these men. It is simultaneously a contestation of the inherent subjective memories of the victims. Their temporality existed by virtue of loyalty to the institution and the nation and tribute to the fallen soldiers. Justice, then, can be found in a coherent narrative of sacrifice for a glorious future. I believe that all these entangled temporalities underline once more that time and intersubjectivity are unbreakable when one is attempting to understand violence of the past in the here and now.

CHAPTER 4

Trauma

TRAUMA HAS BEEN identified as a powerful new language that authenticates experiences of suffering across the globe (James 2004). Many transitional justice practices that aim at societal transformation and social healing also include therapeutic interventions that draw heavily on traumatic assumptions of self and suffering (Hamber 2009; Moon 2009). In Argentina, many victims, mental health workers, legal practitioners, and human rights activists also classified the experiences of abduction, torture, rape, illegal appropriation of infants, disappearance, killing, and survival of the last dictatorship in terms of enduring trauma.[1] The unresolved mourning, the silencing, and the impunity of the atrocities continued to unsettle victims' memories. The lack of accountability, particularly during the 1990s, had been deeply frustrating for many victims and deepened their traumas, causing further action in the form of alternative pursuits of truth and justice. Against this backdrop, the trials for crimes against humanity created real momentum. But this was not without psychological costs.

Although many victims shared an ongoing need to verbalize their traumas, the current practice of testifying in court was often considered "traumatic." This potential for retraumatization was always a compelling concern. For example, a federal judge defined the physical encounter between witnesses and accused in the courtroom as "traumatic"; a human rights activist defined the legal acquittals of defendants as "extremely traumatic"; and a psychologist/ relative of a disappeared described the victims' interrogations by defense lawyers as "traumatic." Trauma was an umbrella term that embraced various feelings such as pain and guilt, but also included commitment and solidarity. But it was more than that. I began to realize that for victims and practitioners in Argentina, trauma had a profound effect on their understanding of engaging with and in the world.

Didier Fassin and Richard Rechtman (2009) have elucidated how an anthropological perspective unravels a moral economy of trauma in many clinical and legal environments in Western Europe. They argue that the traumatized victim has become a culturally and politically respectable figure and ultimately propose that trauma itself has become an "unquestionable moral category" in modern times. In a local context where the locations of dead bodies are deliberately not made known, and those responsible for the killings are at large or remain mostly silent about their illegitimate warfare, I noted that sharing traumatic stories became morally loaded beyond clinical and legal spheres. Likewise, *lo traumático* (the traumatic) transcended the violent experiences of the last dictatorship and the subsequent truth and justice practices. Trauma articulated what everyday morality looked like for many Argentinian victims.

I believe that any inquiry into the lived experiences of transitional justice should first and foremost focus on people's own articulations and representations of their experiences of self and suffering in the (violent) world they engage with and live in (Turner and Bruner 1986, 9–10). *Lo traumático* intersected with local notions of consubjective suffering, open wounds, and spiraling and uncertain temporalities that were all "hooked together by a definable social logic" (Geertz 1973, 404). In practical terms, ongoing verbalizations of repressed memories and anxieties of the victims and subsequent analysis were not restricted to a therapeutic or legal sphere, nor do these practices belonged to liminal times and separate spaces. The feelings and practices concerning trauma were palpable at multiple social sites and even belong to a social life in urban Argentina, where the "working through" of anxieties is a common everyday practice. Sharing and analyzing feelings is a respected social practice in urban Argentina, which has long historical and cultural roots.[2] Although psychoanalysis as a practice belongs mainly to an urban, intellectual, and left-wing middle class, through diffusion of psychoanalytical ideas in local popular media, many Argentinians have internalized psychoanalysis as a social language that provides important everyday answers to suffering (Plotkin 2009, 72–80; Visacovsky 2009, 54–62). Being able to verbalize anxieties has great value for many Argentinians, and is practiced by young and old and by men and women alike.

Several local human rights organizations working with the victims of the last dictatorship have also implemented therapeutic programs since the very beginning. Decades later, during the trials for crimes against humanity, psychologists were frequently in the courts to support witnesses during their testimonies. Although not all these Argentinian therapists considered themselves psychoanalysts, working methods and overall interpretations of the human psyche in the supportive witness programs were greatly influenced by psychoanalytical thinking. Because of the collective nature of the crimes committed, many victims and professionals considered individual therapies inadequate for the task of facilitating the special mourning required of those who suffered the disappearances of loved ones (Hollander

1992, 286). Despite these critiques, victims have continued to practice psychoanalytical therapy individually and also in groups. In general, psychoanalysis continues to function as a practical theory of self for many Argentinians and it has a central locus in their lifeworld.

Although I am hesitant to accept the naturalness of psychoanalysis among a group of people, I do agree that the practice produces important daily metaphors and common practices that interact dynamically with the way people experience everyday life in urban Argentina. The terms "analysis," "working through," "resistance," "denial," "self-defense," "transitional object," and "catharsis" are part of people's everyday vocabulary, especially "catharsis" and "working through," which are quite common daily practices in Buenos Aires. This means that one easily expresses anxieties, and subsequently analyzes them with others. Social life, then, is infused with these reflective practices and allows uncomfortable feelings like pain, guilt, and shame to surface easily. These everyday psychoanalytical considerations were fruitful sources of information on how Argentinian victims experience morality in their everyday world. I believe the latter is often ignored in the analysis of state repression and transitional justice practices in Argentina: not justice but morality was at stake.

In victims' everyday lives trauma is confined not only to devastation because trauma defines an intrinsic aspect of being alive. I believe that from this perspective, trauma becomes an important source of moral comfort. In this chapter, I therefore take up Didier Fassin and Richard Rechtman's (2009) idea of trauma as a moral category, but from a phenomenological perspective. Phenomenological inquiries have recorded how the moral is assembled in various ways and affects the way categories of experience come into being (Schutz and Luckmann 1974, 103). Morality is essential in seeking to understand experiences of justice. I believe that this epistemological "step back" from moral experience can also help to explain the meanings and everyday workings of trauma in various social complexities, including retribution for state repression. Such an analysis can connect us with the various ways in which the "everyday" is experienced. Everyday practices and ideals do not contain a single regime of truth, they always draw on the uneasy coexistence of everyday moralities (Mattingly 2014, 8). Cathartic talk and self-analysis were simultaneously disturbing practices and ideal resources of everyday moral comfort for many victims.

To explain everyday morality, anthropological theorizing has followed the phenomenological arrangement between everyday unreflective moral disposition (i.e., home), moral breakdown, and ethical performance (Zigon 2008). As Jarrett Zigon (2007) has argued, we should not use ethics and morality interchangeably. I agree that both work in various ways defining how a good life comes into being in people's everyday lives. But morality and ethics have worked differently in the case of Argentinian victims. Ongoing ethical performance around moral breakdowns constitutes their everyday reality. One could therefore claim that their lifeworld is arranged in terms of an everyday *reflective* moral disposition. I have described this way of engaging with and in the world as "traumatic home." By "home" I mean to "be at home in a familiar world" in the phenomenological sense of daily existence (*dasein*), which is always in some way familiar (Heidegger 1978, 5).

Without turning a blind eye to the structural inequalities, setbacks, and frustrations arising from the legacies of impunity and denial, in the next sections I provide empirical evidence as to how this everyday assemblage between morality and ethics functions and constitutes the way justice comes into being as an ongoing moral project. I analyze how the traumatic home operates in a local context of psychoanalysis, human rights crimes, and impunity that I hope sheds new light regarding ongoing truth and justice practices in Latin America (Brennan 2018; Collins 2010; Davis 2013; Robben 2018; Vaisman 2017). To better understand how this everyday makeup of moral breakdown and ethical performance works, I believe it is critical to return briefly to local conceptualizations of self and suffering that I termed "consubjective suffering" in chapter 2. At the outset, this way of experiencing trauma follows a logic of subjectivity, wherein the analytical split of the body and the mind and the individual and collective trauma becomes obsolete.

PAIN AND MORALITY

To understand the role trauma plays in altering the way people engage with and in the world, many studies have focused on the rearrangements of temporality in moments of extreme violence and suffering.[3] Traumatic events radically destroy temporal experience between the past and the present, mainly because trauma is understood as an event beyond narration through which the past cannot be consciously incorporated in the here and now (see chapter 3). This idea about trauma and temporality has been dominant for understanding the inherent inability to adequately identify the feelings of trauma in relationship to self. Elaine Scarry (1985) has also shown that with the phenomena of torture, physical pain becomes inexpressible, and she notes not only the difficulty of describing pain but also pain's ability to destroy language. Physical pain, according to Scarry (1985, 5), shatters language because it has no referential content, as it is not *of* or *for* anything. Psychological suffering, though often difficult, has referential content and is susceptible to verbal objectification (Scarry 1985, 11).

I believe that this onset of the unspeakable, the "not referential," and the disruptive turns trauma into a surreal experience. From a phenomenological perspective, one might say that trauma shatters the familiarity of everyday existence. Holocaust literature, such as the work of Primo Levi (1989) and Bruno Bettelheim (1986 [1960]), also draws on the unspeakable to exemplify living with the experiences of the concentration camps. These experiences linger in the unconscious and can suddenly erupt into the present without becoming part of it. Trauma, then, always remains eerie.

In a social world where traumas are continuously shared, it becomes possible to narrate the impossible (i.e., the traumatic) through collective storytelling and shared analysis. I do not deny that for victims of state repression in Argentina, traumatic events like torture and disappearance affected their everyday existence, but instead of an event beyond narration, I observed that victims actively incorporated their traumas into the here and now. Many of these individuals did not make a clear distinction between physical and psychological pain because both constituted their experiences of trauma. This divide between physical and psychological pain follows an ingrained Cartesian separation between body and mind, which does not nearly approach the way suffering and self are experienced in Argentina. The Argentinian understanding of trauma places trauma center stage in a social life that coalesces as a subject-subject division of individual suffering.

Empathic processes of suffering conflate the subject-subject divide of bodily experience and replace the division between self and other by constituting a form of consubjectivity (Kidron 2011, 454–457). As discussed in chapter 3, I discerned a similar process among Argentinians of different generations and with different attachments to the perpetrated violence, a similar process: continuously being with other survivors and relatives whose bodies and minds carried the "truth of trauma" and being surrounded by objects, images, and words that belonged to the disappeared engendered a consubjective being that transcended the body proper, and hence transcended individual traumas. Consubjectivity, in this sense, involves more than a symbolic empathic process of co-suffering: consubjective being implies a conflation of subject-subject. Traumas of perpetrated violence then exist consubjectively through these emphatic processes that merge the boundaries between individual traumas.

Another important aspect of this Argentinian stance toward trauma is that trauma was intrinsic to being alive for the survivors as well as for their relatives. This does not mean that the traumatic experiences were normal in the sense that they were inflicted all the time, or because Argentinians consider rape, torture, and assassination normal practices. Such an argument would be outrageous. The unmaking of trauma as something devastating more accurately suggests a conceptualization of self that is fundamentally incomplete and unknown. In the Argentinian understanding, repressed memories concerning traumas are not hurtful or problematic per se; these gaps in knowledge belong to human life and basically demand ongoing search and analysis without ever reaching closure or cure. In combination with the unpunished crimes, this incompleteness of being turns transitional justice into a project without an end.

To understand the role trauma plays in the way people experience transitional justice, we must therefore look at not only temporality but also morality. The renewed debate on the anthropology of morality can help us to rethink how categories of moral experience come into being in contexts of trauma.[4] Zigon (2007, 133) argues, for example, that many people consider others and themselves moral beings most of the time. Zigon's anthropology of morality heavily draws on Heideggerian phenomenology, which argues that the world one engages with is not natural, but always intentionally pregiven (Heidegger 1996 [1953]).

Heidegger is mostly concerned with how human existence comes into being and differentiates between everyday consciousness and "Dasein." The former is prereflective and inauthentic. The latter is reflective and authentic (Heidegger 1978, 296–298). Everyday consciousness is to be at home in a familiar world without reflecting upon it (Heidegger 1996 [1953], 51). Zigon (2007) has defined this "home" as an unreflective moral disposition, as the way people experience morality without questioning it. One only needs conscious ethical consideration in moments that shake one out of the everydayness of being moral, which Zigon (2007, 136–137) calls "moral breakdown" (using Heidegger's example of when the hammer breaks, one is forced to reflect on the process of hammering).

In his early writings, Heidegger (1993, 19–20) argues that when we lift a hammer, we are enmeshed in a series of meaningful relationships with things and practices. These contexts of meanings are usually implicit in our activities and only become visible when something goes wrong. This is when we "become aware of everything that is connected with the work" (Heidegger 1978, 105). According to Heidegger, this breakdown of implicit meaning is when "Being" reveals itself. Zigon follows up on this revelation of "Being" by stating that moral breakdowns occur in moments of ethical dilemmas in which people occasionally find themselves. During these ethical moments, people are forced to figure out, work through, and deal with a moral dilemma. In other words, people become momentarily reflective. Zigon calls this process of "working through and dealing with" it "performing ethics."

From there, Zigon (2007, 137) makes an important distinction between "morality as the unreflective mode of being-in-the-world and ethics as a tactic performed in the moment of the breakdown of the ethical dilemma." His argument is that performing ethics is moving back home, to once again dwell in the unreflective comfort of the familiar (Zigon 2007, 138). In other words, he describes how everyday moral comfort is disrupted by the liminal process of ethical questioning of the moral breakdown and is reinstated if that process is successful (Csordas 2013, 524). "What is important in the moment of moral breakdown is not 'to be good' or 'to be a good—'but to get back to the unreflective moral dispositions of everyday life. It is having accomplished this return that is considered good, not the act itself" (Zigon 2007, 140).

What is at stake here is this distinction between "morality" as unreflective moral disposition and "ethics" as ethical performance. The idea that everyday consciousness is unreflective becomes rather questionable in Argentina. For many Argentinian victims and practitioners, there exists no successful return to an everyday unreflective moral disposition. Their comfort in the familiar exists paradoxically through ongoing ethical performances of moral breakdowns that largely depend on the local understanding of an incomplete self and the ubiquitous danger of indifference, denial, and impunity.

SOCIAL REPETITION COMPULSIONS

Among the people I came to know in Buenos Aires, Laura Figueroa and Carla Ávila spoke most cogently about the omnipresence of trauma in victims' everyday lives. This was not surprising because both women had long careers as psychoanalysts treating victims of the last dictatorship. Laura's personal history of the disappearance of her father infused her accounts with a tragic immediacy. Twice we discussed at length the victims' prevalent compulsion to talk about the traumatic experiences of disappearance and survival.[5] Laura strongly believed that those who survived must speak for those who are not here anymore. This would prevent anyone from forgetting what had happened between 1976 and 1983. Laura reflected that this implicit rule to speak was more or less a promise detainees made in the detention camps: "If you survived: you ought to tell what had happened." Laura thought that not only survivors but also relatives had a hard time talking about anything else. And although disturbing, this impulse to talk profoundly influenced victims' relationships with others.[6]

Carla Ávila detected similar mechanisms of social repetition compulsions among victims and herself.[7] Carla had survived detention and torture, and we spoke extensively about the difficulties in continuously addressing the traumatic. Based on her own traumatic experiences of survival and loss and those of her patients, Carla said she had become profoundly aware that the fewer words people used to express trauma, the more the trauma resulted in illness. She reasoned that words provided alleviation, and although it was very painful, victims must always put "terror into words." Clearly, Carla did not interpret individual traumas as events that were beyond narration through which the past could not be consciously incorporated in the here and now. Like the shared traumas of the last dictatorship, the repetition compulsions existed as social phenomena. The collective trauma and collective compulsions were not the sum of thousands of individual bodies suffering, but one consubjective suffering.

Repetition compulsion, consistent with the classical Freudian view, is an ungovernable process originating in the unconscious; these repressed memories seek to return to the present, whether in dreams, symptoms, or acting out (Laplanche and Pontalis 1988, 78). I observed at many social sites and among many survivors of detention and relatives of the disappeared that the psychoanalytical processes of repetition compulsion were not individual. Many victims did not experience their traumas through individuality, privacy, and reflexive interiority. Instead, another principle was at work. Originating from the above-mentioned Argentinian understanding of consubjective suffering, ongoing social repetition compulsions melted individual experiences into shared processes of verbalizing traumas.

On another occasion, Carla made an important distinction between a traumatic experience and an original trauma.[8] She explained that the original trauma is the general incompleteness of a person that motivates human life. Each person has this trauma by the simple fact of being thrown into the world through birth. A traumatic experience has other consequences. Both traumas are irreparable and leave eternal marks on the body and psyche, like open wounds that never close. According to Carla, the original trauma of being born/being alive always interacts with the way one lives through subsequent traumatic experiences. A person who has accepted his or her original trauma possesses more tools with which to work through successive traumatic experiences. Living with both types of trauma—although different in origin—requires ongoing speech and analysis. How Argentinian victims experience torture, rape, assassination, and disappearance must be understood in this social world, where the psychoanalytical conceptualization of original trauma and traumatic experience is actively being reproduced.

Contemporary meanings of trauma, from a psychoanalytical perspective, justify and glorify traumas as transformative forces of self. Trauma becomes sacred, or in secular terms, the true giver of a nonrepresentable experience (LaCapra 2004, 262–263). Psychoanalysis, then, is a secular project for learning how to overcome pain through a transformative analysis of self (Speziale-Bagliacca 2004, 13). This notion of transformation, however, must not be mistaken for closure or cure!

Carla maintained that despite continuous verbalizations and reflections, blind spots would always remain. Carla called them the "unnamable holes" that remain forever in a person's life. The traumatic could not be fully put into words because something would always be missing. For Carla, the human desire to understand these unnamable holes will always exist because closure is intrinsically unrealizable. According to Carla, this unachievable desire, in fact, fuels humankind and makes life meaningful. Analysis, then, is an ongoing process of becoming.

Again, from a classical psychoanalytical perspective, these unnamable holes represent the ever-existing unconscious domains of the human psyche. The permanent and unachievable desire to know distinguishes human life from other living organisms. The so-called permanent desire must not be mistaken for human need. From a Lacanian viewpoint, desire cannot be reduced to need since, by definition, there is no relation to a real object (like food or air) independent of the subject (Laplanche and Pontalis 1988, 482–483). For Carla, the inability to fully know one's traumas was familiar and seemed integral to everyday life. Arguably, modern understandings of trauma appear to be largely inattentive to this imagination of trauma as "natural," which is accompanied by the ongoing need for verbalization and analysis.

Carla further explained that victims would always need ongoing repetition around their traumatic experiences. Based on a consubjective notion of suffering, Carla understood these ongoing repetition compulsions in a much more collective way. On a collective level, in every story or piece of evidence, victims were telling of something that was impossible to express individually relating to the crimes committed during the last dictatorship. For Carla, all these bits and pieces reconstructed a traumatic and incomprehensible part of Argentinian history, and, therefore, the possibility of knowing, albeit intrinsically incomplete, existed by means of these ongoing social repetition compulsions.

It struck me that this understanding of trauma differs greatly from a modern medical point of view that mostly pathologizes trauma. The modern inability to conceive trauma as a social and enduring phenomenon is not only based on contemporary ways of managing traumas as individual diseases, it also means that human life should be free from trauma. People like Carla and Laura had no expectations of fully resolving their shared traumas. Alternatively, the constant figuring out and working through of traumas (or in phenomenological terminology "performing ethics") were an integral part of many victims' everyday life. To further rethink trauma in regard to the phenomenological arrangement between the unreflective moral disposition and ethical performances, I believe it is important to take a closer look at how moral breakdowns manifest in everyday life. In the case of Argentina, the manifestation of multiple variations of guilt can be considered as an example. The moral experience of guilt concerning the last dictatorship is a recurring moral breakdown for many Argentinians.

GUILT

Argentinian society is predominantly Catholic, and the subsequent analysis of guilt among victims could also have been done through a Catholic lens (Hardon 2013 [1980]). Notions of Catholic guilt may have been an important moral incentive for some victims with its private confessions and solitary atonements. But the practical outcome of the variations of guilt I encountered in many victims had more to do with psychoanalytic understandings of self. The cleansing rituals of guilt were not solitary and religious in nature; they were social repetitions that were secular in nature. Assigning guilt in Catholic terms to the survivors was problematic for other reasons too. During torture sessions, victims were often coerced into "recognizing" their own guilt and subjugation (Graziano 1992, 166). The junta ideology imposed penance on the "subversives" for being guilty of disrupting God's natural order. The practices of torture and disappearance were therefore not evil, but acts of goodness that would restore God's order (Graziano 1992, 111).[9] These irrational but powerful circular logics of guilt, reaffirming the veracity and necessity of the junta ideology, turned guilt into a hazardous emotional field for many survivors.

In general, I am aware that assigning guilt to victims in Argentina is hazardous and can all too easily turn into wrong assumptions of accountability and blame.[10] Most important, this guilt was not felt toward the military regime and its actors. Guilt was primarily a feeling that concerned the disappeared and their relatives. Although scarce, this is not the first anthropological analysis of guilt and victimhood in Argentina. The moral experience of guilt among the Mothers of Plaza de Mayo, who courageously began to ask where their children were during the years of repression, has been systematically examined (Robben 2000, 87). Antonius Robben distinguishes two main types of maternal guilt—the first, for not being able to protect the child from death—and the second, for not being able to fulfill their maternal responsibility in providing a proper burial. These two types of maternal guilt are still delicate matters in Argentina. Rebekah Park's analysis of survivor's guilt in Argentina also distinguishes two types of guilt in Argentina, hitherto among survivors of detention and torture (Park 2014, 145–146). Feeling guilty for having survived can be interpreted as disloyalty to other detainees who disappeared, or as complicity of the survivors with the military regime in collaborating (forcibly) and sharing vital information about future actions and the whereabouts of others in return for their survival.

The term "survivor's guilt" is widely used in analyses of post-conflict settings and comes from Bruno Bettelheim (1986 [1960]), who survived

Dachau and Buchenwald. It mainly describes the guilt that survivors of the Holocaust felt for having survived. Primo Levi (1989) offers the most thought-provoking modern work on survivor's guilt and on the difficult mandate survivors have to represent the violence they experienced. Levi suggests that his guilt is not solely based on survival, but also on not being able to convey to others the horrors of and death in the concentration camps. Survivors in Argentina also felt guilty for failing to sacrifice themselves for the revolutionary dream of a better and more socially equal Argentina. This dream was not accomplished and continued to burden the next generations of Argentinians.

In discussions with survivors, some openly denied guilt. They thought guilt implied complicity, and many of them had a ready-made story to counteract this form of guilt. For example, one male survivor rejected guilt as a "too Catholic" experience, which he contested based on the Catholic Church's involvement in the atrocities of the military junta.[11] Feeling guilty would undermine his permanent resistance to the Church's complicity. He and other survivors expressed guilt in terms of *compromiso* (commitment) or *deuda* (debt), which released them from the responsibility of survival but not the moral concerns. Each had his or her ongoing working method that prevented a feeling of complicity and accountability, methods that included individual or social therapy and political activism to raise social awareness about the atrocities.

In addition to maternal and survival guilt, during my fieldwork, I also observed other types of guilt among a diverse group of Argentinians with no direct link to a disappeared family member or survivor of detention. Their guilt concerned the unaccomplished revolutionary dream of a better Argentina. They also felt guilty for the relatives who had been unable to properly mourn loved ones and attain a sense of justice due to decades of official impunity and denial.

Luis Noguiera was one of them. He did not suffer the crimes of the last dictatorship in person. Despite Luis's age—he was a young adolescent during the late 1970s—the last dictatorship has been an important source for his fictional writings and motivation for his work defending citizens against contemporary state negligence and misconduct. Luis and I engaged in illuminating talks about the trials and the dictatorship. He once recounted in apologetic tones that he did not get really involved in the armed struggle. In his early adolescence, he rebelled against the dictatorship only by posting pamphlets on walls. In the first months of our acquaintance we never discussed his guilt because I assumed (incorrectly) that he did not feel guilty. It was during a visit to a site of memory that Luis shared his guilt.

The military base, a notorious detention center during the late 1970s, had been turned into a memorial site a few years back. Luis had grown up in this region but had not seen the memorial site, which he considered a small transgression. One morning in April 2010, we drove to the memorial site together. Over a period of several hours, we observed the empty spaces that used to be detention and torture areas, throughout which the guide, Matilda Giachetti, told us horrific survivor stories. When she left for a work meeting with the other guides, Luis and I visited the last military barrack without Matilda's stories. This barrack did not need her stories. It was a small museum, where stories, pictures, and personal belongings of the disappeared were displayed. While living in Buenos Aires, there had been many opportunities to visit sites of memory, memorials, museums, and temporary exhibitions. These places always displayed the legendary black-and-white pictures of the disappeared and their stories in relation to the last time they were seen; this museum, in addition, exhibited personal belongings of the disappeared.

Afterward we sat outside under a tree. I sensed it had been a draining visit for Luis and we started talking about all the things we had just seen.

"We are at a very powerful place, Eva. It really grabs you."

Luis continued by relating a story he had just read about a man wearing a pair of Levi's jeans the day he disappeared. It transported him directly back to the 1970s as he remembered clearly his own teenage desire to have a pair of Levi's. These stories, pictures, and objects at the sun-drenched site of memory in the countryside produced a strange atmosphere between tranquility and unease.

Feeling uneasy, I decided to discuss my reaction with Luis. As had happened during many other moments when I mirrored my own feelings in the field, it was helpful in defining what was exactly at stake. Luis had been silent for some time. I told him I felt a bit uncomfortable because I was having such a pleasant time with him at a memorial site after listening to such terrible stories. Luis nodded.

When I asked him how he felt, Luis searched for words for a few seconds, and then said he felt a mixture of complicity, guilt, pain, and nostalgia. He thought it was a confusing sensation. He started talking about his adolescent rebellion, about his militancy, and his having joined the Peronist Youth Party at a very young age. It was the first time Luis had spoken about his guilt and complicity; I was surprised he used the term *culpa* (guilt). We agreed that it felt different to talk about these issues at a memorial site than at other places; we thought that our words and feelings were fraught with more meaning than usual. After that intermezzo on guilt and dis/comfort, we surprisingly (to me) made an easy shift to talking about our plans for the weekend.

Luis and I talked about guilt again at his home.[12] He revealed that he felt guilty because of his sporadic silence, which he termed "the convenience of remaining quiet." Despite his young age, he explained that his modest rebellion did not mean he was forgiven. As I had still been associating guilt with accountability, mainly because of his young age, I had not expected Luis to feel guilty. His repeated frankness proved me wrong.

Guilt—also expressed as debt or commitment—lingered equally in many conversations. From a Freudian stance, unconscious guilt produces an actual splitting of the ego between the accuser (the superego) and the accused. This differentiation of a critical and punitive agency vis-à-vis the ego introduces guilt as an intersystemic relationship within the self. Feeling guilty is, from the ego's perspective, an answer to the superego's criticism (Laplanche and Pontalis 1988, 414–415). In Argentina, this Freudian internal and individual ethical performance was much more external and social. Feeling guilty in this milieu is not a subconscious individual struggle, but instead serves to function as an imperative moral resource to be a good person.

On another occasion, Matilda Giachetti, whose mother had disappeared, and I also talked about guilt among relatives and activists in Argentina. Besides working at the memorial site, Matilda belonged to the Argentinian human rights organization by and for children of the disappeared.[13] Having studied psychology and anthropology, Matilda spoke as a professional, primarily using hypothetical terms. She told me: "Survivors and people who went into exile cope with questions like: 'Why did I leave?' 'Why did I survive?' 'What have I done wrong that let me live?'" Matilda revealed that parents of the disappeared felt they had failed to protect their children from death and, without a proper burial, this guilt had remained. Matilda further reasoned that the heroic identity of the disappeared and the parents' internalization of their revolutionary struggle made it possible for them to live with their guilt.

After confessing that I sometimes felt guilty during my fieldwork for being too indifferent or not being personally committed, I asked Matilda if she felt guilty. She reflected that when she became a young adult, she had also questioned her *compromiso* to a better world. Her parents had put their lives in danger but what had she done for a better world? She wondered whether perhaps her years of being in therapy, her work at the memorial site, and her exhaustive research on state repression in Argentina stood for her personal attempts to live a moral life.

These commitments and debts characterize long processes of an awakening consciousness, and all these practical variations of guilt have more to do with morality than with accountability. The ability to feel guilt is based on social nearness, empathic processes, desire to make restitutions, and the reciprocal relationship of indebtedness.[14] Jason Throop (2009, 546) has argued something similar with his notion of "co-suffering." Through empathic processes, people can experience the suffering of others through which they can reassure their moral being. Co-suffering is thus not the same as consubjective suffering. The variations of guilt I detected in Argentina revealed both empathic processes: a form of co-feeling of guilt through which one reassures moral being, and the consubjective experience of guilt that made one part of the guilt.

Guilt obliges Argentinians to repeatedly make compensations through truth sharing and remembrance. In phenomenological terminology, they were continuously engaged in ethical performances. Their ongoing practice of sharing and analyzing uncomfortable feelings and excavating truth about the atrocities problematizes the notion of a liminal period of ethical performance that would reinstate the unreflective moral disposition (i.e., home) of everyday life. Luis and Matilda's ethical dilemmas concerning the 1970s were not liminal; instead they were perfectly interwoven in their everyday lives.

Ethnographic analysis of the complexity of guilt in this post-conflict situation shows an ongoing jumble of trauma and reflection. I believe that this is where anthropological insight into experience and morality itself appears, and where we can start to identify certain conditions under which categories of experience come into being, are perpetuated, contested, or transformed (Zigon and Throop 2014, 4). For people like Matilda and Luis, engaging with ethical dilemmas is not a problem that must be solved so as to return to the unreflective moral disposition called "home." Engaging with moral breakdowns and performing ethics is an inherent aspect of being alive. The traumatic home, in this sense, produces the so-called Heideggerian paradox of a *reflective* moral disposition in everyday consciousness. This paradox of being home, while ethically performing, is also reflected in ongoing truth seeking about the atrocities of the dictatorship in Argentina.

IN SEARCH OF TRUTH

During the junta years, people in Argentina were not supposed to denounce the atrocities that were being committed. The military junta tried to implement a social imposition of silence and isolation (Hollander 1992, 285). It is even said that during the last Argentinian dictatorship "sharing" became equivalent to "danger" (Puget 2002). After the regime fell apart, the so-called military pact of silence remained intact. In contexts of secret state repression and legal impunity for human rights violations, evidence on which to make credible accusations is often insufficient (Wilson 1997c, 141–142). Truth obviously matters in ending impunity (Sanford 2012, 368–369). I believe that this structural presence of the unknown is fundamental in understanding how truth seeking can become a vital moral project in victims' everyday lives. Many victims in Argentina consider their truth-sharing practices as important contestations of the silence imposed by the repressive regime. With military officers still being silent about the whereabouts of the bodies and children, this project will always be incomplete.

Important underlying rationales on the recovery of truth stem from the belief that truth regarding the perpetrated violence should engender consciousness and prevent future violence. Particularly in countries where authoritarian regimes have perpetrated atrocities in secrecy, such as in various Latin American and African countries, truth inquiries have often been given preference in the local transitional justice landscapes because in many cases amnesties were granted for the perpetrators or pardons were issued (Hinton 2010, 3–4; Wilson 2001). The South African Truth and Reconciliation Commission is a renowned example of this. The title of the truth commission report *Nunca Más* (Never Again) of the National Commission on the Disappearance of Persons (CONADEP) is perhaps the most well-known Argentinian product of this truth rationale. The report's title belongs to a post-Holocaust ethos that not only recognizes the suffering of the victims but also asserts empathic connections to them and a moral desire to act (Hinton 2016, 26).[15] I detected similar moral desire among various survivors and relatives in Argentina, such as Isola Hernandez.

Isolda went into exile in Venezuela in 1978. After more than thirty years, she returned to Argentina. During my time in the field, we often spoke about her *militancia* (activism), her time in prison, and her enforced exile. As with other survivors, Isolda frequently talked about this traumatic past and her personal guilt for having left the country. She believed it had taken more than thirty years to reach an extensive (and nuanced) understanding of what had happened to her and all the other victims during the repression of the 1970s. Isolda frequently spoke about the court testimonies, written testimonies and novels of survivors she had been reading or listening to, films and documentaries she had watched, and the new sites of memory and exhibitions she had visited. She also pointed out what I really had to see, read, or visit. She continually absorbed these stories of survival and disappearance, and she also kept a diary and wrote fictional stories about the violence. During an interview, Isolda reflected on this infinite stream of traumatic stories in her life. She explained that the last dictatorship was not part of a remote history, but part of the absolute present.[16] She was amazed that she continued listening to these horrifying stories and never felt indifference: "It is not like: well, I have heard it so many times . . . No. It is rather the opposite. I keep looking and looking. In a sense, I believe that I am looking for answers to [questions like]: 'Why did it all happen?' 'How did I get involved?' This search is just part of my life."

Isolda explained that it was very difficult to understand what had happened during these years but, by joining with other survivors and relatives, all moved toward more nuanced understandings. Isolda thought that their ongoing search for *verdad* (truth) was more than a *denuncia* (accusation). Their search for truth was *un canto a la vida* (a hymn to life).

The notion of a permanent and unachievable desire to know clearly echoed in Isolda's ongoing search for understanding about the atrocities. For people like Isolda, this everyday truth seeking and analysis were morally comforting practices—common ways of engaging with a social world of denial and silence. It was considered immoral to stop searching for the truth about the atrocities and the traumas. Put differently, failing to reflect would imply indifference, and that would make her life meaningless, and even nonhuman.

After more than thirty-five years, multiple truth practices and truth productions about the last dictatorship in Argentina are still widespread: forensic anthropologists excavate anonymous graves. Former detention centers are turned into sites of memory, and official memorials are constructed. Family members place memorial stones at street corners where their loved ones lived or were last seen. Libraries and bookshops have large sections on the disappeared and the last dictatorship. Court employees and personnel of local human rights organizations collect legal testimonies at the tribunals. There is a National Bank of Genetics that collects the DNA of family members of the disappeared in order to locate illegitimately appropriated children. People store and exhibit newly found pictures in national databases along with recordings and objects of the disappeared. Museums also dedicate exhibitions to the disappeared, and theaters and cinemas offer plays, films, and documentaries about the violence of the 1970s and early 1980s. There is even a niche in Argentinian music that voices the country's violent past. In general, the social life of victims is marked by this heightened alertness to truth about the state repression of the 1970s.

Their truth seeking has been more than a practice to prevent violence from breaking out anew. Robben (2005, 317) rightly points out that especially with the experience of disappearing people, the recovery of truths about what happened helps victims to cope with trauma and distrust. In this same line of reasoning, Robben (2018) has recently argued that reframing the atrocities in Argentina in terms of "genocide" further helps victims to cope with unresolved mourning. It nevertheless remains unclear why ongoing truth seeking helps Argentinian victims cope with trauma. In my view, the shared ethical performances of figuring out and working through traumas from the 1970s are part of an everyday moral disposition that favors reflexivity. Victims' ongoing searches and contemplations regarding these difficult times are not temporary ethical considerations in moments that shake one out of the everydayness of being moral (Zigon 2007, 136–137). The ongoing ethical considerations constitute victims' everydayness of being moral. It is intrinsically unrealizable for victims in Argentina to fully uncover the truth about the atrocities, not only because those responsible are silent or dead but also because they have a psychoanalytical understanding of self with "unnamable holes." Their everyday moral life becomes meaningful and familiar through these ongoing ethical performances.

As mentioned, the ongoing verbalizations and analysis were not restricted to a therapeutic sphere, and these practices did not belong to liminal times and separate spaces. Rather, there was a sliding scale from formal counseling sessions between therapist and patient, to more everyday forms of free association and working through at home, at a memorial site, at a bar, at court, or at other places where people meet. This not only constitutes trauma as an unquestionable moral category, it also shows how trauma can produce a way of engaging with and in the world where home, moral breakdown, and ethical performances are not separate stages of everydayness and liminality; instead, they form one meaningful totality. This "paradox" is played out on multiple social levels and largely explains, why next to a lifetime of impunity and denial, justice is an ongoing moral project without closure in Argentina.

EVERYDAY THERAPY

I witnessed many Argentinians during their "everyday therapies," but never as clearly as during the times I spent with Ana Luisa Campos. Ana Luisa is a woman in her early sixties. Her brother disappeared in the late 1970s and, like her recently deceased mother, Ana Luisa spent a great deal of her time with people who had undergone similar experiences. The first time I met her, she immediately told me that when other relatives of the disappeared began placing stones in the streets of Buenos Aires, she also placed a memorial stone for her disappeared brother. The next time we met, Ana Luisa gave me a copy of the recording of the day that the memorial stone was cemented on her brother's former apartment. Ana Luisa explained that a friend had digitalized her brother's diary and the scarce information that was available about his disappearance. She appeared very pleased when she told me that the information was copied onto a DVD and made available to the wider public.

Ana Luisa and I often talked about the testimonies we heard in court, and about how she dealt with her painful past on an everyday basis. Ana Luisa reflected movingly on her recent experiences, which she always related to the disappearance of her brother and her deceased mother, who used to walk at the Plaza de Mayo. Once Ana Luisa recounted casually that she was reading a Spanish translation of Paul Ricoeur's (2004) work *Memory, History, Forgetting* with her weekly reading group, composed of relatives of the disappeared. Ana Luisa thought that the reading and discussing of

Ricoeur with other victims had unveiled important uncertainties about their traumatic pasts.

We often discussed problems that arose from listening to the testimonies in court, which had affected our dreams, relationships, and even our appetites. But oddly, we never experienced these talks as disturbing. It appears that being together in these ethical considerations becomes comforting, almost as if it were good to feel hurtful and confused.

After a long period of not seeing each other, Ana Luisa and I arranged to meet at her home during my third field trip in 2012. When Ana Luisa opened the door of her apartment, she told me she had invited Blanca Capellini as well. Because Blanca's brother had also disappeared, Ana Luisa thought it would be good for all of us if she joined in. I feared that Blanca's presence would obstruct an intimate conversation with Ana Luisa, but nothing was farther from the truth. The common idea that self-analysis concerning traumatic experiences is a private matter did not apply in urban Argentina. Self-analysis is a profound social activity.

Ana Luisa and Blanca talked freely that afternoon about what happened after the disappearance of their brothers. Neither woman married, nor had children. Both their mothers walked at Plaza de Mayo and, after their mothers had died not so long ago, Ana Luisa and Blanca continued the struggle of their mothers. They reasoned that what they and their mothers had really missed was mourning. Ana Luisa then paraphrased Freud saying that only when the bodily remains are returned can people start to accept the emptiness caused by the loss of a loved one. For that reason—not having received or buried their brothers' remains—the women indicated that they had never begun the crucial process of mourning.

Blanca said she had also recently placed a memorial stone in front of her brother's high school to inform the next generation about his disappearance. She noted that she had also made a short film containing the little information she possessed about his disappearance. Ana Luisa alerted Blanca to the new archives about the disappeared at Parque de la Memoria, a well-known memorial site in Buenos Aires. She suggested that Blanca send the archive a copy of her brother's story. Blanca told us that she always tried to do everything she could to provide information about her brother's disappearance.

We discussed all their traumatic life events, but rather than feeling depressing our conversation was warmhearted and comforting as we shared tea and biscuits. Without hesitation, Ana Luisa and Blanca both mentioned that it was enormously beneficial to talk about their traumatic pasts. They said that silence sickened, and although the traumatic memories were very painful, sharing them was highly reparative. They revealed that through the constant incorporation of new information they were able to reach vital new understandings. Ana Luisa and Blanca believed that it helped them live more fully day by day. Blanca even said, while smiling, that the conversations kept her head in the right place. It was more than these conversations with other relatives and survivors though: Blanca explained that every time she spoke about her traumatic memories, when she read something, saw something, or heard something related to their traumatic past, it always clarified and repaired something (as if it had filled a hole).

Ana Luisa and Blanca were not the only people to think this way. As mentioned in previous sections, everyday psychoanalytical practices such as "working through" and "catharsis" were normal practices in Argentina. For Argentinians, this ongoing social therapy utterly merges truth sharing and the self-analysis of difficult feelings into everyday life. Conversely, a shared psychoanalytical worldview problematizes certain practices—including "resistance" and "denial"—when the unconscious and the uncomfortable are left unspoken and unanalyzed.

A conversation with three young Argentinian psychologists in their office was educational. They recounted that victims of state repression sometimes refused to talk about their traumatic experiences before they had to testify. In their opinion, it was impossible to testify without psychological guidance and it was a clear example of "resistance" and "self-defense." I was not able to join these therapeutic sessions with future witnesses. Nevertheless, we did participate together in a group session, which was a thought-provoking meeting focused on local meanings of survival, testimonies, and collaboration that illustrated how truth practices, variations of guilt, and ongoing social therapy tangibly shape their engagement with and in the world.

In 2010 I entered a large consultancy room at the office of a local nongovernmental organization (NGO) that works with victims of state violence. Before the group meeting, they had asked me to read a Spanish translation of the *Remnants of Auschwitz: The Witness and the Archive* (Agamben 2000), in which Giorgio Agamben expands Levi's (1989) argument that the saved (the survivors of the Holocaust) must speak for the drowned (the dead) and the inherent inability to adequately narrate the experiences of death. He traces this complicated relationship between witnessing atrocities and giving testimony, which according to Agamben only exists in the potentiality of the unsaid. The people of the NGO had informed me that *lo que queda* (i.e., what remains) would guide our thoughts for the group meeting. Besides the staff members and two psychology students, there were also two women whose relatives had disappeared. After a short introduction, one woman said that she read Agamben during the holidays, and everyone laughed with admiration because she had read the dense philosophical reading in her free time. This unforeseen laughter generated a more open atmosphere that continued throughout the afternoon and set in motion a form of shared free association.

A staff member thought that the book was about inventing a new ethic after Auschwitz. Agamben's writing on testimonies regarding the concentration camps taught her that a testimony is not only about what is said but also about what is not said. The woman was critical of Agamben's notion of the impossibility of verbalizing what happened though. She disliked its implication that the Holocaust was something mystical. Everyone that afternoon agreed that the disappeared provided the truest testimony of all, and Agamben's mysticism was therefore not appreciated in light of their absence. The tangible absence of *los desaparecidos* in the world gave voice to what was real terror to those left behind. By no means had their absence represented a potentiality of the *un*said.

The criticism of Agamben acted as a trigger for one male staff member. He reacted immediately and said that he did not like the parts of Agamben's book pervaded by the suggestion that victims were perpetrators. He confessed that reading it produced many uncomfortable memories. In response, a woman remembered the story of a victim who fell in love with her torturer during illegal detention. The group member was not pleased that the woman was now considered a victim. She reasoned that the woman was a clear collaborator and did not deserve a trial. A younger staff member responded that another ex-detainee had recently been indicted for collaboration during a current trial for crimes against humanity, but she thought that such accusations should not occur. She felt that it blurred boundaries between victims and perpetrators even more.

Another woman, who had been silent until then, joined the conversation. She recounted that she had just remembered the collective testimony of several female survivors in another book. She recalled that she became very angry while reading it. "How could these women get so involved with their torturers?" she asked indignantly. Another reason that reading Agamben made her angry, she said, was that he did not value witnesses' words. This woman believed that analyses such as Agamben's made the concept of violence too abstract, which was regrettable in view of concrete experiences at Auschwitz and the clandestine detention centers in Argentina. A younger staff member recalled a recent documentary on the trials for crimes against humanity in the federals courts in Argentina. She viewed it with several victims, but she did not like it. It bothered her that survivors in the documentary tried to explain why they had collaborated. She explained her feeling of deep discomfort watching innocent victims trying to validate their survival in the detention centers.

After two hours, I asked if the group believed that survivors could speak for the disappeared. Most seemed to agree that survivors can and do speak on behalf of the disappeared. The people at the meeting said they felt that they were indebted to the disappeared and that was the main reason for the current trials aimed at prosecuting crimes against humanity. Then, we all said a friendly good-bye, and one woman expressed very earnestly that she would like to reflect on the issue of guilt at the next monthly meeting.

The Franco-Argentinian psychoanalyst Janine Puget (2002) describes similar processes during her collective therapeutic sessions in the mid-1980s with Argentinian survivors of torture. Although the session in which I participated was almost thirty years later, I was struck by the similarities between the group sessions. Puget describes in detail how contemporary everyday political and social events disturbed the victims, which thus required reflection and subsequently offered insights into previous traumatic experiences. Puget also discusses how, after a violent discussion, one group member said that although he had feared being ejected from the session for being too aggressive, afterward he felt comforted and lighter.

TRAUMATIC HOME

As noted earlier, I gradually began to realize that the legacies of impunity, apathy, and denial—together with all these ongoing verbalizations and reflections on the traumas inflicted during state repression—had a profound effect on the ways in which many Argentinian victims experience moral life on a daily basis. Trauma was central to their lifeworld. The last accounts on "everyday therapies" tie together how ongoing speech and analysis about enduring traumas produce what I have called traumatic home. This means that Argentinian victims are at home in a familiar world that embraces a reflective moral disposition. This underlying everyday morality has been largely ignored in the understanding of Argentina as the "justice cascade" and an important contributor to global trends in transitional justice practices (Sikkink 2010; Sikkink and Booth-Walling 2006). To be able to explain the meanings and everyday workings of suffering in conflict-ridden societies I believe this epistemological "step back" from moral experience is fundamental. Such an analysis can connect us with the multiple ways in which transitional justice is experienced.

The concept of traumatic home not only allows one to rethink the role trauma plays in influencing the way people experience transitional justice practices, it also provides empirical insight regarding the ontological implications of experience. As explained earlier, according to Heidegger (1978, 105), "Being" is revealed once something goes wrong and one is forced to reflect on the breakdown of implicit meaning. Everyday consciousness becomes temporarily interrupted. Zigon's (2007, 140) argument that it is considered good to have accomplished a return to the unreflective moral disposition follows this logic. For many Argentinian victims, as the stories here have shown, it is exactly the opposite—an unreflective moral disposition is unethical. In its place, ongoing ethical performances are considered to be moral, or human for that matter. This is not to say that ethics and morality are identical in Argentinians' everyday lives; the traumatic home simply operates differently; being together in the ethical moment is their everyday moral disposition. The meanings and expectations of transitional justice practices as closure or movement away from the atrocities, like the trial for crimes against humanity, become utterly problematic, or even impossible from this moral stance.

Some might argue that Argentinian victims reside in a permanent state of moral breakdown due to the traumatic experiences of the last dictatorship. On the contrary, I reject this argument because it would undermine Argentinians' familiarity with trauma in their daily encounters. Despite being disturbing, their traumas are also important sources of everyday moral comfort and produce a reflective way of engaging with and in the world.

CHAPTER 5

Disgrace

IN 2007 THE RETIRED lieutenant colonel Ignacio Domín-guez had been prosecuted for crimes against humanity, including having carried out multiple torture sessions and the assassination of a detainee in prison. He stood trial at the federal court in Córdoba. At the court hearings Ignacio felt like a "circus clown" and he deeply questioned the legitimacy of the judges.[1] As mentioned in chapter 2, the indicted military officers and their kin called the trial for crimes against humanity a circus, metaphorically articulating their criticism of the legitimacy and credibility of the human rights politics of the Kirchner administration. Their critiques and concerns were not exclusively motivated by the threat of life imprisonment. What bothered the officers was the public character of the trial. The retired colonel Alfonso Palacios felt that their military honor was completely in tatters: "They drag you handcuffed and treat you as a criminal. They push you in jail and undress your wife to frisk her as if you are an ordinary criminal. It is humiliating."[2] The current "ironic" role of the state as the final arbiter of previous state terrorism was also criticized. Such double standards represented a despicable act of betrayal.

In December 2010, Ignacio declared for the last time in court that he never felt responsible or guilty for the crimes of which he was accused. He stated: "I have the boundaries between loyalty and complicity very clear." Another indicted officer addressed his final words to various victims who had repeatedly criticized the officers for their lack of remorse; the indicted officer explained that feeling remorse was impossible and that expressing atonement would be synonymous with culpability. This double bind of victims' desire for atonement and officers who were incapable of feeling remorse stayed on my mind for quite some time.

Ex-general Videla, the former head of the junta, was also one of the indicted officers standing trial in Córdoba. Videla justified on general terms the repressive methods of the armed forces between 1976 and 1983. His declaration was in line with previous statements about the just war theory and Christian notions of the need to restore the natural order, which the junta had used to justify their state repression. It was not the first time Videla confronted punishment. He had been prosecuted and sentenced to life for the disappearances at the junta trial in 1985 and in 1998 at the trial for the appropriation of minors.[3] In contrast to the previous silence in court (Graziano 1992, 226), this time Videla acknowledged in person that some irregularities and mistakes had taken place in "this imprecise war." Although these were difficult to justify, they had been the result of unconventional subversive warfare, he said. Again Videla did not express atonement for the atrocities he had ordered. Before his closing words on God's justice, harmony, and reconciliation, Videla simply congratulated his subordinates who were currently being prosecuted for their loyalty, except one sergeant: "Sergeant Molina is an *inoperante* [incompetent]."

THESE STATEMENTS OF innocence and loyalty before the verdict were quite predictable. Only a handful of Argentinian officers have publicly atoned for the killings, disappearances, and tortures. Nonetheless, Videla's last words on the "messy" warfare were still newsworthy in Argentina. The local dailies wrote at length about his renewed justification for the violence perpetrated. Videla's palpable lack of remorse was also a great concern in the local media.[4] Among the victims his official declaration again underlined the cruelty of the regime.[5] The officer's explanation opposing atonement and Videla's curious attack on Molina seemed unimportant in light of the crimes that were being prosecuted and were not addressed in the media. But what had Molina done that he needed to correct before the final verdict? Only one small article published in a popular daily described what Molina had done a few weeks before. During a court hearing, the sergeant had asked forgiveness for his involvement in the assassination of an illegal detainee at a detention center.[6] Had Videla called him incompetent for this? Had Molina somehow let his men down by making this public atonement?

At the court victims repeatedly demanded truth and remorse from the indicted officers. But most of the officers kept silent and emphasized their innocence. This lack of remorse from perpetrators is often explained based on the argument that it is simply engendered by retributive justice and also poses an obstacle to truth finding (Bloomfield, Barnes, and Huyse 2003, 104; Payne 2008, 5). In my opinion, this elucidates only to a certain extent why many military officers in Argentina have not made public atonement. Betrayal and the absence of remorse in the courts in Argentina tell a moral story that differs from only strategic considerations aimed to circumvent punishment based on the risk of self-incrimination and the defendant's right to remain silent during court hearings.[7] The key to this lack of remorse was also not merely the assumption that military personnel are machines that are incapable of feeling.

Besides a firm belief in the legitimacy of the violent acts condoned by the state, the nonadmission of guilt in court and prison was also connected with various ways in which the military in Argentina experienced morality on a daily basis. Surprisingly, for officers like Ignacio, atonement would be an act of betrayal. This abandonment of institutional loyalty toward the military in Argentina has been a true disgrace for decades (Miguens 1986, 17). Everyday military principles of loyalty and silence can help us make sense of how justice for state repression (and its lack) comes into being in Argentina. In our theorizing, we often tend to look at the unfamiliar to make sense of military life. But the understanding of everyday military moralities materializes not only in its differences with civilian principles (or oddities to the ethnographer) but also in its (sometimes uncomfortable) similarities (Van Roekel, forthcoming). Military morality is not composed by one regime of truth, but is also a moral messiness.

JUST WAR

Contemporary Argentinian history is laced with frequent, prolonged intervals of military rule. Civilian rule and military dictatorship alternated in cycles of violence (Robben 2005). A militarized society in the first part of the nineteenth century played an important role in establishing strong ties between the armed forces and the emerging nation-state.[8] As in many other Latin American countries, the military as an institution had been central to the formation of national identity and citizenship in Argentina, where, until the early 1980s, joining the military was highly valued (Potash 1971; Rouquié 1983). The polished boots, the impeccable uniform, and the short military haircut were important cultural manifestations of a privileged class (Van Roekel and Salvi, forthcoming). The military lifeworld was one of elite advantage and power.

Beginning in the 1930s, Argentina underwent various military coups and governments that owed their office to the sword rather than the ballot (Verbitsky 2005, 193). Military regimes' hostilities toward civilian rule, its union-busting tactics, and even the efforts to silence any expression of dissent and free speech were not new to Argentinians, but the scale of terror that accompanied the junta policies of the 1970s was new (Brennan 2018, 19). The Argentinian military played a decisive role in politics and nation building, but it also had a mythical role in society as the "ultimate savior" in turbulent times. Argentinian military officers became the "Church's soldiers," who fought against the enemies of Christ. From this perspective, brutal military intervention was the only adequate way to save the fatherland from internal enemies, such as communist threats. It was believed that the spread and implementation of such ideologies would cause the country to fall into permanent chaos and disorder. Brutal military actions against guerrilla warfare were therefore seen as necessary actions to maintain the natural order and manifestations of loyalty, obedience, and professionalism that were endorsed and sanctioned by members of the Catholic Church (Badaró 2009, 78). The Argentinian commanders believed that they had the constitutional right *and* duty to defend Argentina's cultural heritage (Robben 2005, 179–185). The enemy could be an armed guerrilla, but also "someone who spreads ideas which are contrary to Western and Christian civilization." The elasticity of these terms made everyone suspicious in the early 1970s and further reinforced the righteousness of a (imagined) moral crusade in all quarters of society (Graziano 1992, 126). Anyone could be *chupado* (sucked up) by the regime.

Theories of just wars and moral crusades during unconventional wars and internal conflict are not uncommon in military life.[9] But the entanglement of mysticism and counterinsurgency among the Argentinian armed forces in the 1970s was remarkable. The junta ideology was entrenched in Christian ideas of the natural order in which the absence of unity was perceived as a true defect that needed to be corrected at all times. From this perspective, (violent) disagreement and strife were not inevitable liberal practices that constituted a political community, but dangerous flaws of humankind that required correction. Keywords within this unity doctrine were "peace," "harmony," and "obedience." God's creation was the ultimate manifestation of this natural order, and the source of any disorder (such as "subversion") was a sinful disruption that needed to be overcome (Graziano 1992, 110). This allowed any violent intervention to be justified based on God's law.

For decades the "just war" theory in the Argentinian armed forces clearly guided the shared belief that nothing the military did was evil because it was in accordance with (or in protection of) this natural order. The Argentinian military junta simply modernized these formulations in the 1970s: preservation of the natural order meant eliminating "subversion," which became firmly established as a key military responsibility. All concerns about ethics, human rights, due process, constitutional hierarchies, and division of power were simply subordinated to this urgent moral crusade (Graziano 1992, 110–111). From this perspective, torture and disappearance were not evil, but—in a perverse twist of reasoning—acts of virtuousness. As in the mid-1980s, many middle-rank officers still believed that their successful performance during the repression reinforced their honor and their image as good soldiers (Waisbord 1991, 164). Not *genocidas* (genociders) but "sacrificial lambs" had been wrongfully prosecuted in Argentina's courts. Many still believed that they possessed the right and obligation to make decisions for the masses. This heroic self-identification has largely become anachronistic and is shared by hardly anyone in Argentina today (Van Roekel and Salvi, forthcoming).

Forty years later, however, the ideals of "harmony," "sacrifice," and "obedience" still echoed in many of my conversations with indicted officers and their kin in Argentina. They were "political prisoners" as well as victims of the last dictatorship (Salvi 2012).[10] Besides a strategic play to circumvent accountability, acknowledgment of the victim-perpetrator seems to indicate a general approval of the attractive idea that something of the human resists all forms of moral destruction (Fassin and Rechtman 2009, 97). The victimization of perpetrators, by themselves or others, recognizes that they too suffer because of the atrocious acts and dismisses the existence of evil in what it means to be human. Such a view rejects the possibility that we can be monsters.

During my conversations with the indicted officers "just war" and processes of victimization only somewhat explained why many military officers were not feeling guilty about the crimes they had committed. Their rejection of accountability and remorse was a jumble of additional reasoning and other feelings. By getting close to several indicted officers and their kin, I noticed that there were cracks in their narratives of the divine and privileged role of the military in Argentinian society and their new status as victims of the dirty war. The many silences and euphemisms I observed in private spheres were entangled with disquiet and trouble. Other stories and alternative explanations emerged, which only provided moments of moral comfort to their unease.[11] They were reluctantly aware that they were no longer a powerful and untouchable elite, but unbecoming officers with demoted status in society and the armed forces (Van Roekel and Salvi, forthcoming). I believe it is necessary to analyze the way these military officers perceived what they did in relation to what was valuable to them (Tudor 2001, 142)—not by embracing one value, but by looking at multiple relations, values, and ideals to elucidate why they seldom atone for what they did.

Years of military training and combat shape alternative ways of engaging with and in the world (see chapter 2). Militarism as a model for behavior has experiential logics that take different local forms, while still displaying fundamental underlying similarities such as patriotism, esprit de corps, and due obedience (Gusterson 2007, 165). Among the (mostly) retired military officers who stood trial in Argentina, this militarist model of self had survived. I am well aware that these men were more than well-trained officers or devoted members of a moral crusade. The indicted officers were fathers and husbands who lived in the midst of many individuals who continued to tell them that what the military did was right, and also sometimes kept their secrets (Natarajan 2018, 309). Political ideologies and everyday military moralities opposing atonement and revealing information about the atrocities clearly transcended the logics of their barracks and their (spiritual) battlefields.

During my fieldwork with the indicted officers I became part of closed-off sociomilitary circles that held quite conservative ideas on class, family, gender, and the Catholic faith (Waisbord 1991, 161).[12] These moral codes were very distinct from the moral standards held among victims and human rights activists, which ambiguously embraced incompleteness and chaos in their intentions to live a good life. As argued in chapter 4, everyday moral practices and ideals are not constituted by one regime of truth, but rather draw on the uneasy coexistence of everyday moralities (Mattingly 2014, 8). Moral experience from a military perspective is also an uneasy coexistence of everyday moralities that embrace harmony, loyalty and obedience, recognition, and silence. Disgrace emerges when officers systematically do not (or cannot) meet these values, ideals, and convictions.

Ignacio's Tears

One austral summer morning in 2010 I joined Aldo Domínguez for another prison visit to his brother Ignacio. After a thirty-minute drive northwest, we entered the military base. Alongside the road a new cohort of soldiers was marching fast in strict file. Spacious green meadows alternated with the old-fashioned military barracks. In the meantime, Aldo was telling me that the military prison was formerly used for disobedient rank-and-file soldiers or for military officers who had committed crimes violating the code of military justice. After his participation in the military uprisings against the former trials of military personnel during the second half of the 1980s, Aldo also served time in this prison. I could hear in the way he spoke that he was proud of his actions. Now the prison was fully occupied by military officers who were indicted or convicted for torture, assassination, disappearance, and the appropriation of babies.

As we turned our car onto the sandy trail, two young military officers stopped us. They saluted Aldo with a slightly pleased look on their faces; I could see they knew each other, but strict military protocol limited their enthusiasm. They inspected the trunk and our papers, and everything seemed fine. Aldo had previously explained that this prison had rather lenient visiting hours as well as frisk policies that were more polite compared to those at civilian prisons. Besides shortages of prison cells, the argument by which the indicted officer-prisoners were transferred to these more lenient prisons was their older age and need for more medical attention. Not only convicted officers older than seventy or those with medical problems were incarcerated in the military prison. Ignacio, in his mid-fifties, was still in good health, as the last time we met.

After parking the car under the trees in a nice green setting, we walked toward the one-story building that looked a bit like a *finca* (farmhouse).

Ignacio and his wife Valeria were standing outside waving behind the wire fence. After the lenient security checks, Aldo greeted his brother affectionately and continued saluting other inmates. The cells were grouped around a canteen-like space. Many cell doors were open, allowing inmates and family to walk in and out freely. Crowded with family and friends, a buzz filled the large room. The tables were loaded with food and drinks. When I first arrived, most of the men and women were slightly hostile, but after Aldo's charming introduction they accepted my presence.

Because all the tables were taken, the Domínguez family headed toward the fenced garden. Ignacio was already busy arranging seats and drinks. His grandson was playing with a plastic gun. His wife Valeria lit the candles on a birthday cake. Valeria explained that although they had already had a party at home, they wanted to celebrate their granddaughter Carolina's birthday with her grandfather. They sang two birthday songs and Carolina blew out the candles. Everyone shouted, "Happy birthday!" They looked happy for an instant, but soon Ignacio and Aldo became absorbed in dense talk about politics and the current trials. Family life continued behind the wire fence in ways similar to home. The women were cleaning up and the children were playing in the garden.

As an anthropologist interested in the "political prisoners" I was able to join the male conversation that afternoon. Ignacio said that there were few novelties. His lawyer had told him that the judges were deliberately delaying the proceedings. Ignacio was convinced that the judges knew that what they were doing was wrong, but they did it anyway. He did not say why, as if this were a tacit truth we all shared, but I was unaware of it. When asked what he had been doing here besides waiting, Ignacio said that he was taking his prison days like an army cadet in the old days: "We have a strict and demanding routine: we get up early, do some sports, and drink *mate* (herbal tea) together. After lunch we do another round of exercises and around 18:30 we play cards, have dinner, and go to bed. The days pass quickly, very quickly."

Ignacio's prison stories were often persuasive in presenting a likable image of a man who was being prosecuted for crimes against humanity. He seemed well aware that it was difficult to undo known evidence of throwing people alive out of airplanes to let them drown, or torturing people with *picanas* (electric prods) to orifices—facial to genital. Like Ignacio, many indicted officers often had persuasive monologues aimed at convincing me, the "Dutch anthropologist," that they were actually very decent military men. They all said that they had fought a war for a just cause, and they all believed that they were illegally incarcerated. One officer once asked rhetorically: "How can it be possible that Ignacio and I were sent to Croatia with the UN Blue Helmets, received several military decorations, and now we are seen as the worse criminals?"

Other officers gave copies of their court declarations, and they showed pictures of their families. As an officer's wife looked at the picture of a happy family event, she asked: "Does this look like a torturer, a monster?" Their stories provided quite a different version from that I was receiving in the courts, the media, and the shocking testimonies of the victims. That afternoon in prison Ignacio also remembered something else that had happened the previous Monday: "It was around noon and we suddenly heard a band playing military marches. They played the hymn of the march of *San Lorenzo* just outside our pavilion on the other side of the fence. We all headed towards the fence and listened. I could not withhold my tears, Eva; it was incredible."

Again I was enveloped in a tacit truth that I did not understand. Assuming wrongly that he was trying to say that he felt sorry in some way, I asked Ignacio why he had cried. Ignacio replied that listening to military marches encouraged him, and particularly *San Lorenzo* always kept up his morale, he said. "It makes us always feel really proud; imagine listening to them in here!" The melodies brought back memories of being a soldier and expressed a kind of nostalgia that gave Ignacio a boost of energy. Ignacio's account of his unexpected tears deeply surprised me; much more than the repetitive stories of glory of having saved the country from chaos. I was even more surprised that he had been so eager to share it with me. Was he trying to convince me of the imagined injustice that had befallen him? Or was he trying to explain something else to me?

An attempt to understand perpetrators may be seen as a form of justification, but if we want to understand the extremes of human capabilities we must turn to the "dark territory" of motivations and meanings of those who perpetrate (Clendinnen 1999, 81–82). Although such reciprocal field processes can be deeply uncomfortable (Van Roekel, forthcoming) no matter what their motivations in sharing their life stories are, I agree that we must always try to understand how people experience their lives under the conditions in which they find themselves (Bickford 2011, 95).

REMORSE

There exists a stubborn military myth that soldiers are trained to fully repress negative feelings, to act without any hesitation, and to become like a small cog in a huge machine with the final aim of killing (or being killed) in order to defend the homeland. This rhetoric of emotional repression is still present in many military handbooks. A commonly used Argentinian handbook of the military academy also states that fear, panic, confusion, and loneliness will only interfere with combat; instead physical and emotional resistance is mandatory.[13] Perhaps in moments of fierce combat, or during secret intelligence operations such emotional "lapses" might occur, but these so-called emotional voids are more episodic than permanent. Similarly, those who execute violence would stop thinking. Alexander Hinton (2016, 31), in his work on perpetrators of the Khmer Rouge in Cambodia, has termed this as "thoughtlessness, a failure to think." Perhaps it would also have been easier to imagine the Argentinian indicted officers as thoughtless and emotionally void, but there was abundant reasoning and feeling going on among them. Aldo's repetitive and intense opinions, for instance, about the few military confessions in Argentina regarding the crimes committed during the last dictatorship are worrisome and intriguing at the same time. I think that we should never reduce or take away people's mental capacity. We may not agree with its content or even find it outrageous, but this does not mean it is absent.

Aldo deeply disapproved of the few loose-lipped officers who had spoken about their involvement in the crimes against humanity. I asked him why it was wrong for these men to speak openly about their wrongdoings? It seemed a virtuous thing to do when many victims in Argentina are still urgently looking for answers about their disappeared relatives. But Aldo remained unforgiving of these "hypocritical" fellow officers. Once he said: "A good soldier always obeys, and cannot feel guilty for innocent lives that have been lost."[14] I was startled by the resoluteness of his answer. When I asked him if he thought it was really impossible that an officer could ask for forgiveness, express remorse, and reveal what had happened regarding his actions under orders, Aldo reasoned that it was "unmilitary" to atone. For Aldo, the military officers who had confessed did it for political reasons and personal convenience, as human beings (as if different from military beings) were always full of interests. A good military should suppress this at all times. This military exceptionalism in outstanding (unhuman) behavior was often Aldo's benchmark in judging right from wrong. He was also confident that he would never break down, as had these few officers before the local media or the courts. If he had done something "barbaric" during war that called for remorse, he would never, never repent, he said. "Although things could have been done better [in war], I know of no genuine military that really atones." Remorse was immoral to him. Despite Aldo's continuous efforts to let me into his local moral world, I still had a hard time in making sense of this so-called natural lack of remorse.

Aldo also spoke constantly about *espíritu de cuerpo* (esprit de corps) and the corresponding chain of command. Together with his son Eduardo, who was an active captain in a military tank division, we more thoroughly reflected on responsibility, remorse, and military morals during one late afternoon in a cramped apartment.[15] They talked extensively about *espíritu de cuerpo*. This was the true cohesion that existed within a group: all its members had to fully identify with having the same nature. Noticing my

incomprehension, Aldo compared *espíritu de cuerpo* with a family or an oper-
ating room: "Everyone has the same function, executing different duties but
with the same objective, and everyone knows that success depends on
everyone, and failure is [the] failure of everyone. It is like a body, and if you
lose an arm, the body will not function properly, not even to speak of losing
your head."

A well-functioning military *espíritu de cuerpo* followed a rigid chain of
command. Father and son argued that officers and soldiers, in the heat of
combat when bullets fly, cannot argue with their superiors as to whether
they should or should not fire their guns. They simply follow orders. Their
handbooks and military justice codes even condemned deliberate obstruc-
tion as a betrayal punishable by imprisonment or the death penalty.[16] Guilt
only emerged when one executed wrongly, or as Eduardo explained: "In
the moment of executing an order, your thoughts and actions are for a common good. . . . I will only feel guilty if I did something that I was not
ordered to do."

According to the regulations, their commanders in chief were always
responsible for what was done or not done. After some beers, cigarettes, and
a whiskey our conversation became less formal. I had dropped my mental
list of questions earlier because the conversation was going smoothly. But I
was still not convinced that codes of due obedience, esprit de corps, and the
chain of command were capable of fully ruling out guilt. They also did not
seem to explain why there were troubled undercurrents in conversations
with officers who had fought the war against subversion. I became a bit irritated and I pushed the conversation:

EVA: During the period of subversion there were orders that should not
    have been executed, right?
EDUARDO: It's more about due obedience than guilt. I mean, they may order
    something that I might . . .
EVA: Indeed, when they give you an order . . . that seems inappropriate, do
    you still execute it, or do you enter into a crisis of consciousness?
ALDO: You do not follow, no . . . that makes General Balza a hypocrite and
    a coward!
EDUARDO: No, if it's not good, no . . . what happens is that you are not told
    what the intention or purpose of such an order is . . . then what is the
    parameter to decide [what to do]?
EVA: . . . Can you imagine that there are officers that live today with guilt?
EDUARDO: No, I think not. . . . Can one feel guilty for collateral damage?
    Yes.
ALDO: Sometimes behind collateral damage things are hidden which have
    been evaluated (negatively), but are still executed. . . . You ask us if

these guys feel guilty . . . beyond doubt, in this unconventional war a lot of them took advantage in a context without rules. . . . They deserve to feel guilty, beyond doubt.

The conversation about guilt was a double bind: feeling guilty was possible (even desirable) and was not possible for the militaries that fought the "unconventional war" in the 1970s. Having followed orders would cancel out remorse, being responsible for collateral damage and military wrongdoing were an impetus for guilt. In brutal state repression "without rules," remorse becomes a moral minefield. Competing moralities and parallel frames of reasoning constitute an uneasy emotionality among the military. Everyday morality never follows one regime of truth. Despite acknowledging the moral ambiguities concerning evil orders and remorse, to reaffirm their disapproval of atonement, Aldo and Eduardo fell back on the characteristic confession of Captain Scilingo in our conversation, not as a role model, but as an antitype: "There are examples . . . like Captain Scilingo. He spoke of the death flights; perhaps some things are true. [But] Scilingo got cash for it you know. Repenting afterwards is just too late. [Scilingo] was a corrupt crook before; he did not break down because of guilt."

There are multiple explanations concerning why perpetrators come forward: remorse is only one of them; apologia and heroic justification of the violence and economic reasons in the form of exchange payment may also have triggered confessions from military officers in Argentina (Payne 1999). Not only in my conversation with Aldo and Eduardo did the military confessions provoke strong reactions.[17]

Scilingo's public confession about the death flights hit like a bomb nationwide in the mid-1990s. He had been involved in two death flights and spoke about it with Horacio Verbitsky, a journalist and president of the Center for Legal and Social Studies (CELS), who published the account in the book *El vuelo* (translated in English to *Confessions of an Argentine Dirty Warrior*, 2005). President Menem immediately accused Scilingo of being a criminal, and warned other former torturers and killers to confess to a priest (McSherry 1997, 263). General Balza's mea culpa in the mid-1990s was another antitype. The commander in chief of the army had publicly acknowledged that no officer or soldier was obliged to obey orders that were immoral or that departed from military laws or regulations, indirectly agreeing that the armed forces had systematically exceeded in their use of violence. This acknowledgment met with bitter disapproval in large sectors of the armed forces. Balza's recognition that "blind obedience is unacceptable" was in turn unacceptable to many officers. Army officers were not supposed to take public positions about internal affairs without clearance (McSherry 1997, 265–266; Robben 2005, 419n31). Whatever the reasons may have been for

Balza and Scilingo, to Aldo and Eduardo the officers were the antiheros of the armed forces. Their public stories of remorse and forgiveness were acts of disloyalty.

Aldo and Ignacio also introduced me to the retired colonel Alfonso Palacios. He had been an active military officer between 1976 and 1983, and like Aldo he was not held responsible for crimes against humanity. Despite his retirement, his commitment to the military remained strong. We had lengthy conversations during which he always expressed his preoccupation with the "political prisoners" in military prison. His study was stuffed with books about the subversion of the 1970s, military textbooks, and old catechisms. Alfonso really liked to talk about politics and Argentinian history, especially about the years of political violence, the state repression, and the Malvinas/Falklands War. One afternoon I wanted to talk with him about military ethics and military education.[18] Alfonso gave me a worn dark-blue book he had used in military school more than thirty years ago. During his years as an army cadet his teachers and superiors always directly or indirectly referred to this book, he said. Although our conversations hardly ever became very emotional, I noticed that the book had sentimental value to Alfonso. He had disposed of most of his schoolbooks, but he kept this little handbook, and said: "This is like revealing the psyche of a military. . . . It is the origin of what it means to be a military. It shows that command is not a mere authoritarian act, but that it has an entire system behind it."

This military origin myth elaborated mostly on the chain of command. True command was the action that the superior executed toward his subordinates, aimed to direct, persuade, and influence in such a way as to obtain their voluntary obedience, confidence, respect, loyalty, and active cooperation in the performance and fulfillment of the mission.[19] Another commonly used Argentinian handbook on the chain of command as well as the military justice code also mentioned this naturalness of duty, the superior's responsibility, and obedience.[20] It clearly stated: "If a soldier withdraws from corporate loyalty, he places himself outside the army."[21] Alfonso's handbook also echoed Aldo and Eduardo's interpretations of *espíritu de cuerpo*. It reasoned that esprit de corps was the emotional state of a military organization, which could only be achieved when individuals fully identified with the corporate values, interests, and objectives and adopted them as their own. This unity would make them feel proud and satisfied about shared successes and depressed about shared failures.[22] The handbook stated an explicit list of feelings and physical sensations that were firmly disapproved of, including pain, hunger, fatigue, and fear. Another list stated that trust, faith, discipline, and honor enhanced positive human behavior and military spirit. Remorse and guilt were not mentioned at all in the entire handbook.[23]

Powerful moral myths about military loyalty and due obedience do not provide an unambiguous script for the experience of remorse among the military in Argentina. Militarism does not simply cancel out feelings such as remorse for violence committed under command, it is just spelled out differently.[24] Manifestations and the meanings of remorse always vary in time and space. Nancy Scheper-Hughes (2007, 179–182) offers an interesting overview of (lack of) remorse, diverging from Renato Rosaldo's exploration of a headhunter's rage instead of remorse after violent death, and Colin Turnbell's ethnographic account of the atonement of a Pygmy hunter's excessive greed. Scheper-Hughes's own analysis of how white South Africans make sense of black and colored suffering and the overall lack of remorse by those who orchestrated Apartheid violence further diversifies the meaning of remorse. Such overarching moralities may be significant, but they are definitely not totalizing (Zigon 2008, 163). Years of military training and everyday moral codes had shaped alternative understandings of violence and the self that made the experience of remorse a double bind. But when speaking privately, troubled undercurrents remained, and the officers were often less convinced than some of their superiors about the unconventional methods they had employed during the last dictatorship.

RECOGNITION AND MARGINALIZATION

The Argentinian armed forces formerly belonged to very influential groups, but in the mid-1980s they were progressively pushed to the margins of the state.[25] Since 1983 there has been a substantial antimilitary tendency in Argentinian society, and people have increasingly begun to perceive the armed forces as their enemy and not as their ultimate savior.[26] Many indicted officers, however, still embrace the old principles of militarism, influence, and privilege that no longer fit in the context of their substantial loss of power and social status (see also Bickford 2011, 35). This loss of power and recognition was omnipresent in the military lifeworld.

Medals, insignias, military parades, and honorable burials after death in combat are important military acts of recognition and respect.[27] But such palpable signs of institutional and state recognition were almost absent for the indicted military officers in Argentina. Official acknowledgments for this generation have become very scarce. A decade of several interventions by the national authorities, such as pulling down the paintings of General Videla and General Bignone from the Patio of Honor at the National Military School and expropriating the Higher School of Mechanics of the Navy (ESMA), brought about rather the opposite. The retired navy captain Rafael Arabelleda bitterly disapproved of the *Espacio por la Memoria y para la Promoción y Defensa de los Derechos Humanos* (Space of Memory and for Promotion and Defense of Human Rights) in his former navy school, the ESMA.

Before the school was converted to a notorious illegal detention center in Buenos Aires during the dictatorship, it was a prestigious military school. Rafael always avoided passing the ESMA building; he could not stand to see it anymore. It was a too tangible expression of a long process of sociomilitary decline that began in the 1980s and reached a bitter end with the trials for crimes against humanity. For people like Rafael, turning warfare into crimes against humanity, and patriotic saviors into *genocidas* represented deliberate destruction of the armed forces. As with the trials in the 1980s, the prosecuted officers again felt abandoned by their institutions, their superiors, and the state.

Their demoted status contrasts starkly with the privileged position of the armed forces that lasted for almost two hundred years in Argentina (Frederic 2012, 224–225). (Imagined) recognition of the generation that fought the war against subversion emerged in private or even secret spheres. Besides my being a potential advocate for their cause, my visits also palpably demonstrated to the military that some people out there still wanted to listen to their interpretations of the violence and the current trials. This acknowledgment should not be underestimated. Knowing that there was still interest in their stories implied that they were still considered worthwhile, important players in global military-political affairs (Bickford 2011, 20). I was definitely not the only one visiting the indicted officers in military prison. An Argentinian journalist who published a book on Videla (Reato 2012) also visited the inmates in prison. A former *guerrillero* (guerrilla) also visited the officers. His visits were much appreciated by the indicted officers because he had declared on national television that besides the current prosecutions of military personnel, he too should be detained and prosecuted. Once a Venezuelan right-wing activist also went to military prison. He believed that Cristina Fernández de Kirchner and the now late Hugo Chávez both attacked the traditional values of the Latin American continent with their left-wing politics (see chapter 3). The unexpected military march of *San Lorenzo* also expressed the military attachment to recognition. The melodious expression of acknowledgment resuscitated, at least momentarily, their fallen reputations.

Eduardo and Aldo Domínguez also reluctantly shared their resentment of the declining prestige of the armed forces in Argentina.[28] In discussing it, Eduardo recalled nostalgically the last big military parade in 1991 at Avenida Libertador, a large avenue in Buenos Aires: "[Back then] the streets were full of people. Now such celebrations do not exist anymore. Outside Buenos Aires you might see people still cherish the national flag, but the media only voice the negative military experiences of the 1970s."

Aldo was convinced that this social decline started, more or less, after the Malvinas/Falklands War in 1982: "Since Alfonsín, policies hit hard because of fear and anger for new military coups. . . . [By then] military power was greatly minimized. [Due to political decisions] salary cuts and no new armaments [were provided]." For both father and son, after these financial cutbacks the armed forces lost their capacity to carry out their constitutional missions. They were now unable to protect their homeland. Noting that all this was somehow harmful in a personal sense, I asked them why. They explained that financial and symbolic scarcity run against their military vocation. They had reached rock bottom as a military institution. Aldo admitted reluctantly that the children of generals had told him they felt deeply ashamed of having a father as general, because they had not defended their military institution during the current trials. "If a general is not defending us, who will?" Eduardo asked in response. They both thought that the current absence of their superiors was very dishonorable. The generals should speak up and defend their subordinates who were facing prosecution.

The bitter comments about institutional disgrace have a longer and more complicated history than the silent generals in the courts. During the last dictatorship, the generals of three forces (army, marine, and air force) competed in the pursuit of power, which produced disgraceful fractures in the internal regime; likewise, the junta had not been able to control its subordinates, it had failed in a stable political economy, and on top of all that, it had caused the Malvinas/Falklands defeat for starting a war unprepared.[29] This combination of tremendous and even immoral military flaws had left Argentina's armed forces in tatters. Bitterness about losing both wars, but especially the Malvinas, always lingered in conversations with the officers.

For many officers, the Malvinas/Falklands War was the final blow against the ruling military government (Marchesi 2005, 177). For ten weeks the Argentinian and British forces fought over the archipelago in the South Atlantic. Patriotic sentiment was the last resource of credibility and political legitimacy for the military regime. More than 14,000 poorly trained soldiers with timeworn armaments were transported to the islands. The British forces were much stronger and, on June 14, 1982, Argentina surrendered. The junta saw no option but to hand over power to an interim regime. During the hostilities, 3 islanders, 649 Argentinian soldiers, and 255 British soldiers were killed (Guber 2004, 14). More than 1,000 Argentinian soldiers were wounded. Upon their return they were largely ignored by the Alfonsín regime (Espiniella 2009, 225–226).

In the social and political chaos of the first days of democracy, the legacies of the disappeared weighed much more heavily than the violent defeat by the British. The returning soldiers were not cared for because of participating with the culprits who had caused so much damage and suffering during the illegal state repression. Many soldiers and officers felt doubly devalued—for the state repression and the Malvinas. Soon the Malvinas

War became an "absurd war and its 'glorious soldiers' poor souls abused by their superiors. Neither the state nor society offered them any kind of recognition" (Guber 2008, 124). The Argentinian Federation of Malvinas War Veterans indicates that more than 460 war veterans committed suicide (Espiniella 2009, 220).[30] Malvinas veterans are a small group of retired officers that since 1994 have publicly struggled for recognition and commemoration of the soldiers who were killed and injured.[31] The process of lack of recognition has reinforced a sense of marginalization, betrayal, and disrespect among this generation of officers.

The indicted military officers and Malvinas veterans alone did not experience marginalization and disgrace; their families also lived in these conditions.[32] An unreciprocated desire for recognition transcended the prisons and protest sites. As alternative symbolic acknowledgments of fallen soldiers, veterans and their families are organized in the *Círculo Militar* (Military Circle), the social club for military families in Buenos Aires. Victoria Herrera de Quiroga, for instance, once invited me to a book-launch party at the *Círculo Militar*. An Argentinian historian had written a book on the guerrilla attack on a military barrack in La Tablada in 1989, where Victoria's husband had died in combat. The book voiced a military version of the violent events, and Victoria was invited as a guest speaker. A small crowd of retired military officers, wives, and other interested *porteños* (inhabitants of Buenos Aires) listened quietly to Victoria's emotional account of her husband's death. Afterward, a well-known retired officer spoke on behalf of the men who fell that day, and at the end of his talk, all the men in the audience rose and saluted in honor of the officers who had died in combat. Their voluntary salute was a serious matter.

On a larger scale, at the nearby Plaza San Martin, the National Commemoration of Victims of Terrorism in Argentina is organized since 2005; there the deaths caused by the left-wing attacks during the 1970s are commemorated, while at the same time those who fought against the subversive war are praised for their courage. Besides smaller ceremonies at the *Círculo Militar*, I participated twice in this largest public event among a miscellaneous crowd of military families, supportive conservative right-wing groups, and relatives of victims of terrorism. The military street protests were very different from the human rights rallies I had become familiar with. Once I shared this commemoration with members of *hijos y nietos de presos políticos* (children and grandchildren of the political prisoners), a small activist group composed of those with family ties to the indicted military officers.[33]

Although the event was about the commemoration of the victims of terrorism, the organizers had invited a member of the Association of Lawyers for Justice and Harmony.[34] The middle-aged lawyer made a strong plea criticizing the trials for crimes against humanity and the illegitimate treatment of the political prisoners. After applause and affirmative cheering, several victims spoke about their loss, and the quiet public lit hundreds of candles. The victims covered their faces and carried black-and-white pictures of the soldiers and civilians who had been killed. Speakers blasted folk music with lyrics about the Formosa guerrilla attack in the northern part of Argentina. At the back a screen displayed pictures of guerrilla attacks of the 1970s and pictures of children and civilians killed.

Standing in the crowd listening to several speeches commemorating the victims of terrorism, I asked Federico, whose father was being prosecuted, why they were not wearing their *hijos y nietos* shirts as they had done the year before. Federico replied that the organizers of the annual event ordered them not to wear their shirts because they did not want to merge issues. This event was only for the victims of terrorism, and not for the political prisoners. For Federico and the others it was all the same thing. His friend Consuelo had been less obedient. Her grandfather was being prosecuted, and she was defiantly wearing her *hijos and nietos* T-shirt. Federico warned her, but Consuelo said she did not give a damn. She recounted with a satisfied smile that journalists had even recorded her shirt on camera. After the commemoration, which lasted for two hours, no one lingered on the streets, but dispersed quickly into the neighboring cafés. Consuelo went with some other children to the temporary campsite of the Association of Relatives and Friends of the Political Prisoners of Argentina, another family-based organization for the imprisoned military officers.[35]

This smaller protest at a nearby plaza was principally against the trials for crimes against humanity. For several days, spouses of prosecuted officers had set up a temporary demonstration camp at Plaza de Armas, in front of the Ministry of Defense. Besides some improvised tents and black-and-white pictures of the guerrilla attacks, hundreds of white crosses were placed in the ground to commemorate each officer who had died in prison in past years. The patch of grass looked a bit like a soldiers' war cemetery (see figure 4). Emphasizing their role as housewives and mothers, the women wore aprons depicting the Argentinian flag behind painted black bars, figuratively emphasizing their role as housewives and the injustice that had befallen their husbands. Most of them were very reluctant to talk; only two women acknowledged that they had never imagined protesting like this in public for days, and they emphasized their role as decent military housewives and mothers. Every afternoon two young offers lowered the national flag from the tall flagpole in front of the Ministry of Defense, and folded it carefully. Although the daily ritual was not even remotely related to the indicted officers, all the children and wives at the camp watched straight ahead in silence. These informal and indirect practices of recognition and commemoration restored, in some sense, their fallen reputations.

Figure 4. Indicted officers' symbolic war cemetery, Buenos Aires

Alfonso's Silence

Alfonso Palacios and I had another long talk in his study at home.[36] It was again a persuasive conversation about a just war and the unconstitutionality of the current trials. When finalizing our conversation, Alfonso emphasized once more that in each war, including the Malvinas, there were disappearances:

> Here in Argentina, they really exploited this figure of the disappeared, you know. It somehow has become a death impossible to transcend or recover from. . . . The mothers of soldiers of the [torpedoed] cruiser *General Belgrano* [in the South Atlantic] were never able to bury their sons. . . . After an assault on a bar, mothers could not bury their sons and daughters. The remains of these youngsters were only pieces of flesh and at that moment there was no such thing as DNA identification.

It was not the first time that afternoon that the disappearances came up; only at the end of our conversation did I ask Alfonso about the deliberate practice of disappearances in Argentina. He stumbled over his response: "Well . . . what do I know . . . I do not know . . . I should think this over . . ."

After this short silence—it was not more than a few seconds and a few stumbling words—Alfonso quickly resumed his discussion of the political and economic interests of the figures of the disappeared and the unconventional warfare of the guerrillas in Argentina. Again he justified their military actions that had used the unconventional methods of the guerrilla warfare, which created an irregular warzone that did not respect military law. Alfonso's compelling words about the politics of the disappeared were persuasive, but I noted that his silence had articulated something else.

In Argentina, military officers have hardly ever openly admitted their wrongdoing, even less their involvements in the crimes committed. Within the corporate structure of the armed forces and its frames of fraternity, blame and accountability are hardly ever assumed in person. They are often absolutely silent about it. Such persistent silence can turn the violent past into a "non-event" (Payne 2008, 194). To me, Alfonso's silence did not seem to be deliberate amnesia. He had somehow communicated, without words, a certain discomfort about their military actions. Moreover, Alfonso's stumbling words were not a strategic gap in public discourse (Fijii 2010, 239; Treacher 2007, 291). His unforeseen silence seemed rather a moment of "conflicting feelings" (Sheriff 2000, 117). By probing about the deliberate practice of disappearing opponents, Alfonso accepted that something had been wrong with the functioning of the military institutions since *aquellos años de plomo* (these years of lead). Malfunctioning during the last dictatorship had not only damaged the military institution but also directly affected the officers' sense of self which they rarely put into words.

Silence is not meaningless, and it does not erase violent events from the past. In its multiple forms, silence became an important trope in the understanding of everyday morality among the military. We should not neglect these spaces between words. Silence, however, is often undertheorized, mainly because of Western epistemic perspectives on life, which has affected intellectual attention by drawing it mainly toward speech (Crapanzano 2004, 52–53). Explosive speech that is generated in one sphere may be proportional to silence in another sphere (Sheriff 2000, 128). I am aware that there are many different forms of silences, with different meanings, motivations, and outcomes. Whatever value or strategy is awarded to silence, I believe it is meaningful to analyze it.

Like Alfonso, other officers I spoke with had reluctantly accepted that various "procedures" had gone profoundly wrong between 1976 and 1983. I did not always follow their moral reasoning. Violence can be morally categorized and judged differently from one's expectations. Taking a human life seems to be, at least to me, the worst crime, or at least more immoral than theft. But for officers the assassination of a group of guerrillas was a moral act, but raiding the apartment of a disappeared couple was immoral. I often thought these responses were rhetorical and used as a way to justify their killings. Inga Clendinnen (1999, 91) argues something similar when quoting Himmler in a speech where he states that the slaughter of a thousand men is a decent act, whereas stealing a watch from a corpse is reprehensible. For the indicted officers, rape, torture, and corruption belonged to immoral warfare. These war crimes had to be punished by a military tribunal. Then there was another category of violence that they had perpetrated, which was beyond their moral framework: the military officers I spoke with were unable to explain the disappearances, the death flights, and the appropriation of newborn children. Although they never felt responsible to be formally prosecuted, some officers, like Alfonso, did express disquiet. Corporate shame seemed an important locus to understand the way these officers made sense of these inexplicable atrocities. With the experience of shame—whether individual or collective—one did not do something wrong, but something *is* wrong: one recognizes having fallen short of the moral standards of being. Feeling shame therefore becomes a matter of existential moral foundations that are being thrown into question, rather than being something one has done wrong (Tudor 2001, 186).[37] I believe that moral wrong being is helpful in describing the military lifeworld for the generation of officers that fought the war against subversion.

Shame

In October 2009, the former head of the junta, now late ex-general Videla allowed me fifteen minutes of conversation in prison.[38] I was not a jurist which made the prosecuted general curious about why a Dutch anthropologist was studying the trials for crimes against humanity. His judgments concerning the violence and the trials were a contradictory mixture of just war theory and societal scapegoating. The state repression had been necessary and therefore justified, but at the same time sinful. Videla wanted to emphasize that on March 24, 1976, the Argentinian armed forces overthrew the government of Isabel Perón and assumed power with every intention of exercising it indeterminately, but *with* political consent. Videla still seemed very confident about their violent intervention. He considered Operation Independence, and the subsequent military coup legitimate military actions. He added determinedly: "It was an elected government that issued a decree that handed over power. They knew it would be war . . . they wanted it [war] . . . and big mistakes are made in each war. And I am not talking about a dirty war, all wars are like that."

In our brief conversation, Videla differentiated the junta successes and failures firmly between the military and the political; they had won the military cause, but had lost the political one. He routinely said that he took full responsibility for all that had happened. Again his acknowledgment revealed little affective depth. This overall responsibility for wrongs has little meaning to the victims: nothing was acknowledged in person or clarified concretely. Videla continued that he never gave orders to implement a systematic plan to steal newborn children: "I never gave such an order, it just happened and those men had to do something with it. Only afterwards was it officially decided that they would be adopted. . . . At the time of our legal case that was not important. There were so many accusations of torture, murder and kidnapping. These few babies were not seen as something important at all." Videla further reflected that only years later did the practice of forced adoptions become a systematic plan. He finished by saying that Argentinian society was guilty. When I responded by asking Videla if he thought that the armed forces were the scapegoat, he nodded reservedly in agreement.

In 2012, the Argentinian conservative journalist Ceferino Reato (2012) published his controversial book *Dispoción final: la confesión de Videla sobre los desaparecidos* (Final disposal: Videla's confession about the disappeared). The book is based on twenty hours of interviews in a military prison with the former junta leader. The pages show a similar acknowledgment of military failure in warfare procedures. Videla had experienced the disappearances during the last dictatorship as a "bad aftertaste," and he had therefore chosen to leave a revised version of this past so history could reverse the trouble that was bothering his soul (Reato 2012, 28–32). What was his trouble and why did he desire reversal? In the book, Videla admitted responsibility for four mistakes—the coup itself, the resistance to a political opening, the disappearances, and the institutional failure to delegitimize the systematic plan of child kidnapping (Reato 2012, 205). Besides a contribution to "history," Videla supported the indicted officers on the basis that they were not able to defy orders due to the logic of due obedience (Reato 2012, 34–36).

Many indicted officers maintained decisive tones (both spoken and written) and used euphemisms like "excesses of war" to admit immoral warfare. Talking about war crimes with officers in more personal vocabulary was not only a strategy it was also inappropriate. Alfredo Scilingo, in his confession to the journalist Horacio Verbitsky (2005, 154) states likewise that he always referred to the methods he was ordered to carry out in terms of "detaining," "interrogating," and "eliminating" the enemy. It was too hard to say "kidnapping, torturing, and murdering." As in the absence of personal imbrications in the crimes, self-assessments were also hardly verbalized by the indicted officers in Argentina. The empathic openness and exchange I managed to establish with several victims were almost unimaginable with the indicted officers. They hardly ever confided their hardships and discomforts.

By the time of my second meeting with the retired navy captain Rafael Araballeda, his officer friend had recently been incarcerated.[39] Knowing that Rafael belonged to a submarine division during the last dictatorship,

I asked him if he feared prosecution. Rafael firmly indicated no, and with confidence he said that he had a clear conscience; he had done nothing wrong. I remember that these statements of innocence often sounded like justifications for the crimes. With active engagement and growing acquaintance, however, their perspective regarding knowledge of these wrongs emerged. During the conversation the topic of the Malvinas/Falklands War arose again. For Rafael it was really a fatal blow: "It was a true disgrace." The war against the subversion was fought wrongly, but the Malvinas had brought another difficulty, which had worsened the social decline of the armed forces. Rafael thought that guilt remained for not having executed both wars correctly. He explained: "Military men should be experts in the management of violence. . . . The state must only provide us with orientations, and we must employ the minimum of violence possible to reach the objective."

Finding another opening that afternoon to talk about the immoral warfare of the 1970s, I asked Rafael specifically about the death flights and his judgment of them. He considered the death flights terrible. In the same self-assured voice, Rafael continued that the disappearances in general were one of the biggest mistakes of the military. He said: "It shows an enormous lack of responsibility and is deeply shameful." He quickly added that if he had been ordered to do such a thing, he would have refused firmly, and he condemned his superiors: "There is a great amount of naivety or arrogance, thinking that people who committed [these crimes] would escape punishment; it is dishonorable arrogance."

A few months later Rafael and I met again. Asking his opinion about sudden public interest about commemorating the Malvinas/Falklands War and its veterans in Argentina,[40] Rafael vehemently shouted: "It is a military shame!" He was definitely not referring to the current commemoration. Rafael again explained that the Malvinas/Falklands War had been an ill-equipped and disorganized military operation that had ended in brutal defeat by the British. I asked Rafael: "What about the practices of disappearing subversives, the death flights, and the illegal adoption of babies. Is this shameful in a military sense as well?" Rafael firmly refuted the idea of a systematic plan for stealing babies, but he agreed that these interventions were badly executed and a *vergüenza* (shame) for the armed forces. "How could [the junta members] think that these wrongs would not end up becoming apparent?" Rafael's straightforward answers about the shamefulness of their actions during the dictatorship were unusual. If the disgraces of the subversive war were to be openly acknowledged, a more common practice among the indicted officers was to acknowledge them in terms of sacrifice. Many middle-rank officers still believed that they had to pay for all the societal sins emerging from the unconventional war methods and political chaos (Waisbord 1991, 169). This shift toward martyrdom rather fortified moral superiority and military exceptionality (Graziano 1992, 225). Rafael's shame sounded different though.

I once asked Aldo if he felt *mal* (bad) for things he had done in the past.[41] He explained: "There have been things that we could have executed better, this is what the Americans call 'review after action,' the Marxists call it 'auto critique,' and others call it a 'consciousness exam'; such things are always [practiced]." By then I knew that rape belonged to these "excesses" that required "review after action." Rape was a taboo and only once did I talk about rape in the illegal detention centers. When Aldo brought up the topic, I was stunned to have a conversation about it.[42] For Aldo rape at the detention centers was not a systematic crime; their justice codes and Catholic faith firmly prohibited it, he said. Aldo was never ordered to do so, but he admitted that rape in the detention centers had happened. He tried to explain it from his viewpoint. The conversation that followed was not thoughtless or emotionally void. They had never imagined the enemy as human, let alone female, he said. "You always constructed an ugly enemy in your mind, but suddenly we were confronted with attractive young women." Aldo admitted reluctantly that terrible sex crimes had been committed, but they were not systematic. He further reasoned that other women constructed sustainable relationships with military officers after their detention. When Aldo used me as an example of his enemy at an ambush and explained that some women had offered their bodies hopefully in return for freedom, our conversation became so odd and uncomfortable that we changed topics.[43] I must admit that it felt better *not* to discuss these topics in such personal ways. In contrast to the everyday morality of speech and analysis, we *tragamos el sapo* (swallowed the frog).

SWALLOW THE FROG

When Ignacio Domínguez and his fellow officers faced their verdict, Ignacio said that the time had come to swallow the frog. The retired lieutenant colonel Leopoldo Cardoso also said that the victims would need to swallow the frog as he was convinced that after the Kirchner regime there would come a "revenge of revenge," hinting at new transitional practices and setbacks that would undo the life sentences. Noticing my unfamiliarity with the frog metaphor, Leopoldo explained: "It means that when you do not like something, you still have to accept it." Neither men told me exactly what the frog represented to them. But I understood that instead of talking, one had better keep quiet. Swallow the frog was a recurrent trope in my conversation with the indicted officers; it transcended military life and was embedded in broader social histories and everyday moralities.[44] It was Victoria Herrera de Quiroga, whose husband died in combat in 1989, and two

children of military officers who taught me that military officers had different ways of dealing with private matters.[45] Victoria's husband was killed in
a guerrilla assault.[46] The military chaplain who married them had already
warned Victoria: marrying an officer may mean an early parting. Victoria
had been quite used to her husband not being around often, and he spoke
little about what he did at work. Victoria said she became accustomed to not
asking.

Silence and the military in Argentina have a particularly infamous history. During the dictatorship the phrase *silencio es salud* (silence is health)
often appeared in television and radio advertisements, and was published in
local newspapers (Payne 2008, 183). It supposedly referred to the large
amount of traffic pollution in Buenos Aires, yet indirectly indicated that
it was safer to keep quiet about the anomalies at night, the violence on
the streets in broad daylight, and moreover that one should never criticize the
dictatorship or denounce the crimes that were being committed. The notion
that silence was "healthier" nestled in Argentina. After the regime handed
over power in 1983, *el pacto de silencio* (the pact of silence) was implemented,
which ordered the military to keep quiet about the anomalies that had been
committed during the last dictatorship. The meaning of silence quickly
became synonymous with the secrecy and concealed facts about the repressive years.

During the 1990s, the meaning of silence extended to broader connota-
tions against public action and political protests, favoring the private and
the personal (Chauvié 2009, 4–5). The social preference for silence and privacy was a clear reaction to the flamboyant culture of protest in Argentina
(Robben 2005, 61–63). Ever since, victims and human rights activists have
contested and condemned this military silence. In particular, the concealment regarding the whereabouts of the disappeared and appropriated
children produces outrage and disbelief among victims. Why not tell where
the bodies and the children are? Why not tell how someone was killed in an
ambush?

Silence not only implies strategic amnesia or indifference; it can also be
a moral resource. Argentinian soldiers should keep silent about anomalies
and never take information outside the organization that affects the army's
prestige (Guber 2008, 126). Silence would be healthier for the indicted officers in Argentina, providing a beneficial alternative, obliterating the past
through deliberate disengagement (Payne 2008, 183). Such persistent orders
to be silent would provoke a general avoidance of speaking about personal
wrongs to others among the military (Bill 2006, 664–665). But I believe
that too often we seek refuge in the binary between civilian life and military to clarify (or justify) officers' ways of dealing with the personal and the
emotional.

Michael Jackson (2013, 225) cites Wittgenstein's "whereof one cannot speak, thereof one must be silent" not to propagate silence, but to be wary of judging human actions (thoughtlessly) in categorical terms. I believe we need to be wary of adjusting monolithic theorizing to the military pact of silence. Captain Scilingo confessed because he felt tormented. He was convinced that most of those who went through the ESMA or participated in the death flights were haunted and that they struggled to talk about it or not (Verbitsky 2005, 156). Although providing piecemeal bits of truth, several officers have come forward since 1983, and others have admitted military wrong being on their terms.

When I met two adult children of former generals, these ambiguities between speech and silence became more knowable. Javier Isla was a former member of the guerrilla organization *Montoneros*. His father was a high-ranking military officer during the last dictatorship. Javier went into exile after he was illegally detained and severely tortured for years. His brother, also a militant, disappeared. As in many Argentinian families, the oppositional ideologies and traumas had ruptured their family. But Javier's father never spoke a word about it.[47] He had gone through the mourning process all alone. He never talked about the loss of his son. They never spoke about Javier's exile either. Only recently had there been a turning point, said Javier. A few years ago the entire Isla family had been invited to the inauguration of a new memorial stone for a group of people who disappeared in Mataderos, a popular suburb in the southern region of Buenos Aires. That was the place where Javier's brother had been seen for the last time. Javier had been really surprised his father wanted to go. "They called my brother's name and my father raised his hand and even shouted ¡*presente*! (present). Tears ran down his cheek."

Rosario Barrera Albornoz also never spoke with her father about the dictatorship, during which he was an important admiral. In 2010, he was under house arrest awaiting trial for more than three hundred offenses, including the appropriation of fifteen children. Before my visit, Rosario's sister took their mother for a walk to avoid upsetting her. Work and family life remained separate. It was again a very controlled and distant conversation in which the admiral admitted that the military had been out of control and committed grave mistakes. When we walked back to her apartment, Rosario said that after his retirement in the early 1980s her father had been very depressed, but kept silent. He never learned to talk about the personal, she said. Rosario was used to it. The talking cure has been scarce among the military officers in Argentina. Many officers did not consider it healthy to talk.[48] Rosario's father did go into therapy briefly, but quickly decided it was not beneficial.

MEN AND MONSTERS

Extreme violence flourishes by dehumanizing subjects and quantifying actions up to the point that human beings lose their distinctiveness (Bauman 2002, 129). The idea that war (as practice and discourse) itself pushes the levels of good and evil to unimaginable extremes and turns ordinary people into murderers—to the extent that they forget their enemies are human beings—remains strong in much of our thinking about how people can commit atrocious crimes (Fassin and Rechtman 2009, 90). Dehumanization makes little sense in the story of Javier's father though. Hypotheses at this level of generality regarding why people commit evil crimes are too difficult to maintain when one investigates multiple stories of perpetrators (Clendinnen 1999, 112). Dehumanization does not provide an all-encompassing logic of human conduct in violent times. There are gray zones where violent conduct is motivated by dehumanizing practices, ideologies, and interpersonal exchanges at the same time. We somehow want to categorize the perpetrator in one way or another. Why can people who perform inexplicable atrocities not be nonhuman automatons, ordinary fathers, monsters, and victims at once in our theorizing?

We tend to overlook the idea that various moralities and self-images coexist uneasily in perpetrators' lives. In the endeavor to understand or make a convincing argument, we often reduce our findings so that life looks comprehensible, logical, and, in the case of understanding perpetrators, bearable. But all-encompassing theories and catchy concepts do not come near to morality in everyday life. How we engage with and in the world is a messy reality that can be confusing, hypocritical, and immoral at times, while at other fleeting moments it can be perfectly clear, genuine, and moral.

CHAPTER 6

Laughter and Play

AT THE BEGINNING of my fieldwork in Argentina I worked briefly with a local research team on a project to evaluate the trials for crimes against humanity. The main objective was to investigate the efficacy and consequences of a program that implemented police protection and psychological assistance for future witnesses. One day, Ariadna Villalba, a fellow researcher, and I were evaluating reports from different tribunals in Argentina. During a short break we talked about the disappearance of a witness named Julio López. By that time the story of a new disappearance in Argentina had reached mythical proportions.

Julio López, a construction worker, was illegally detained during the last dictatorship. In 2006 he testified at the first trial for crimes against humanity in La Plata. He disappeared one day before the tribunal announced the verdict for the main defendant, the former police officer Miguel Etchecolatz. Although police squads searched for weeks, Julio López never returned; until today those responsible for his disappearance remain at large. The disappearance of Julio López set off many rumors and conspiracy theories. Conservative right-wing groups within the police forces, who were alleged to be opposed to the current trials were the first to be held responsible. The disappearance also fostered internal disputes within the human rights groups: the oppositional sectors accused the current Kirchner government, whereas the co-opted human rights organizations said not the government but the sectors that escaped government control should be held responsible for López's disappearance (Van Drunen 2010, 234).

What happened to Julio López and who is responsible for this new disappearance remain a mystery today, and another disappearance has gone unpunished. During a time, after decades of impunity, when justice is being served with regard to the disappearances, the disappearance of Julio López has an extra sting. But instead of speculating on what happened to López or who was responsible, Ariadna asked me if I had read the latest periodical column "Day by Day," about the disappearance of Julio López in the local magazine *Barcelona*. Without waiting for my answer, she quickly stifled a laugh, and said that I would probably not understand it anyway: and Ariadna was right, I was quite puzzled and found myself asking what could be so funny about the disappearance of Julio López?

Playful Worlds

When I began this research I did not expect laughter to be important in the way people experience justice in Argentina. It seemed insignificant to the larger story because there were so many other urgent issues to discuss. But any deep comprehension of violence requires liberation from official memorial culture by including irony, shock, and black humor (Huyssen 2001, 39).[1] Understanding humor in the context of López's disappearance asks that *Barcelona* readers bypass political correctness and submerge themselves in an immoral world of apathy, double standards, hypocrisy, impunity, denial, and indifference. The magazine's humor regarding the dictatorship and the current trials was about the double binds in the search for truth and justice. The ambiguities and inconsistencies about the violence and injustice were always central to the jokes. After my initial puzzlement, it made sense to follow up on humor and laughter about violence.

Traditional and contemporary work on protest and resistance has repeatedly demonstrated the political importance of having fun (Graeber 2009; J. Scott 1985). Sons and Daughters for Identity and Justice against Oblivion and Silence (H.I.J.O.S.) *escraches* (public shaming action as a form of alternative justice) and the micro counterperformances of the indicted officers in court exemplify these forms of spectacular politics and hidden transcripts. This humor and play is not lighthearted or pointless, but at once unsettling and meaningful. In taking a critical approach to Mikhail Bakhtin's (1968) carnival, humor and play about violence and impunity carry the power of inversion, which makes the playful also utterly serious. Without idealizing and turning a blind eye to what laughter and play obscure (willingly or otherwise), these playful forms temporarily create an upside down world in which social and political hierarchies are overturned, unacceptable behavior is tolerated, and power is stripped of strict rules of respect. The carnivalesque, for that matter, is a playful space in which to test new ideas and contest stubborn truths and in which utopian ideals and everyday life merge and stimulate action and change (Gardiner 1993, 34).

We should never underestimate the power of jokes, laughter, imaginative play, comics, satirical columns, and ironic smiles in the ways people engage with and in the world. These playful moments are not only strategic, magical, or artificial; humor and play are also altered forms of consciousness that have real effects on people's experience of the world (Jackson 2013, 16–17). We should therefore always try to seize the value of play as an important cultural factor in social life (Huizinga 1970, 22). Kathleen Stewart (2007, 69) even argues that ethnographers should always wire directly to jokes, sometimes skipping content altogether. Laughter and humor are indeed vibrant moments, comparable to art, through which one becomes immersed in meaningful experiences (C. Wright 2010). Laughter and play are not about explaining the world, but about a fleeting immersion in it. However, laughter and play about atrocities and impunity are complicated matters. To be able to become immersed in these playful worlds, I needed context and content. To connect with the laughter on contemporary mockery and play in Argentina regarding state violence, besides familiarity with the history of political violence and state repression, also required comprehensive knowledge of recent political scandals and controversies concerning the local political elite.

I believe that play (in all its imaginary forms) powerfully ties together how justice in contexts of violence and impunity is being imagined, bodily enacted, and advocated for in confusing ways. In play people create fleeting moments that accept uncertainty and confusion about justice as a practice and ideal. It embraces the double binds and ambiguities of violence and impunity in everyday life. Play taps into these troubles, immoralities, and contradictions instead of explaining them away or justifying them. It is in these everyday playful moments addressing violence that we can most perceive and feel the ambiguities and structural inequalities underlying transitional justice categories such as impunity and accountability, retribution and restoration, justice and revenge. The jokes voiced opinions and experiences that were often situated at the edge of what was morally accepted and what was not. Laughter and play about violence were often saturated with ethical hazards in terms of entitlements, double-sidedness, and the potential for offense. Consequently, play was hilarious for some, but deeply offensive for others. Understanding jokes, play, and laughter about impunity, torture, disappearance, amnesia, humiliation, and indifference requires profound knowledge of the matters being ridiculed.

TORTURE AND SURVIVAL

One morning in May 2010, I witnessed a testimony that was quite different from usual at court.[2] The witness was María Eugenia Sosa, a middle-aged woman who had survived torture and detention at the Higher School of Mechanics of the Navy (ESMA), the largest detention center in the city of Buenos Aires. Normally, court testimonies were serious matters, but this time the legal procedure became animated. People in the public gallery muffled some giggling, as María Eugenia spoke with remarkable wit about her painful memories of abduction, torture, and detention, without saying much about what had actually happened to her. She was kidnapped in 1979 and detained in the ESMA. María Eugenia remembered with a big smile that one of her kidnappers was a fat guy, "but maybe that was my impression as I was much thinner back then!" With another grin, she explained that revealing too many details of the torture she suffered would be too cruel to the public. Before María Eugenia erupted in laughter, she added: "I [have] already live[d] 30 years with this [experience], and it cost me two properties in psychoanalytical therapy!" indirectly satirizing victims' widespread practice of seeking therapy, and the current distressing experience of listening to victims' testimonies. As she recalled all the people she had seen in the ESMA, María Eugenia apologized with an ironic twist in her voice that she always first remembered the ones who survived and then those who had died. The public laughed with her.

María Eugenia told the tribunal that after her release from the ESMA, she slept in a sitting position for five years because she imagined seeing the men who had tortured and detained her all the time outside of her window, as they were still at large. She could easily identify some of them sitting in front her at court. During cross-examination, a lawyer apologized for asking about her horrific memories. With another laugh, María Eugenia waived his apology aside, and said ironically that her detention at the ESMA was still much worse than this interrogation. The loss of identity and loss of any form of human condition was a sensation that remained with her for a long time: "Even in democracy I had these panic attacks. I would go to the nearby hospital and just sit there. People would ask me what was wrong, but I could not really tell . . . sleeping really gave me the creeps. . . . But I hate to be a victim!"

Her laughter and unexpectedly funny gags definitely took the edge off her testimony. Her wit at court was quite extraordinary. Because of this or for some other reason, María Eugenia's recollections of the crimes did not persuade the defense. One defense lawyer questioned her use of a memory card containing the names of detainees during her testimony. Another lawyer even accused her of being a liar, referring to previous slightly different statements María Eugenia had given in the past twenty years regarding her detention. The lawyer asked the tribunal to disqualify her testimony because it had been contaminated by other victims' stories; she had made it impossible for the judges to prove that her memories of her detention were genuine. I noticed an anxious atmosphere among the human rights public for a few seconds, but the judges did not disqualify the testimony. Only one judge asked a question about how long she had been detained in the ESMA. Before answering his question, María Eugenia recovered her wit and responded swiftly: "In the building or in life?!" On her way out of the courtroom she quickly stuck her tongue out at one of the defense lawyers.

Finally among friends and family she asserted that she had been fighting against tears in the courtroom.

LIKE MARÍA EUGENIA, many victims, time and again, shared their distressing stories, in the courts and elsewhere. Some testimonies about torture, illegal detention, death, and disappearance were told only once. But most stories of survival and disappearance were told by many and more than once. Some did this with an ironic twist, arguing that all children of the disappeared and survivors always have troubles and problems. They laughed about their traumas and social repetitive compulsions. Offensive to outsiders, gallows humor often underlines the conflicting moral values that people attach to jokes about violence and suffering (Kidron 2010). It enables distancing of oneself from what produces pain and indignation, and instead makes one laugh, and somehow free oneself—by means of play—from bothersome things (Pedrazzini 2010, 85). Humor then, functions as a deliberate psychological mechanism that turns suffering into serious play.[3] It thus helps survivors and relatives mitigate the intensity of the traumatic stress. Humor can also be a form of catharsis that allows survivors to explore the relationship between jokes and consciousness (Freud 1960). Humor, like dreams, not only helps people cope with trauma but also tends to expose repressed memories (Oring 1984, 4–7).

But the coping and purgative effects of humor do not sufficiently explain all kinds of playful framing of atrocities and genocide. Gallows humor about the Holocaust, for instance, allows victims to explore the incongruities and ambiguities between hegemonic commemorative narratives and familial lived experiences (Kidron 2010, 432). By mocking mainstream testimonial and therapeutic practices, victims contest what is morally accepted and rejected within hegemonic discourses about the Holocaust, which enables them to live with multiple contradictory dualities (Kidron 2010, 443). People struggle with trauma on numerous levels and within entangled temporalities, aside from the individual trauma inflicted upon them in the past.

In her work as a psychoanalyst among victims for years, Laura Figueroa had also listened to innumerable accounts of torture, survival, disappearance, and death. During all these years of counseling, Laura had learned that some survivors could never forget that they had been in a detention center.[4] Their traumas had influenced everything in their lives; they could hardly talk about anything else, and their survival identity had significantly shaped the relationships with all their friends, lovers, and children. Many survivors had unstable relationships with people who had experienced the same; divorce and separation were quite common. The survivors with children faced a dilemma concerning whether they should or should not tell their children about their survival. Speaking openly and explicitly about their survival might be too confrontational, but at the same time they were also afraid of unconsciously placing their children in a negative position by not telling them about their traumas. These issues were discussed repeatedly during therapy. Besides these social instabilities, survivors suffered professional and financial instabilities such as job loss. Sometimes children of the disappeared and children of the survivors experienced similar problems and came to Laura to discuss their troubles. Laura always coped in a professional manner, she said, but sometimes she came home thinking she could not tolerate it anymore.

When she discussed the risk of retraumatization, Laura also employed humor in her therapies with survivors and relatives. This was often the only way to access people's traumatic experiences, Laura said. Clearly echoing a Freudian stance, humor translated the victims' traumatic experiences into something expressible. For Laura herself, humor was a necessary escape while working with survivors and relatives; otherwise fatigue would take over. If she were to become too seriously involved in victims' traumas all the time, Laura thought she would become paralyzed and of no help. Humor was her way of entering and leaving the traumatic past with the victim, and it allowed her to avoid becoming a carrier of suffering. These lively jokes and spontaneous laughter functioned on a daily basis as a kind of cathartic relief, and a way to explore the traumas of torture and survival.

But then Laura's humor took a different direction. She suddenly laughed out loud, when she remembered that coming home after a day's work she had shouted at her partner, a human rights lawyer working at the trials: "Enough, enough, I do not want to hear anything anymore from a victim-survivor!" The humor indirectly criticized the repetitive nature of victims' testimonies and therapies. Without this dash of humor working with victims would be impossible, she said. Laura's laughter about the talking cure in which she was actively taking part revealed contradictory dualities between morally accepted opinions and what people sometimes actually felt while listening to these repetitive memories of torture and survival. Survivors' humor was thus about coping not only with the traumas or entering the past without risking retraumatization but also with the dominant practices that people should employ in treating their traumas and achieving forms of justice.

Impunity and Amnesia

In 2010, approximately a year after hearing about the column about López in *Barcelona* for the first time, my eye accidentally spotted a copy in a kiosk and I intuitively remembered Ariadna's muffled laugh. On the back page the headline said: "August 2nd: National Son of a Bitch Day." Underneath were nine black-and-white photos of military officers involved in current trials for crimes against humanity, each captioned "Happy Son of a Bitch Day." Automatically I assessed that this hinted at the commercial excesses of these contrived celebrations, such as Secretary's Day and Teacher's Day, which both occur in September. After months of doing fieldwork and trying to understand what violence and justice meant for the victims and the indicted officers, the ugly depicted faces of these notorious military officers made me stifle an almost inaudible laugh. Becoming part of a confusing world in which the boundaries between friend and foe, truth and denial, and accountability and impunity, became more blurred every day made *Barcelona*'s humor more familiar. It is said that laughing at jokes requires the internalization of certain values and beliefs (Apte 1985, 17). The internalization and hence endorsement of humor should imply complicity and belonging. Approving of a joke would then mean acceptance of a moral point of view on a certain matter which creates solidarity (Buckley 2003, 5). But humor about violence is not always about inclusion and exclusion. Humor about collective forms of violence is often against clear-cut social boundaries between them and us.

After that moment at the kiosk, I started reading *Barcelona* more often, especially the López column as I flipped through the other pages. All the columns had a similar format: detectives were searching for Julio López in unlikely localities, or were asking well-known people if they had information about López's whereabouts, which for different reasons had been head-line news in Argentinian newspapers. One column, for example, began by stating that the detectives had nothing to do, and instead of continuing their investigation they decided to download the award-winning Argentinian film *El secreto de sus ojos* (The Secret in Their Eyes).[5] The central theme of this fictional story is the pursuit of alternative justice and its moral predica-ments for victims when a legal system fails to achieve justice in murder cases. The story, although fictional, is intimately tied to the political history of Argentina where for decades the human rights abusers of the dictatorship walked freely because of the amnesty laws. What happens to people when impunity rules for such a long time? In the film this central theme of impu-nity is taken in another direction when the husband of a murdered woman kidnaps the perpetrator and detains him for years in a shack in his own gar-den. He took the right to punish into his own hands.

The López column describes the detectives as they watched the film's exaggeratedly well-known scenes—starting with a dynamic view from the air over the entire city, and reaching a very close shot of people at the Tomás A. Ducó football stadium in a popular neighborhood of Buenos Aires. In the stands, the detectives observed several repressors who had abducted people during the last dictatorship. Subsequently, they thought it wise to visit the stadium; perhaps they could finally discover an accomplice who knew something about the most famous disappearance during the democracy. However, no one knew where López was. The columns always ended like this: López was not there or no one knew where he was, which indirectly emphasized current political cover-ups, denial, and impunity regarding this new disappearance.

The next piece comes from a López column and narrates Cristina Fernández de Kirchner's journey to Paris to attend a protest march for Ingrid Betancourt, the French Colombian politician, who had been kidnapped by the Revolutionary Armed Forces of Colombia (FARC) guerrillas and was still in their hands:

> Sunday, April 6. President Cristina Fernández travels again to Paris. . . . During the protest march for Ingrid Betancourt, she asks for Julio López. It seems that the FARC has nothing to do with his disappearance. [The former fashion model and French President's wife] Carla Bruni does not know anything either and instead they start babbling about purses. The [Argentinian] minister of economics asks the directors of the Paris Club if they know anything. No one knows.[6]

The *Barcelona* columns on López deal with explosive matters of social accountability regarding old and new versions of impunity and structural indifference among the ruling classes and powerful elites in Argentina (see figure 5). This refers mainly to the double-sidedness of the current human rights politics of the Kirchner governments. *Barcelona*'s main criticism was that the Argentinian elite, such as the first lady and subsequent president Cristina Fernández de Kirchner, who proclaimed that they defended human rights, too often forgot about or were (deliberately) indifferent to López's disappearance.

Barcelona's humor is clearly morally incorrect and pokes fun at all official and social institutions, including the government and the Church, as well as at the former repressive regimes, and now even the human rights organizations (Fraticelli 2008, 117–124).[7] The magazine was established in the aftermath of the economic meltdown and political crisis in 2001–2002. Since then, *Barcelona* has questioned the current conditions of democracy, the unequal power of the ruling classes, and the lack of accountability and social justice in Argentina. Their articles were part of a growing response that criticized the subsequent Kirchner governments and their "opportunistic" human rights policies.[8] By offering alternative readings of human rights politics, *Barcelona* ridiculed the structural lack of accountability and general amnesia among the local media and the ruling classes in Argentina in regard to the "most famous disappearance in democracy"—Julio López—which very much resembled the decades of impunity for and denial of the disappeared (see figure 6).[9]

Ridiculing existing double-sided discourses about state violence, accountability, and social injustice in Argentina is not something recent. Print humor has a long history in Argentina: satirical magazines had already

Figure 5. Cover page of the satirical magazine *Barcelona*

emerged during the mid-nineteenth century, and not always without risk. Graphic mocking humor was quite dangerous in a country recovering from almost two decades of violence, chaos, and impunity (Foster 1989, 61).[10] It offered alternative versions of ongoing contradictions, inconsistencies, and injustices. What many of these satirical publications in Argentina had in common was their attempt to demystify and denounce cherished beliefs of the official ruling classes (Foster 1989, 37).[11] *Barcelona* often dedicated cover

Figure 6. Satirical board game about the search for Julio López

pages and news items to mocking López's disappearance and the trials for crimes against humanity, and to ridiculing elite members of the human rights organizations and the former repressive regimes.[12]

Fernando Carrizo, an editor of *Barcelona*, made it very clear that the publication was not a humor magazine.[13] Their journalists were first of all serious writers who, with acid undertones, informed against official accounts of the ruling classes. Their work carried the power of inversion where the playful was at once utterly serious. According to Fernando, *Barcelona* mocked everything and everyone as long as it had a purpose, but it mainly mocked the media and exposed contradictory discourses of the long-standing and new ruling classes. The López column emerged out of the critical observation that López's disappearance had quickly ceased to be news. The columns were clearly not intended only to amuse the urban middle classes; Fernando belonged to progressive groups that in general supported the human rights policies, but he reluctantly acknowledged that *Barcelona* had to depict the sinuous sides of the Kirchner administration and the human rights movement.

Barcelona used any excuse to talk about López. The political demand for López's appearance should have been widely communicated by the Argentinian human rights organizations. However, due to their close alignment with the Kirchner government, for whom López has not been a priority, they did not repeatedly mention this new disappearance during their public events in the same way they always did by shouting the slogan "¡30,000 desaparecidos, ahora y siempre!" (30,000 disappeared, now and forever!). Paradoxically, according to Fernando, this apathy among the human rights groups concerning a disappearance was also a "repugnant circle of silence." In addition, *Barcelona* mocked the disappearances of the last dictatorship and questioned the current political use of the figure of the disappeared by the government and eminent members of the human rights organizations. Fernando indirectly referred to the recurrent presence of mothers of the disappeared with white scarves at public events. After some years under Kirchner rule, Fernando halfheartedly had to acknowledge that today a noncritical, idealized, and clean vision of the human rights organizations was simply unsustainable.

Fernando's arguments opposing the current apathy about López's disappearance and the political use of human rights and the disappeared represented a far-reaching unease about social accountability and hypocrisy that, even after thirty years, was still clearly apparent among the urban classes in contemporary Argentinian society. Mainly using humor to reveal their criticisms, they reluctantly admitted the awkwardness of some of the human rights policies of the Kirchner governments and the new forms of social injustices, indifference, and impunity.

Print humor about indifference and amnesia concerning previous violence and current injustices was practiced not only by progressive criticasters. In 2006, another mocking magazine materialized: *B1: Vitamina para la memoria de la guerra en los 70* (B1: Vitamin for memory about the war of the 1970s). The magazine also criticized general amnesia except for this specific period of Argentinian history. *B1* mainly reclaimed a promilitary and rightist ideology that favored the military repression of the late 1970s, an ideological disposition that had attained a small niche in the contemporary public sphere. For instance, *B1* was not sold at the kiosk, so I got a stack of issues from a military wife.

While flipping through pages, I noticed that the conservative humor magazine also denounced the latest inconsistencies of the Kirchner governments. Being less layered and complex, *B1*'s articles, graphics, and manipulated photographs of the Kirchner governments were more direct denouncements of hypocrisy. What was most telling about *B1* was its contestation of current interpretations of historical events and of responsibility and blame regarding the political violence and state repression. The title of the magazine hinted at the risk of vitamin B1 deficiency, which is commonly linked to cognitive problems such as Alzheimer's disease, a form of dementia. The magazine's aim was therefore to "fortify" memories of Argentinians about the political violence of the 1970s and reinstate *la teoría de los dos demonios* (the theory of two demons), indirectly satirizing the fact that the Kirchner government and the human rights organizations had, in their historical representations, severely played down or even omitted accounts of revolutionary violence such as assaults, abductions, and bombings. The cover page of the magazine always depicted four large white pills clearly marked "B1," which could slow down this malicious forgetfulness. Laughing about impunity and hypocrisy allows momentary acceptance of the double binds of memory and accountability that seem inevitably present in Argentinians' daily lives.

Happiness

Restorative justice tends to promote harmony and forgiveness, whereas retributive justice endorses disagreement and revenge. But the emotional overlap of revenge and justice is much messier. Transitional justice theories tend to ignore how people who are deeply immersed in restorative and retributive practices live out forgiveness and revenge. How and why people experience revenge and forgiveness (or not) should therefore be looked at from an integrated view of social mores and personal feelings both within oneself and in one's relations with others.

Restorative justice as an ideal has had few repercussions among the survivors and relatives in Argentina. Harmony and forgiveness have not been ingredients for the way justice emerges in Argentina. At the same time, many victims in Buenos Aires displayed a kind of everyday ethos against revenge. Revenge was a bad and inappropriate feeling. Revenge belonged to the uncivilized—meaning the officers who tortured, killed, and caused the disappearances. For instance, Ana Luisa Campos, whose brother disappeared, always asserted that she never felt revengeful.[14] When she saw the indicted officers for the first time in court, she had mixed feelings that she dared not analyze, and she was unable to put them into words. When a notorious general of the regime was finally sentenced to life imprisonment, first Ana Luisa cried. But then she felt something that for the most part resembled *venganza* (vengeance)—the feeling that justice was finally being achieved.[15] Still faithful to shared analysis, Ana Luisa apologized for not venturing to analyze her feelings resembling revenge when this general was finally sentenced to life in prison. She then reasoned that her revenge had not been unleashed because, fortunately, a legal institution had allowed her to contain her feelings and she was able to feel happy. I noticed that the laws of retaliation and forgiveness among victims were different in principle from the biblical sayings "an eye for an eye" and "love your enemies." Their laws stood instead for the pursuit of *alegría* (happiness) that reigned when justice had finally been served. Happiness became central to the way Argentinian victims experienced and interpreted retribution and restoration in the courts and beyond.

IN JULY 2010, Tomás Olivera and I met at a noisy coffee bar near Tribunales, the city's judicial district.[16] Tomás, a committed human rights lawyer, belonged to an important civilian organization that was pushing for the proceedings in several trials for crimes against humanity. He was highly appreciated among victims and activists for his work. Having been just an ordinary boy from Mataderos, a popular neighborhood in Buenos Aires, he never imagined becoming a lawyer. His political activism emerged when he was in secondary school during the 1980s, and led him to study sociology. During this initiation into the social world of academics, revolutionaries, and intellectuals he became increasingly acquainted with people who had survived detention and torture during the authoritarian regime. They inspired him to join their political struggle for justice and against impunity. Listening to all these stories of human rights abuses, Tómas had a kind of epiphany: law was fundamental in changing social reality and he became a dedicated law student.

In his previous work at a law firm, Tomás filed many cases for reparations to families of the disappeared. During this period he heard many individual stories of loss. At that point in Tómas's life, the intangible idea of the disappeared now became a cruel human flesh-and-blood reality. He felt very weak and angry, he said, especially knowing that the criminals were still walking the streets of Buenos Aires as free individuals. This idea generated real *odio* (hatred). I did not pursue the issue, but I remember that Tomás hastened to say this was not the kind of hatred that cause one to inflict criminal offenses. I then confronted him with an existing accusation—mostly among right-wing conservative groups—that the trials were a form of *venganza*. Tomás rejected this firmly. *Venganza* implied the infliction of similar harm on the person who injured you. The survivors, relatives and human rights activists never tortured, abducted, or starved anyone, and they did not appropriate other people's children; they only used the National Constitution and the Criminal Code to judge these criminals for what they had done.

Revenge was indeed a nonexistent feeling among victims. I asked Tomás why he thought victims in Argentina had not carried out acts of vengeance. He promptly replied that there had been *escraches* by H.I.J.O.S. as well as spontaneous fistfights between notorious torturers and some victims. Why did Tomás answer my question on the absence of vengeance with the *escraches*? I remember being confused about his reference to *escraches*. Other survivors, relatives, and activists always emphasized that *escraches* were peaceful and playful searches for alternative justice while impunity ruled for decades. Was there an overlap of retribution and play that I was unaware of?

In 2018, I received an email from a woman whose parents disappeared, which was signed *Justicia, Memoria, Verdad y Alegria!* (Justice, memory, truth and happiness). One online post of the human rights organization of the children of the disappeared H.I.J.O.S. in February 2012 also reasoned: "Being happy is our only revenge."[17] It stated that happiness was the best way to demoralize and undermine the repressors. In a Bakhtinian manner, not carnival but happiness has become a central locus of justice for many victims. But this reversal of revenge and happiness did not exactly communicate the opposite of what was meant or was functioning as a substitute for silence (Fernandez and Taylor Huber 2001, 5; Hutcheon 1994, 44; Kibler 2005, 464). That would blind us from seeing the playful at the expense of what it entails for the people involved. Happiness did not communicate the opposite or substitute inappropriate (or silenced) revenge. Happiness actually *was* what many relatives and survivors felt during the trial proceedings, particularly after the sentences. Happiness countered the image of a lifeless, depressed victim and this reference to positive feelings and being alive was their real triumph.

The trials were indeed a real celebration after years of waiting and carrying out creative projects to overturn the amnesties (Seidel 2011). Their playful resistance of the human rights organizations in Argentina have for decades produced and encouraged positive feelings through drumming, chanting, jumping, singing, *mate* (herbal tea) and *asado* (barbecue), fireworks, costumed figures on stilts, flags, graffiti, and colorful clothes. The demonstrations of March 24 celebrating *Día Nacional de la Memoria por la Verdad y la Justicia* (National Day of Memory for Truth and Justice) were archetypal. Twice I witnessed dozens of colorful *murgas* (popular bands of street musicians) with dancing adolescents and deafening upbeat rhythms. Plaza de Mayo had turned into one big street party. Colorful flags and banners covered the blue sky, and street vendors were almost invisible behind their ambulatory barbecue sets due to the thick smoke of all the sizzling sausages. These "street parties" with their carnivalesque character and playful features, were creative forms of effective resistance used to continue redefining how to deal with the sinister past, fight amnesia, and claim social justice (Strejilevich 2010, 238–239).[18] They were playful spaces in which to test new ideas for a new world.

This spectacular protest is serious and fun at the same time. Not only do these playful acts lie somewhere between structure and agency, contesting everyday power relations that are understandable responses to moral and legal systems that are incapable of addressing the grievances of its people (Goldstein 2003, 271–272). *Escraches* also have real effects on how people experience the world, thus temporarily turning a lifetime of suffering and impunity into happiness.

Together with Emilio Váldez and some of his friends, I could feel for myself why and how happiness and fun were central to the trials for the crimes against humanity. Emilio, in his early twenties, was active in a left-wing activist group. He had asked if I wanted to join them for the opening festivities of a new trial, where the former police officer Luis Patti and de facto president Reynaldo Bignone were indicted for crimes against humanity. Patti was quite a notorious figure. During the dictatorial regime he worked on the police force. In the 1990s he turned to politics and became the mayor of a small provincial town. Patti had already faced several trials during the Alfonsín government in the mid-1980s, but no verdict was ever reached due to the amnesty laws that had been issued in 1986 and 1987. Although the trials were finally prosecuting notorious figures like Patti, some "justice" matters could not be addressed between the four walls of the tribunals.

One block away from federal court, we all sat on a patch of grass just outside the building in a provincial town that comprises the huge geographical area of the *conurbano* (greater Buenos Aires). Around us local journalists were already filming and photographing the extraordinary preparations for the street event. Members of H.I.J.O.S. were unloading speakers from a bright orange school bus and hanging dozens of tiny flags and colorful balloons with *juicio* (trial) and *castigo* (punishment) on the trees and fences. Just a few meters away from the federal court, several photos mocking Patti were put in place, depicting him in the notorious black-and-white striped prison uniform. There were also *verdad* (truth) and *justicia* (justice) games for children (see figure 7), such as hopscotch, and instead of a ring toss, plastic handcuffs were substituted, toward different counters figuring the armed forces. Other games mocked the indicted officers, such as game of darts with Patti's face in the bull's eye (see figure 8), and a tin-can toss for the most severe punishments. The games were also fun for adults to play, and we all laughed when a man's dart hit Patti's nose. The laughter engendered a very jolly atmosphere.

At the back of the patch of grass they were also grilling *choris* (sausages) and toasting *pan* (bread), for the popular treat of *choripan* (grilled sausage on a roll) indirectly situating the protest class-wise. The practice of eating *choripan* during protests belongs to *el pueblo* (people, used to address the working classes) in Argentina (Auyero 2003, 85). This "popular" smell of greasy sausages and smoke was now penetrating our hair and clothes. A slogan above the makeshift barbecue stated: *Si al chori, no al Patti* (Yes to chori, no to Patti), indirectly ridiculing the suspect's last name by using "Paty," a well-known mass-produced hamburger brand in Argentina that is often sold at street events. Commonly known among Argentinians, *choris* are more delicious than the manufactured Patys. While standing in line for a *choripan*, we overheard that the court session had finally begun: an ill Luis Patti, tucked into a blanket, was carried into the courtroom on a stretcher. This news produced a harmonious wave of indignation and laughter among the people in line. A young man thought that Patti staged his illness. He said it was "outrageous!" smiling as he did so.

During the first recess, a group of lawyers joined us for lunch; Tomás was one of them. We discussed the formal court session and Patti's "pathetic" entrance. Tomás was delighted and commented that the huge demonstrations during Juan Perón's presidency used to be like this, with wine and *choripanes*. Assuming incorrectly that I was following Tomás's line of thought on the *argentinidad* (typical features of Argentina and its people) of popular street demonstrations, I shared with them that I was about to go to another demonstration of the military officers and kin, near the Ministry of Defense. Their justice event at court that day represented the demonstrations only of the human rights groups in Argentina. Protests of the conservative right-wing and the military were of very different order and incentive. Tomás replied immediately that the military always accused *el pueblo* of coming to the demonstrations only for the food and drinks. He disapproved of this opportunistic interpretation of their popular street gatherings.

Figure 7. Truth and justice game, San Martin

By the time we had eaten our *choripanes*, we reeked heavily of smoke and sausages. Wiping his mouth with a napkin, Tomás asked if I needed a ride back to Buenos Aires. Accepting his offer, I asked him to drop me off at Plaza de Armas just in front of the Ministry of Defense, where a handful of loyal retired officers, military wives, and children of indicted officers were protesting. Being a man with a sense of humor, Tomás hardly repressed

Figure 8. Dartboard with Luis Patti as the bull's-eye, San Martín

a satisfied smile, asking rhetorically: "Are you going to see these *fachos* (fascists) with the smell of our *choris*?"[19] With boyish rebellion Tomás added that he wanted to join me. He found it extremely funny that a foreigner, happily smelling of the sausages from their justice celebration, was about to enter the territory of the military. It was a clear inversion of power and influence. The popular aroma of *chori* at a modest military protest emphasized via smell the marginalized position of the armed forces that now had to accept researchers into their midst (Frederic 2012).

Victims' grievances about the last dictatorship in Argentina have been unaddressed by the legal system for a very long time. But the trials for crimes against humanity did not make previous "subaltern" humor practices obsolete (J. Scott 1985). The playful resistance against impunity in the form of "street parties" simply moved to the federal courts in Argentina. Victims and human rights activists continued to have fun and be happy as they were used to, perhaps even more than before, considering the many truth and punishment games mocking the Patti trial. Why is it then that such forms of "subaltern" play are still used by victims of state violence and human rights activists of different generations in Argentina, when official legal actions have currently been implemented to respond to their injustices? Why do they still turn to street parties, serious parades, and *escraches* when retribution is being made?

The emotional imbrication of justice is a complicated matter that does not fit neatly into transitional justice categories such as forgiveness and revenge, impunity and accountability, and has more to do with social mores and subjective experiences of righteousness. I believe that happiness with its playful contours became a central manifestation of moral superiority and triumph among survivors and relatives in Argentina. This is quite the opposite of the logic of a "head for an eye" in the Cambodian genocide (Hinton 1998), where justice only exists through exceeding reciprocal violence. This happiness is neither carefree nor pointless. Happiness is a serious incentive and further allows survivors and relatives to live with trauma as an everyday moral resource. The serious celebration of trauma turns it into something positive and something to live for.

HUMILIATION

In December 2010, returning to Córdoba to observe the verdict of an important trial for crimes against humanity, I had the opportunity to spend some time again with the retired lieutenant colonel Ignacio Domínguez and a dozen indicted officers and their families, just before the judges announced their verdict. Ignacio had been prosecuted for murder and torture, and after the court had heard all the witnesses and defendants, the prosecutor demanded a life sentence for him. Finally reaching the end of the trial, Ignacio's prospects about the outcome had reversed completely. A few months earlier he had still seemed convinced that he could prove his innocence; his declarations in court about the just war they had fought against the guerrillas and about the workings of military due obedience, in his view, were rock-solid answers to prove his innocence. Just a few days before his own verdict, Ignacio took notice of fourteen life imprisonments that had been pronounced at two trials for crimes against humanity at other federal courts across the country. Not surprisingly, these recent life sentences had caused Ignacio's previous confidence and courage to plummet; his slight hope for a more lenient sentence had now diminished to almost zero. It seemed as if he were finally resigned to incarceration for life. It was quite strange to see a normally fierce and warlike officer this way; his dread seemed almost unbecoming.

After the final words of an indicted general, during a long recess, Ignacio's memories drifted to a time when he was still a young, carefree parachutist, and none of the crimes for which he was being prosecuted had occurred yet. The function of positive memories in easing anxieties and stress was not what caught my attention though. Ignacio's gallows humor did. As a man with a boyish streak, Ignacio also made several jokes that afternoon. He boldly calculated, for instance, when he should swallow his first tranquilizer. "Only a quarter of a pill," he said sarcastically, because he did not want to fall asleep; he was thus indirectly making fun of the snoozing older officers during the long court sessions. On and off, he poked fun with his fellow indicted officers about their proximate "guillotine" and their "execution by firing squad." He ridiculed their situation as one in which they, the "evil officers," were about to receive, in his opinion, exaggerated and unlawful punishment by a dishonest and biased tribunal.

At some point during the afternoon loud music started coming from the streets. A few hours earlier, members of H.I.J.O.S. were unloading speakers and constructing a makeshift stage, and now the sound volume of leftist protests songs had increased to a maximum. The indicted officers started talking about rumors that the human rights organizations present at other verdicts had burned cardboard silhouettes of the indicted officers. Their faces showed that they deeply disapproved of this symbolic cremation. Not being able to escape from the pulsating beat, the rock music bothered all the indicted officers and their families. One woman confessed that she really loathed the "human rights music," and added with pronounced irony: "As we too are having great fun down here, we should also start dancing!" Her grotesque body movements, in which she parodied the human rights *murga* dance bands, provoked laughter among some indicted officers. At that point, other indicted officers entered into uncontrollable peals of laughter and another woman joined the awkward dancing. Afterward Ignacio almost begged the lady to repeat her imitation of a witness who was exiled in France and a few months earlier had traveled to Córdoba to testify. While imitating with noticeable pleasure the witness's testimony about kidnapping and torture, the woman exaggerated her Spanish with a heavy French accent, and Ignacio entered into the boisterous laughter, which was contagious, so everyone joined in.

A few hours later Ignacio received a sentence of life in prison. I realized—after being immersed in their sour play that afternoon, with all the jokes and laughter—to some extent what it meant for Ignacio to finally face the factual inability to act from his current weak position, a social position that he was quite unfamiliar with and reluctant to accept. The idea that he would officially be a perpetrator of crimes against humanity, or a genocider, had been difficult to swallow. During the past months, from prison, Ignacio had still ruled his family as a patriarch and spent his unoccupied prison hours working out, so as to be fit and energetic as a decent soldier would be in preparing for combat. He had tried to convert his experiences of the battlefield into the legal reality of the trial for crimes against humanity, but he had failed. I believe that Ignacio had never imagined he could become a weak man, abandoned by his institution and superiors, and no longer able to protect his family and fellow soldiers from injustice and humiliation. He had modified his previous armaments into the officially permitted weapon "the microphone" to defend their military actions during the last dictatorship, but it had not produced any change in the course of contemporary Argentinian history. Ignacio had to acknowledge that he had become a powerless man, abandoned by his superiors and his fatherland, and about to spend his life in prison for crimes he did not feel responsible for. Such weakness and legal absurdity did not fit in Ignacio's lifeworld. Making fun about it was what was left for him: "Execution by guillotine!"

When physical aggression is forbidden by law, or simply impossible or undesirable, it can be replaced by the tragedy of making one's enemy small, inferior, despicable, or comic, which, in a roundabout way, enables one to achieve the enjoyment of overpowering the other (Freud 1960, 102–103). Frustration because of powerlessness is overcome by ridicule, although the latter has little effect on the actual balance of power.[20] It is argued that ridiculing the despised other is more than a psychological necessity, or something springing from a subordinate position: this humor is also a form of belonging in a deeper sense. Laughing with others involves camaraderie as one engages with prior moral and political beliefs (Buckley 2003, 199). The approval of a joke, as in shared laughter, is a symbolic form of accepting a moral viewpoint on a certain matter and, consequently, it constructs a sense of solidarity (Buckley 2003, 5). When one laughs about thorny matters such as accountability for state crimes, including torture and disappearance, does it mean one automatically approves of certain moral viewpoints? Does all shared laughter routinely construct solidarity? I am skeptical about this moral simplicity and determinist view. Laughter and jokes do not routinely involve moral positioning; such play can also yield to everyday moral confusion. Laughter and play may be significant, but they are definitely not totalizing. Sharing humor in a post-conflict setting is beset with everyday moral confusion, uncertainty, and inconsistency.

MORAL MESSINESS

In October 2013, in the Netherlands, I assisted at an international conference on humor and violence in Latin America. I had just presented the aforementioned field observations made at the Patti trial and during the time I spent with Ignacio and the other indicted officers before their verdict. My main argument was that, on a daily basis, seizing humor and play in the field had an important role in understanding the way people experience transitional justice in Argentina. My direct mention of having become immersed in these playful worlds may have been too straightforward and "ethnographic" to the conference participants, who consisted primarily of literary critics. In particular the reference to laughing with indicted officers was deeply insulting to two middle-aged Argentinian scholars who were noticeably aligned with the victims. They judged the act of laughing with military officers as distasteful and offensive; moreover, as I had not presented a solid theoretical frame, they even questioned the working ethics of the research.

The play and laughter I had experienced with the indicted officers, in a sense, was a field narrative illustrating broader thematic discomfort about complicity and accountability in Argentina. I nevertheless realized then that social acceptance was limited regarding what was funny and tolerable and what was not when the topic was state violence among Argentinian victims and people loyal to their cause. Beyond words, the suddenly uncomfortable atmosphere at the conference again effectively depicted an internalized ambiguity about accountability and complicity, which is quite characteristic of societies recovering from collective violence. I was back in the field, feeling deeply uncomfortable about the research and my position in it. Had I misunderstood the humor and play for lightheartedness that had little meaning? My laughter may have demonstrated a blind spot and a failure to fully grasp what many victims in Argentina continue to live through. Understanding is always partial. The impossibility to know fully belongs intrinsically to social life, including the manifestations and meanings of play and laughter.

Humor and play can be deeply offensive and unpleasant. How do people actually negotiate the perilous everyday terrain that lies between humor and offensiveness (Lockyer and Pickering 2005, 3–4)? Should certain forms of play and humor therefore be blocked? Is censorship sometimes warranted, even if it goes against the right to freedom of speech? Is it taboo or simply an act of freedom of speech to mock the disappeared or survivors of torture, as it is with Muslims, women, or black people (Kuipers 2011, 68)? Is it wrong per se to laugh or joke with people who are considered evil? There are no straightforward answers to these questions. The meanings of humor, play, and laughter depend heavily on context, the identity of the person producing them, and the recipients (Lockyer and Pickering 2005, 9).

Humor regimes unlock entitlements to humor (Kuipers 2011, 69). These regimes are the unwritten rules stipulating who can joke and laugh about what. The boundaries involve declaring some topics off-limits and are infused with power relations. Foreign ethnographers who engage with "evil" seem not to be entitled to laughter. But such stipulations about entitlements to laughter are overthought. Humor, play, and laughter are often unforeseen and ephemeral, and not premeditated. At the particular moment of an impulsive joke or during unexpected bouts of laughter, laughter and play about delicate matters fleetingly embody the social condition of moral confusion concerning accountability for and complicity in deep wrongs.

In the field I visited prisons many times to talk with the indicted military officers of different ranks. Quite often these afternoons were cheerful familial gatherings with typical Argentinian food, smoking, sodas, and the usual extended conversations. Ex-general Jorge Rafael Videla sometimes joined his subordinate officers at lunch or for a talk. Once a friend of Ignacio's took me to Videla's new cell. After exchanging casual greetings with the ex-general and his wife, the small corridor-shaped cell turned out to be too small for four adults and I found myself pressed against a wall with some funny cartoons glued on it. Never being prepared for casual conversation with the former head of the Argentinian junta, I stutteringly asked, with a slight dash of irony, if he had been decorating his new cell, while pointing to the cartoons before me. Videla laughed in return, and said a previous inmate was responsible for the childish wall decorations. After some more insignificant babbling about his new cell and laughter, I left them to their weekly prison get-together.

In prison this sense of fun and camaraderie often hung in the air. These teasing moments revealed a great deal about how easily one can fall into the military avoidance of talking about serious matters such as military involvement in the atrocities being prosecuted, and instead making fun of hardship, discomfort, and evil. Temporarily adopted into this social world, I had become part of their complicity in silence and the accountability that comes with it. My not addressing these issues made me undoubtedly a part of their "circle of silence" and therefore responsible for social neglect regarding serious matters. This is not to say, however, that shared laughter and having fun with the indicted military officers meant moral belonging to a group and moral positioning on matters like state repression and the trials for crimes against humanity.

Laughter and play in a post-conflict setting produce not only the social creativity needed to live with trauma and impunity but also with everyday moral confusion and social uncertainties about accountability and complicity as well as an acknowledgment of the *imaginary* social boundaries between "us" and "them." *Barcelona*'s humor was perhaps the most remarkable and most premeditated in addressing the messiness of accountability—such as the contemporary impunity and hypocrisy among the ruling classes in Argentina to which the human rights movement, to some extent, belonged during the Kirchner governments. All these playful forms are understandable responses to the uncertainties and inconsistencies people face in Argentina, during times when legal systems were incapable of addressing the grievances of victims as well as when official justice is being done. But above all, the laughter and play of relatives, survivors, and the indicted officers and their kin created fleeting moments in which the uncertainty and confusion about state violence and transitional justice as a practice and an ideal were accepted. In a sense, one felt not revenge or forgiveness, happiness or trauma, restoration or retribution, impunity or accountability, but all of these and none of them simultaneously. I believe that in laughter and play we can best feel the ambiguities and failures of transitional justice—not by explaining them away or by providing answers and solutions, but simply by becoming immersed in and part of it.

Ultimately, it was not *what* the joke or the laugh represented or communicated in a roundabout way, but *what* these playful moments did and meant for victims and military officers in particular—sometimes quite ephemeral— circumstances. One might still argue that these playful moments did not alter the distressing situations encountered by the victims and the indicted officers, but simply reproduced power relations and structural inequalities. These criticisms, however, neglect the significance of play in the lifeworld. Laughter and play about violence turn out to be more than catharsis, cultural resistance, moral belonging, or moral confusion. Play smoothly brings contradictions together in one (fleeting) meaningful experience. Social phenomenology has largely neglected the structure of play, but play also constitutes the way in which we engage with and in the world. Whatever form or whatever kind of play, when it comes to violence, any thorough understanding of it requires local knowledge of the content and context of a given joke and laughter. I therefore hesitate to produce a single explanatory model on the function of play in post-conflict settings. We should always localize laughter and play, thinking about why it emerges and how it affects the way people live every day.

Each joke and bout of laughter must be thought through anew.

CHAPTER 7

Where Justice Belongs

IN EARLY 2011, the tribunal had subpoenaed Armando Flores to testify about the kidnapping and assassination of the well-known Argentinian writer Rodolfo Walsh by a *grupo de tarea* (task group). It was the third time he had been asked to testify about this crime. The witness was in his late sixties, but looked older. Although he was trembling a great deal, I jotted down that his voice was remarkably clear and militant. His testimony lasted only forty-five minutes. The witness mainly described the conditions in which he found the house of Rodolfo Walsh: the building looked as if it had been bombed, the walls were perforated with bullets, and furniture was scattered in the garden. Before leaving the stand, Judge Bernardo Martínez asked, as usual, whether the witness had anything more to say. After expressing his criticism about the crucifix displayed in the courtroom, saying it had intimidated him because of the Catholic Church's complicity with the military regime, Armando looked straight into the courtroom and said, "This is for the children and grandchildren of the defendants: 'Where are the bodies, where are the children, and where is Walsh's last manuscript?'"

Normally, at the end of their testimony witnesses addressed these final words about the location of the disappeared remains and the appropriated children of the disappeared to the indicted military officers present in the courtroom, or to the armed forces in general. Surprisingly, Armando had addressed his words to the children and grandchildren of the indicted military officers. That night I discussed with my life companion the potential implications of this generational transmission of accountability for crimes against humanity regarding the future of justice for the human rights crimes. Matías agreed that many children of the military must have heard violent stories when they were young. But these children had probably not interpreted these stories as crimes, he said, but as normal practices during times of violence.

Had Armando somehow reinterpreted the generational transmission of memories of violence? Was accountability for perpetrated violence now also being transmitted to future generations? A year later I was able to ask Armando about it. He had carefully prepared his appeal regarding the whereabouts of the bodies and the children of the disappeared to the children and grandchildren of the military. Armando insisted that they had the opportunity *and* the duty to share these truths. They possessed vital information and were accountable for keeping it secret.

Uncertain Justice

Perhaps the peak is over, but the trials for crimes against humanity in Argentina have not yet ended. Besides ongoing trials and appeals against verdicts, there are still new cases to be tried. The stories in this book were fleeting moments in this enormous legal process of trying to achieve justice for the crimes committed during the last dictatorship in Argentina. Armando's final words at the end of my fieldwork resonated strongly as I wrote up my findings. His idea of the transmission of accountability further pushed my reflections on the transitional justice trajectory in Argentina toward uncertainty and infinity. Framing the trial for crimes against humanity in Argentina as "retribution" or "transitional justice" seemed sillier every day. If listening to the (embodied) memories about human right violations involves (re)traumatization for the victims and their children, and if the children of the perpetrators are also accountable for keeping atrocious crimes secret, then the prosecution of the perpetrators cannot lead to any form of closure. How, then, can we be faithful to those who made us transform our understanding and reconcile their knowledge with academia (Jackson 1995, 156)?

In the field, human actions and events do not always fit into the categories and concepts we use in trying to capture social life. Uncertainty about what would happen after the trials came to an end were common in Argentina's courts; nobody really knew what would happen next. I once discussed the possibility of a new general pardon or a new amnesty law with my dear friend Luis Noguiera, a passionate novelist. We discussed it on a street corner in Buenos Aires, using the appropriate determined gestures and raised voices. In 2010 a potential new era of impunity was unimaginable for Luis. After our friendly but heated quarrel, I took his ardent opinion for granted and went home, believing there would be no more place for impunity and denial regarding the crimes of the last dictatorship in Argentina. When Luis visited me in the Netherlands a few years later, we remembered our fight and had to agree that anything was possible in Argentinian politics. Luis had a harder time accepting it.

In 2015 Mauricio Macri, the son of an influential Italian businessman (Franco Macri), and former mayor of Buenos Aires, won the presidential elections. Thus began a new neoliberal era with its own political controversies, such as the notorious "Panama Papers" concerning millions of offshore entities and containing the personal financial information of wealthy individuals, including Mauricio Macri. Although Macri had pledged that the trials for crimes against humanity would continue while he campaigned for presidency in 2015,[1] eight months after having won the election financial cutbacks in the judiciary were implemented and various areas of investigation linked to the crimes of the last dictatorship were discontinued, especially those inclined to expose the roles of businessmen and other civilians during the state repression.[2]

When I returned for a brief fieldtrip and family visit in early 2016, these recent changes in politics and policies were palpable in almost every conversation. For example, Carla Ávila and I met at a coffee bar near the psychology department of the University of Buenos Aires. The rain that afternoon reflected our depressing discussion. Carla felt as if we had spiraled in time, again listening to resurrected stories about the "dirty war" and "fuming revolutionaries" having wildly attacked innocent Argentinians. Pleas to prosecute key figures of the armed guerrilla groups were also gaining ground again. She had never imagined that these stories and claims would become salient again. I noticed that her sense of justice was again at stake. Macri's interpretation of state terrorism in terms of a "dirty war" was not mere rhetoric. These revamped discourses paid lip service to versions of the violent past against which Carla had struggled for so long. Furthermore, they were accompanied by policies and debates that might favor the convicted officers. Macri's discourse and policy outcomes are new traumatizing denials of victims' suffering. The trials for crimes against humanity may have generated fixed punishments on paper, but the practical outcome of incarcerations of the convicted military personnel and the nature and scope of accountability are again being debated in Argentina. The familiar demand among victims and human rights activists: *cárcel común perpetua y efectiva* (common jail for life) seems less certain than it did five years ago.

During the same fieldtrip I also met Aldo Domínguez. I asked him if they were appealing his brother's life imprisonment. He said that Ignacio was not discouraged and they were continuing their struggle. They had merely revised their strategy. The Argentinian penal code states that in the case of illness or old age, convicts are permitted to receive house arrest instead of imprisonment.[3] Sometimes this also applies to younger convicts who have health problems. To be entitled to these fundamental rights, various convicted military personnel opted before the court to frame their prison conditions (ironically) in the context of the universal character of human rights and humanitarianism. During the Kirchner administrations, it had been increasingly difficult for convicted military to access these rights.

When Macri assumed power, many convicted officers tried to convert prison time into house arrest and to benefit from a civilian law—Ley de 2×1.

In 2017 the Supreme Court in Argentina implemented this 2×1 law, which benefited various convicted officers sentenced for crimes against humanity.[4] The law states that the time a convict spends in prison before being sentenced is counted twice. This means that two years of preventive detention (before and during the court proceedings) counts as four years of detention after the sentence is issued. In this case, a convict with a prison sentence of ten years would thus already be released after six years. Because of the complicated nature of the trials for crimes against humanity in which hundreds of crimes are prosecuted simultaneously, many officers have been in detention for years without a sentence. The structural impediments of the justice system in Argentina became an advantage for the convicted officers (Van Roekel and Salvi, forthcoming). But the Supreme Court ruling was not unreciprocated.

The applicability of the 2×1 law for crimes against humanity was widely questioned by local human rights organizations. I was not in Argentina at that time, but in online newspapers I read that the streets of Buenos Aires were once more filled with thousands of protesters headed to the Plaza de Mayo. The protestors were from human rights groups, survivors, and the relatives of the disappeared. People were chanting the common protest lyric: "Como a los nazis, adonde vayan los iremos a buscar" (Like the Nazis, wherever they go we will find them).[5] I also read a new refrain: "Nunca más un genocida suelto" (Never again a genocider free). Six days later, the National Congress gathered to approve a new law that would undo the potential consequences of the Supreme Court ruling in favor of possible new benefits of the 2×1 law. In just twenty-three hours and forty-four minutes—one of the fastest parliamentary procedures in Argentinian history—both chambers approved Law no. 27.362, with only one vote against, declaring the 2×1 calculation for crimes against humanity inapplicable.[6] The social and political controversy concerning the legal appeal for reduced years in prison reignited a nationwide debate concerning the accountability of members of the armed forces for state terror in the 1970s—a debate that continues today (Van Roekel and Salvi, forthcoming).

In November 2018 I was able to meet Ignacio at his home. This confirmed once more that a life sentence in common jail was not a fixed matter. It had been more than eight years since we saw each other in court just before Ignacio received a life sentence. Ignacio explained how he managed to receive house arrest on appeal. His poor health was the main reason, he said. Despite the recent dismissal of 2×1, with Macri still in power and a recent shift toward the conservative right in the region, Ignacio still had high hopes that he would soon be free. New amnesties and general pardons were again on the military agenda. Ignacio was less optimistic about his superiors: they betrayed the "political prisoners" for abandoning their struggle. I noticed his bitterness when he mentioned that he preferred not to see them in the military hospital where he went for regular health checks.

On my way back from this visit, I thought about Carla's deep worries two years earlier. A firm sentence of life imprisonment was not a guarantee of justice. Concerns about how to address this ongoing uncertainty on multiple levels about the aftermath of state violence and human rights violations in Argentina led me to analyze the affective processes of justice without predicting determinate consequences of the trials for crimes against humanity. Indeterminism fits better with a phenomenal approach. The anthropology of experience shares with phenomenology a skepticism toward determinate systems of knowledge (Jackson 1995, 160). I share a similar preference for holding on to the untidiness of everyday life and showing how people, replete with feelings, are engaged in a material existence and enmeshed in the complexities of their social worlds (Wilson 1997a, 15). I have done so by moving back and forth between anthropology of emotion and social phenomenology as they contribute to, but in a sense go beyond, contemporary debates on transitional justice and human rights violations in Argentina and other societies that struggle with accountability for and remembrance of state violence and human rights violations. This concluding chapter revisits the debates on transitional justice and emphasizes why I am skeptical of the range and applicability of this concept to describe and analyze the trials for crimes against humanity in Argentina. Instead, phenomenal justice examines the ways people define and experience feelings that engender social processes concerning atrocities, human rights abuses, and injustices that do not always fit in a transitional phase from conflict to settlement. With some final considerations on feelings and the lifeworld, the chapter ultimately addresses the issue of where justice belongs.

FEELINGS

Contemporary theorizing often assumes that violence and trauma are conditions that must be overcome. In departing from this view, transitional justice as both a theory and a policy has therefore often been ineffective in disclosing alternative assumptions about what trauma and violence mean and do to people whose lives have been affected by atrocities and by truth and justice practices. Future theorizing on violence and its aftermath would benefit from a thorough revision of this liberal utopia. For many Argentinians, the idea that truth and justice practices bring closure to trauma is an immoral thought—and even unimaginable in their social world where legacies of impunity and denial endure and can easily resurface. For survivors and relatives of the disappeared *dolor* (pain) and *deuda* (debt) must not be overcome, but instead must yield important moral resources in their daily lives to counter social indifference and potential setbacks of justice. As they continuously search for and speak about truth as well as share pain and guilt without ever reaching a definite conclusion, victims and activists reaffirm an everyday mode of moral being. Without arguing that their feelings are consistent or fixed in content, I came to understand that their pain and guilt were not transient or curable, yet taken to be defining conditions of existence (Kleinman and Desjarlais 1995, 180–188). The trials for crimes against humanity are another realm for the reaffirmation of this moral being.

The naturalness of violence, for that matter, works in similar ways for the indicted officers. By acknowledging *vergüenza* (shame), various indicted officers reluctantly accepted they had been wrong to employ violence. But this was rarely manifested for various reasons. Silence and loyalty were defining conditions of their existence. *Tragar el sapo* (swallow the frog) is not only an act of denial or deliberate amnesia. Violence belongs to their social world and comes with moral codes that only difficulty fit with civilian social mores. The act of confessing or publicly atoning is an immoral demand, and for some officers it is an impossible task. We may not agree with the content of this moral reasoning, or even find it outrageous, but that does not mean we should ignore it.

Impunity has been indicated as the major driving force of truth and justice practices in Argentina. I do not deny that impunity and the revived discourses and practices that again question, deny, and silence victims' injustices and traumas are key to the transitional justice landscape in Argentina. But from an affective stance, another underlying cause of this local "justice cascade" can be found in the way victims experience trauma as "home" vis-à-vis the stubborn silence of the military. Such an overall conclusion, pointing to psychoanalysis and militarism as explanatory frames of meaning, is always tempting. But again I am hesitant about this conceptual determinism. Although there were profound desires for otherness, the analysis of individual cases showed ambiguous everyday experiences regarding the traumatic home and *tragar el sapo*. These included Nora and her reluctance to repeat the story of the disappearance of her son David, and Scilingo and Molina who rejected the pact of silence and the critique against remorse, and publicly confessed the atrocities. Competing everyday moralities partially constitute the ideals and practices of truth and justice, which creates a messy field of feelings. I believe that it is in these affective in-between spaces where one feels the ambiguities and inconsistencies of life.

Despite a predominant intellectual gaze within transitional justice theory toward remorse, revenge, and forgiveness, these feelings were not suitable for defining experiences of justice and truth or retribution and restoration (or lack thereof) in Argentina. Forgiveness, remorse, and revenge were all inapplicable, albeit on different terms. These feelings and their related retributive or restorative practices originate from a desire to end conflict and suffering. But for many victims forgiveness solves the traumatic consequences of torture and disappearance. This resolution goes against the ways in which they define existence and being alive. The practical outcome of retribution worked out differently. *Alegría* (happiness) was their way of engaging with retribution. For many victims justice actually became synonymous with this local mixture of trauma and happiness. One might think this form of alternative justice would be awkward in a trial, but in Argentina's courts the formal and the alternative blended together quite easily. The military had a harder time accepting justice on these terms. For them, the locus of trauma and happiness made the trial into a circus. In return, their Christian ideal of agreement, harmony and silence, and military criticism of remorse continue to produce outrage among the victims. These various feelings in the courts were not existential facts, but ambiguous sources and uncertain outcomes of intersubjective engagements.

LIFEWORLDS

Researching and thinking for more than a decade about feelings and violence, I now realize that violence does not destroy sociality (or the social structure of the lifeworld). Studying morality involving dark themes powerfully confirms the intersubjectivity and sharedness of how we engage with and in the world. Conflict communicates how intersubjectivity and morality work in the ways we engage with and in the world. Lifeworlds in conflict would actually be what continually activates the justice cascade in Argentina. An anthropological return to the lifeworld is then practical and urgent.

The question of the universality of experience has long bothered anthropologists. By blending social philosophy and ethnography, anthropology has widely contributed to the existential question of what it means to be human. I very much welcome the recent return to phenomenology and the lifeworld in anthropology.[7] These anthropologists provide valuable countercriticism in regard to the alleged intellectual pointlessness of the descriptive introspectivity of phenomenology. According to these criticisms, the lifeworld would be too fixed and the structures of experience would leave too little space for contestation and change. But if we look at "how lifeworlds work" (Jackson 2017), we do not blindly accept fixed structures. We must simply keep asking: How does morality look? What does the social mean? How does time work? How is the body experienced? These analytical steps back are not pointless; they stimulate thinking in new directions toward contemporary theories of how people suffer on their own terms and how justice (and injustice) looks in our world today. I encourage such "phenomenal" inquiries that can change the course of urgent societal debates. Contemporary migration, new forms of economic and digital warfare, and increasing climate change are worrisome developments that produce new injuries and injustices and will require clearing in the future. We should not automatically frame these considerations in terms of transition from conflict to agreement, from injury to cure, and from injustice to justice, but as infinite ideals and practices in which people try to make sense of the world and make life more livable, even in dark times (Ortner 2016).

I see various potentials for phenomenological anthropology in rethinking contemporary and future conflicts, injustices, and their aftermaths, in their multiple and unexpected forms. First, we must always question anew how the lifeworld works for people whose lives are permeated by violence and injustice, and how these are connected to larger structures and processes of inequality and precariousness. Second, I believe it is in the fleeting moments of laughter and play that we can most feel the ambiguities, uncertainties, and inconsistencies of the structures of "being." Laughter and play allow us to feel the cracks and fissures of the ideals of moral life and how these play out in everyday life. Third, representations of the ways we engage with and in the world definitely require narrative styles that convey the complexity and moral messiness of social life. Besides the indispensable roles of ethnography, poetry, and fiction in describing how people feel, we might want to look for other forms of mediations that inform us about life in the phenomenal sense. We need new modes of telling stories about violence and injustice because we still have a long way to go in reaching new pathways to knowledge that accept the idea that life is not an abstraction.

Acknowledgments

Ethnography is a social activity. We all know that. Without the minds, bodies, and voices of so many people this ethnography would not have been accomplished. Above all and before anything else, I want to thank everyone in Argentina for all the time they spent sharing their lives with me. As I have decided to maintain anonymity, I will not name them, but without them this book would not exist. Thank you.

Next, I thank all my colleagues in the Department of Cultural Anthropology at Utrecht University. Your critical comments and reflections on previous drafts and persistent belief in the research that underlies this book have been the engine for more than a decade of fieldwork and thinking on violence in Latin America. I especially want to thank Ton Robben and Hans de Kruijf who supervised this project on Argentina from beginning to the end. I am grateful for all their thorough comments and firm belief that thoughts simply need time to mature. At crucial moments both have guided me into the right direction. I would also like to thank Kees Koonings, Martijn Oosterbaan, and Carmen Pérez Pérez for their insightful comments on previous drafts, and Marie-Louise Glebbeek for her initial encouragement to continue in academia. I want to thank individually Tessa Diphoorn, Katrien Klep, Yvon van der Pijl, Floortje Toll, and Nikkie Wiegink for being inspiring colleagues and caring friends.

I also want to thank all the members of the interdisciplinary PhD-student forum for research on Latin America at the Centre for Latin American Research and Documentation in Amsterdam. Our discussions always helped to put emerging insights into regional perspective. I want to thank Willem de Haan from Vrije Universiteit Amsterdam for allowing me to present my first findings from the field at an early stage and for encouraging me to bring this project to a fruitful end. I also thank my new colleagues in the Department of Social and Cultural Anthropology at Vrije Universiteit Amsterdam for offering their warmth and confidence in this project, and the time to finish this book. Lastly, I want to thank the late Marieke Aafjes for sharing her Argentinian knowledge and putting me in contact with her Argentinian friends. You left this world far too early.

I also want to thank all my inspiring colleagues and dear friends in Argentina. Buenos Aires now feels like home because of all the people who have helped me throughout the entire research project. First of all, I would like to thank all those who belong to the different nongovernmental organizations, the tribunals, and other governmental institutions who have been working determinedly on the trials for crimes against humanity and commemorative practices. Their persistent help and guidance have been extraordinary. Second, I especially want to thank Sergio Visacovsky at the Institute of Economic and Social Development (IDES) for his warmth and guidance during my fieldwork. I am also very grateful to all the other colleagues at IDES during my several stays in Buenos Aires. My special thanks go to Lucila Dallaglio. Likewise, I want to thank Alejandro Isla for allowing me to work at the Latin American Social Sciences Institute in Buenos Aires during one of my stays.

I want to thank Mario Ayala, Sabina Frederic, Celeste Perosino, Mariano Plotkin, Sebastián Rey, and Valentina Salvi for sharing inspiring conversations and their critical comments on my emerging ideas about the trials for crimes against humanity and the meanings of trauma and perpetrator hood in Argentina. I thank Eliana Depino and Melina Di Frabizio for their cheerful support and wonderful help in transcribing the interviews. I also want to thank Peggy Visser, the cultural attaché of the Dutch Embassy at the time of my fieldwork. I thank Ram Natarajan and Katja Seidel for sharing fieldwork in Buenos Aires. We did not and do not always agree, but that makes anthropology such a stimulating field of study and fulfilling way of life. I want to thank Eliana de Arrascaeta for her bright and original insights on Argentinian history and for helping me with the Spanish translations. Finally, I want to thank Beatriz Santos for being an amazing support and dear friend.

This book could also not have been completed without the marvelous support of the editorial team at Rutgers University Press, especially Lisa Banning. Our smooth communication made the world of publishing much less frightening. I also want to thank Karen Ann Faulk and two anonymous reviewers for taking the time to read all the chapters and providing illuminating comments that improved the book.

Finally, I want to thank my family—Gerrit van Roekel, Mariet Paes, Anne van Roekel, Koen Hornman, and Lou and Fien Hornman—they keep me going without losing sight of what really matters. My special thanks go to my mother, Mariet, who from the very beginning became the backbone of my research and writing. Without her I would never have come this far. I also want to thank my family-in-law in Argentina for their ongoing support: the late Julio Cordiviola, Mariana Cordiviola, Hernán Cordiviola, Kika Cordiviola, Maria del Piero, and Antonio Esposito. But above all, I want to thank Matías Cordiviola. Since the very first time we met in Buenos Aires, his love and care have been magical. Leah and Bruno are the greatest gifts and living results of that. Sharing our life is as unpredictable as it is breathtaking.

Eva van Roekel
Rosmalen
February 2019

Glossary

a flor de piel. Close to the surface, a phrase that means an experience is very recent

antes y después. Before and after, a phrase that describes important moments in time that mark a difference

aquellos años de plomo. A commonly used phrase to describe the last dictatorship (literally: these years of lead)

argentinidad. The typical features of Argentina and its people

blando. Weak, used among the military to describe the weak civilian body

canto a la vida. Hymn to life

Carapintadas. Military rebels of the 1980s in Argentina (literally: painted faces)

Casa Rosada. Pink House, office of the president of Argentina

choripan. Grilled sausage on a roll

chupado. Sucked up, used to describe the clandestine practice of detaining and disappearing people during the dictatorship

compañero/a. Comrade, generally used among survivors and human rights activists

conurbano. Greater Buenos Aires

deber de la memoria. Duty to remember, a much-used phrase among survivors of the dictatorship

desaparecidos. Disappeared, used to designate the people who disappeared during the dictatorship

despacho. Office at the tribunals

duro. Hard or tough, used to describe military bodies

en carne propia. In the flesh

escrache. Public shaming action as a form of alternative justice

espíritu de cuerpo. Esprit de corps

fachos. Deriving from fascists, used to refer to the military and the conservative right

genocida. Genocider, a person who participated in genocide

grupo de tarea. Task group, referring to the teams of operatives during the last dictatorship

herida abierta. Open wound

hijos y nietos de presos políticos. A small activist group formed by the children and grandchildren of the political prisoners (i.e., indicted military officers)

inoperante. An incompetent person

juicio y castigo. Trial and punishment, a term much used among victims to demand punishment and the imprisonment of perpetrators of the dictatorship

juicios por la verdad. Truth trials, which began in La Plata in the 1990s, subpoenaed perpetrators to speak about the crimes without facing penalty

kirchnerismo. The period and style of governance during Nestor and Cristina Kirchner's mandate (2003–2015)

las últimas palabras. The last words before a verdict is announced

mate. Herbal tea

Montoneros. Peronist militant group engaged in the armed struggle against the dictatorship

murga. Popular band of street musicians

Nunca Más. Never Again, title of the CONADEP truth commission report

pacto de silencio. Pact of silence, commonly used to describe the military silence regarding the crimes committed between 1976 and 1983

picanas. Electric prods, used during torture sessions

poner el cuerpo. To put one's body on the line, a local expression that means to be committed to a social cause, and to assume bodily risks

porteños. Inhabitants of Buenos Aires

presente. Present, often shouted to remember and identify the people that disappeared during the dictatorship

prisión perpetúa. Life imprisonment; in Argentina this means twenty-five years

pueblo. People, used to address the working classes

quincho. Thatched-roof area, often used for barbecues

silencio es salud. Silence is health, a common expression during the military regime to imply that it was safer to keep quiet about the violence

siluetazo. Artistic act of drawing silhouettes of the disappeared

teoría de los dos demonios. Theory of two demons, a political discourse that equates revolutionary violence with illegal state repression

testigo-víctima. Witness-victim

tragar el sapo. To swallow the frog, a local expression meaning not to verbalize your troubles and anxieties

verdad y justicia. Truth and justice, a common phrase used among victims of the dictatorship

Notes

Chapter Prologue

1. I have anonymized almost all the names of the people I talked to in the field. The names of those with public profiles have not been altered.

Chapter 1 Phenomenal Justice

1. Interview with Carlos Espinosa, October 6, 2010, Buenos Aires.
2. For two decades legal scholars, historians, political scientists, and applied professionals have had a leading role in the establishment of transitional justice as a new field of academic and applied science (e.g., Bloomfield, Barnes, and Huyse 2003; Elster 2004; Hayner 2002; Kritz 1995; Roht-Arriaza and Mariezcurrena 2006; Teitel 2000).
3. See, for instance, Hayner 2002; Kritz 1995; Roht-Arriaza and Mariezcurrena 2006; and Rotberg and Thompson 2000.
4. See, for instance, Arthur 2009; Barahona de Brito 2001; Lichtenfeld 2005; Skaar 2011.
5. Some studies on transitional justice have looked into unconnected feelings such as pain, vengeance, or remorse and have only assessed them from the perspective of the victim or the perpetrator (Doak 2011; Jelin 2010; Mendeloff 2009; Minow 1998; Payne 1999).
6. In the previous two decades feelings have taken an increasingly central place in social theorizing. See, for instance: Bandes and Blumenthal 2012; Davies and Spencer 2010; Finkel and Parrot 2006; Gregg and Seigworth 2010; Karstedt, Loader, and Strange 2011; Wharton 2009; Wulff 2007.
7. See, for instance: Heelas 1986; Hochschild 1979; Middleton 1989; Wierzbicka 1999.
8. There have been attempts to reduce the lack, or even absence, of agency in conceptualizations of feelings by introducing the concept of "emotional dissonance." The main criticism of this is that people do not conform automatically to rules governing emotions (Martin and Doka 2000, 58).
9. Seminal work in the anthropology of emotion has delivered insightful and detailed descriptions of feelings in people's daily lives without framing it in abstractions, such as *Veiled Sentiments* (Abu-Lughod 1986), *Never in Anger* (Briggs 1970), *Body and Emotion* (Desjarlais 1992), *Unnatural Emotions* (Lutz 1988), *The Heart Is Unknown Country* (Rebhun 1999), *Knowledge and Passion* (Rosaldo 1980), *Death without Weeping* (Scheper-Hughes 1993), and *Managing Turbulent Hearts* (Wikan 1990).
10. Understanding feeling as a combination of conscious and physiological aspects dominates the interdisciplinary field that studies feelings (Frosh 2011, 18; Gieser 2008, 305; Laird 2007, 14; Scherer 2005, 699).

11. MRI means magnetic resonance imaging, together with PET scans (positron emission tomography), and CAT scans (computerized axial tomography) are used in neuroimaging, an area in cognitive science where human behavior, including emotions, is 'made visible' in the brain.

12. Ethnographic reliability and verification lie in the repetition of this social procedure (Mead 1964, 55).

13. Once I asked the son of an indicted military officer who sat next to me in court what he had been doing. He answered that he had spent the whole night watching World War I documentaries. Children of the disappeared instead often watched films on local human rights issues and social justice.

14. Many anthropologists have written powerful and detailed narratives about feelings from a person-centered approach (Behar 1996; Briggs 1970; Rosaldo 1989). This focus on a few individuals (though always intersubjective) is a common and valid practice in the anthropology of emotion.

15. To protect the interlocutors as much as possible, besides changing their names, I also decided to avoid explicitly referring to the trials for crimes against humanity in the chapters, as many events as well as names of defendants and witnesses circulate in (digital and print) official and media documentation.

16. To understand these aspects of experience that people find difficult to put into words, metaphors have been widely investigated (Bruner 1986, 21; Csordas 1994, 16; Kövecses 2005, 2; Jackson 1996, 9).

17. See, for instance, the work of Francine Lorimer (2010, 100) and Tanya Luhrmann (2010, 213) regarding how reflexivity helped gain an understanding of emotions in the field.

18. Vincent Crapanzano (1980) does exactly this in his ethnography about the life of Tuhami, a Morrocan tile maker, and his relationship with a she-demon. Using an interactive mode of narrative, Crapanzano raises the dilemma of the "reality" of an interlocutor's personal history and the "truth" of autobiography. By explicitly addressing their otherness, the text suggests the way in which Tuhami's life history is reconstituted through the fieldwork negotiations between the anthropologist, the interlocutor, and the field assistant.

Chapter 2 Things That Matter

1. Interview with Carla Ávila, July 21, 2010, Buenos Aires.

2. A study of the reports on human rights violations in Guatemala has shown that the Guatemalan legal apparatus particularly demanded decontextualized and legalistic reporting of the events. The outcomes of these human rights reports were therefore "individualized, a-cultural, deracinated and . . . universalistic" (Wilson 1997c, 157).

3. Trials can easily be understood as liminal spaces with different rules for acting and interpreting meaning from everyday life (Turner 1986). I must admit that framing the trials as a "ritual" has been persuasive. But the experiences in the courts of my Argentinian interlocutors and friends did not seem liminal. Liminality implies a period of isolation with at least the expectation of a postliminal phase. Without denying the performative processes during court hearings, everyday life and ritual were just too intertwined. There was no prospect of or desire for an after-phase, the courtroom was not a liminal place, and the verdict was not a closure.

4. A study on a therapeutic world has shown that generosity and small attentions were not the stuff of the medical chart. They were the undocumented exchanges that did not belong to the official scope, but thoroughly shaped the world of therapeutic care (Mattingly 1998, 22).

5. Interview with Victoria Herrera de Quiroga, August 2, 2010, Córdoba.
6. Interview with Ana Luisa Campos and Blanca Capellini, March 15, 2012, Buenos Aires.
7. Interview with Bernardo Martínez, March 15, 2012, Buenos Aires.
8. Recent studies have shown that victims have become relevant participants in retributive justice across the globe (Englebrecht 2011, 144; Letschert and van Dijk 2011, 3–5; Pham et al. 2011, 284).
9. Interview with Laura Figueroa, June 18, 2010, Buenos Aires.
10. Interview with Laura Figueroa, July 2, 2010, Buenos Aires.
11. See the report *Acompañamiento a testigos y querellantes en el marco de los juicios contra el terrorismo de Estado. Primeras Experiencias* (2009, 33–38).
12. See the report *Acompañamiento a testigos y querellantes en el marco de los juicios contra el terrorismo de Estado. Estrategias de intervención* (2008, 27).
13. This so-called subject-subject conflation in bodily experience often occurs between healer and patient. Simultaneous sensuous experience produces sensory knowledge that replaces the division of two or more subjects into a particular consubjectivity (Sieler 2015, 147).
14. For example, Carol Kidron (2011) discusses how the descendant of a Holocaust survivor frequently heard her father whimpering in his sleep. She never asked why he was crying, but these experiences influenced her later reframing of her father's crying as Holocaust-related.
15. Interview with Laura Figueroa, July 2, 2010, Buenos Aires.
16. See Article 384 on the examination of witnesses (*Código procesal penal de la Nación* 2005, 108).
17. Interview with Elena Brodowski, June 24, 2010, Buenos Aires.
18. Future witnesses were not required to wait in the hallway outside the courtroom at all tribunals. Each trial and each court had its own rules for the entrance of future witnesses.
19. Ari Gandsman (2012) argues that many Mothers and Grandmothers of Plaza de Mayo share the rhetoric of having lived the last dictatorship *en carne propia* (in the flesh) and therefore their own bodies have become literal and physical vessels of remembrance. He refers, for instance, to a radio interview with Hebe de Bonafini, the well-known leader of the the Mothers of the Plaza de Mayo, in which she criticized written missives. Bonafini stated that for mothers of the disappeared, putting their bodies on the line was the best message.
20. For numerous visual examples of silhouettes, see Longoni and Bruzzone (2008).
21. Chapter 3 elaborates in more detail the theory of the Forum of São Paulo. In brief, it proposes that in 1992 most of the left-wing factions in Latin America gathered at a forum in São Paulo where they agreed that the armed struggle of the 1970s and 1980s had failed. Hence these factions decided to opt for political trajectories and democratic elections. According to Argentinian followers of this theory, the current trials for crimes against humanity initiated under the Kirchner governments are part of this assumed left-wing conspiracy.
22. Letter to the author written by Ignacio Domínguez, July 24, 2010, Córdoba.
23. Law 26.472, ratified on December 18, 2008, by the Argentinian legislative authority.
24. Anthropological studies of military embodiment have mainly focused on the military body in combat or training. A welcome exception is Salih Can Açiksöz's (2012) article about disabled veterans of the Turkish army.
25. Article 18, "Nature and Extension," of the Argentinian penal code discusses the competences of each court and states that trials should be conducted by judges and tribunals that correspond to their jurisdictions (*Código procesal penal de la Nación* 2005, 35).

26. Before the amnesty laws were implemented, similar disapproval existed in the early 1980s (Waisbord 1991, 159–160). A corporatist tradition had profoundly affected civil-military relations in Argentinian society. Many officers thought that civilians were not able to fully understand, and were even opposed to, military codes, rules, hierarchies, and institutional dynamics.
27. Interviews with Laura Figueroa, June 18, 2010, and July 2, 2010, Buenos Aires.

Chapter 3 Time

1. In 1973 the infamous clandestine death squad (the *Alianza Anticomunista Argentina*), secretly allied to the government, initiated a counterinsurgency to wipe out a wide range of government opponents.
2. Besides the *Nunca Más* report of the National Commission on the Disappearance of Persons (CONADEP 1984), for further comprehensive overviews and detailed analyses of the last dictatorship and transitional justice and reconciliation processes in Argentina, I recommend Crenzel (2010), Feitlowitz (1998), Jelin and Kaufman (2004), Lichtenfeld (2005), Malamud Goti (2000), Nino (1996), Robben (2005), Taylor (1997), and T. Wright (2007).
3. For detailed analyses of memory in Latin America, see: Crenzel 2010; Jelin and Kaufman 2004; Klep 2012; Levin and Franco 2007; and Van Drunen 2010.
4. Interview with Laura Figueroa, July 2, 2010, Buenos Aires.
5. See the edited volumes of Argentinian scholars of an interdisciplinary field that works on memory and the last dictatorship and departs from the notion of conflicting pasts and multiple voices: *La cambiante memoria de la dictadura* (Lvovich and Bisquert 2008) *Memoria(s) y política* (De la Peza 2009), and *Pasados en conflicto* (Mudrovcic 2009).
6. This emphasis on the personal and the affective in the way victims of state repression remembered has been crucial to the understanding of the memory landscapes in countries of the Southern Cone (Achugar 2008; Oberti 2009; Sarlo 2005).
7. Interview with Nora Ortega de Sánchez, October 8, 2010, Buenos Aires.
8. In 1995 General Balza apologized publicly for illegitimate warfare during the military regime. For detailed analysis of this public mea culpa, see J. Patrice McSherry's (1997) work on officers' confessions in Argentina. This public apology of a military officer will be discussed in more detail in chapter 5.
9. Interview with Nora Ortega de Sánchez, October 8, 2010, Buenos Aires.
10. Parque de la Memoria is the largest commemorative park of the last dictatorship in Buenos Aires and was opened to the general public in 2007. It is located in the northern region of the capital city, next to the Rio de la Plata. For more information, see, accessed March 18, 2014, www.parquelamemoria.org.ar.
11. The story of the disappearance of Negrito Avellaneda and his parents Floreal and Iris is well-known in Argentina, and thus pseudonyms would not have anonymized them sufficiently. Because I think that the story is key to understanding Nora's entangled temporalities, I decided to include the story without altering their names.
12. In Argentina *herida abierta* not only referred to the last dictatorship. Other violent events were also considered *herida abiertas* in local media and casual conversation. These included the Malvinas/Falklands War, which killed more than six hundred Argentinian soldiers in 1982, the bombing of the Argentinian Israelite Mutual Association (AMIA), which killed eighty-five people and injured hundreds more in 1994, and the death of almost two hundred people in a fire at the nightclub República Cromañón because of official negligence in monitoring safety measures. These victims and survivors often spoke in similar terms and turned to practices similar to those of victims of the last dictatorship.

13. On the illegal adoptions of the children of the disappeared as *herida abierta*, see "No se trató de conductas ocasionales," *Página12*, April 11, 2012.
14. The metaphorical understanding of an open wound is not restricted to Argentinian victims. In his article "Mourning and Melancholia" (1917), Sigmund Freud had already introduced a parallel between an open wound in body tissue and psychic suffering to address the infinite processes of mourning.
15. Other studies have also shown how conspiracy theories are significant interpretative frames of current complex sociopolitical operations (Bickford 2011, 161; Boyer 2006, 331; Jamil and Rousseau 2011, 248; Marcus and Powell 2003, 331).
16. There were two kinds of conspiracy-driven inclinations—a total, almost paranoid, discourse about a rigid, eternal, and invincible conspiracy, and a partial discourse about concrete denunciations of a plot, with identifiable individuals and institutions, which can be neutralized (Bohoslavsky 2009, 20).
17. For more information on the theory of the Forum of São Paulo, see, accessed October 12, 2012, http://www.unoamerica.org/unoPAG/principal.php.
18. A study of Uruguayan military memory has shown that military officers in Uruguay have only recently acknowledged the possibility of a plurality of truths and interpretations of the past, which has been an important change in their institutional rhetoric (Achugar 2008, 206).
19. Interview with Alfonso Palacios, October 22, 2010, Buenos Aires.
20. FAMUS is no longer active. For information on CELTyV and complete memory, see, accessed November 19, 2015, http://www.celtyv.org.
21. Interview with Aldo Domínguez, June 22, 2010, Buenos Aires.

Chapter 4 Trauma

1. This chapter has been adapted from Van Roekel (2018b).
2. Since the late nineteenth century, psychoanalytical practice and psychoanalytic thinking are important characteristics in the lives of many urban Argentinians (Hollander 1992, 284–285; Puget 2002; Robben 2005, 345; Súarez-Orozco 1990, 369–370).
3. See, for instance: Caruth 1996; Das 2007; Felman 2002; Good 1994; and Stolorow 2003.
4. Seminal works within this "anthropology of morality" include: Csordas 2013; Mattingly 2014; Zigon 2008; and Zigon and Throop 2014.
5. Interview with Laura Figueroa, August 18, 2010, Buenos Aires.
6. Interview with Laura Figueroa, July 2, 2010, Buenos Aires.
7. Interview with Carla Ávila, May 11, 2010, Buenos Aires.
8. Interview with Carla Ávila, July 21, 2010, Buenos Aires.
9. Chapter 5 will further explore the role of just war theory and Catholic notions of punishing the guilty with regard to the justification of state terror among the indicted military officers.
10. Guilt and victimhood in contexts of collective violence are a well-studied field in the social sciences and humanities (Branscombe and Doosje 2004; Cordner 2007; Nutkiewicz 2003; Striblen 2007).
11. Interview with Fabián Bianchi, June 24, 2010, Buenos Aires.
12. Interview with Luis Noguiera, October 8, 2010, Buenos Aires.
13. H.I.J.O.S. stands for *Hijos por la Identidad y la Justicia contra el Olvido y el Silencio* (Sons and Daughters for Identity and Justice against Oblivion and Silence).
14. For the relation between guilt and morality, see: Armon-Jones 1986, 53; Lickel, Schmader, and Barquissau 2004, 52; and Tudor 2001, 180.
15. On a less formalized scale, *el testimonio* (testimony) in Latin America has become another—though controversial—political and literary genre that co-constitutes

forms of justice by telling truth about the witnessing of injustices and suffering (Beverley 2004).

16. Interview with Isolda Hernández, September 28, 2010, Buenos Aires.

CHAPTER 5 DISGRACE

1. Letter to author from Ignacio Domínguez, July 24, 2010, Córdoba.
2. Interview with Alfonso Palacios, October 22, 2010, Buenos Aires.
3. The Full Stop Law and the Due Obedience Law did not cover court cases linked to the illegal appropriation of children. As a result, military officers, including ex-general Videla, have been prosecuted for crimes committed as a result of abducting children and altering their identities (Lichtenfeld 2005, 4).
4. "En su alegato final, Videla reivindicó la represión y justificó sus métodos," *Clarín*, December 22, 2010; "Videla fue condenado a prisión perpetua e irá a una cárcel común," *La Nación*, December 22, 2010; and "El dictador volvió a reivindicar sus crímenes," *Página12*, December 21, 2010.
5. Victims of the Khmer Rouge also considered perpetrators' public responses on due obedience and remorselessness extremely unacceptable (Hinton 2005, 277).
6. See the newspaper article, untitled article, *Clarín*, November 10, 2010.
7. For a defendant's right to silence, see Article 296 (*Código procesal penal de la Nación* 2005).
8. For detailed analyses on the intertwinement of the military and politics in Argentina, see: McSherry 1997, 36–38; Plotkin and Zimmermann 2012a, 27; Potash 1971, 402–404; and Rouquié 1983, 65–67.
9. "Just wars" or "moral crusades" existed not only in the hearts and minds of Argentinian military officers in the 1970s. Among retired military officers of World War II and the Vietnam War similar belief systems of just wars and moral crusades existed in the United States (Brunk, Secrest, and Tamashiro 1990, 87–88).
10. Many military officers and their kin described the prosecuted members of the armed and security forces as "political prisoners." I use the term here without implying any moral or political opinions.
11. Graham Dawson's (1994, 22) notion of "subjective composure" discusses similar dynamics in the constructing of masculine identities among British soldiers. The stories soldiers tell not only construct favorable formal and coherent narratives but also "compose" a version of the self that can be lived with in relative psychic comfort.
12. Among Vietnam combat veterans, besides military education, military training, and combat experience, a long-standing military family heritage also strongly affected officers' moral codes (Singer 2004, 380–381).
13. See *Ejército Argentino* (1968, 14, 62, 120–123).
14. Interview with Aldo Domínguez, June 22, 2010, Buenos Aires.
15. Interview with Aldo Domínguez and Eduardo Domínguez, March 23, 2012, Buenos Aires.
16. Article 667 states that ostensible resistance or disobedience of a service order communicated by a superior will be punished by imprisonment, or if in the presence of the enemy, by the death penalty or indefinite imprisonment. *Código de Justicia Militar*, Buenos Aires, July 4, 1951. Published in the official gazette, August 6, 1951.
17. For detailed descriptions and analyses of these officers' confessions, see: Badaró (2009, 311), Hershberg and Agüero (2005, 20–21), McSherry (1997, 263–266), Marchesi (2005, 202–204), Robben (2005, 351–352), and Salvi (2012, 274).
18. Interview with Alfonso Palacios, March 30, 2012, Buenos Aires.
19. *Ejército Argentino* (1968, 2).

20. Article 514 of the Argentinian code of military justice, in force between 1976 and 1983, states that when a crime is committed because of the execution of a service order, the superior who gave the order will be the only person responsible, the inferior will be considered an accomplice only if he exceeds the order during its execution. *Código de Justicia Militar*, Buenos Aires, July 4, 1951. Published in the official gazette, August 6, 1951.

21. See *Arte de mandar* (Gavet, Brito, Narváez 1996, 72–84). This book about a French officer in the Napoleonic army has often been consulted by the Argentinian army (Badaró 2009, 224, n. 78).

22. *Ejército Argentino* (1968, 6).

23. *Ejército Argentino* (1968, 14–15).

24. The machinelike approach to emotion and the military has been widely critiqued among anthropologists (Ben-Ari 1998, 33–46; Higate 2001, 448–449; Katz 1990; Kilshaw 2008, 232–233; and MacLeish 2012, 54–58).

25. This process of marginalization is well described in: Frederic 2012, 229–230; Payne 2008, 6; and Waisbord 1991, 160–162. The increasing social neglect and marginalization of the armed forces in Argentina became an important moral resource for internal processes of military victimization (Badaró 2009, 335; Guber 2008, 124; and Lomsky-Feder 2004, 99–100).

26. McSherry (1997, 33) and Norden (1996, 104–105) describe this slow reversal of symbolic authority of the military in Argentinian society.

27. Acts of recognition by superiors, colleagues, and the state are important symbolic practices in military life (Açiksöz 2012, 9–11; Ben-Ari 2005, 658–659; Bickford 2011, 120–124; MacLeish 2012, 59; and Waisbord 1991, 159).

28. Interview with Aldo Domínguez and Eduardo Domínguez, March 23, 2012, Buenos Aires.

29. For the role of the Malvinas/Falklands War in the marginalization of the armed forces, see: Guber 2008, 120; Frederic 2008, 19; L. Martin 2010; and Waisbord 1991, 164–197.

30. Since 2012, EAAF (the Argentinian Forensic Anthropology Team that has been excavating and identifying the bones of thousands of the disappeared) has been appointed to identify ninety soldiers who were killed in the Malvinas/Falklands War and buried in anonymous graves.

31. Accessed July 17, 2018, www.federacionvgm.com.ar.

32. Studies of German military life have revealed similar situations for military families in post–World War II Germany (Bickford 2011, 157; and Livingstone 2010, 213).

33. *Hijos y nietos de presos políticos* was founded in 2009. Participants were all children and grandchildren of members of the armed forces who were being prosecuted in the current trials for crimes against humanity. They considered themselves the new victims of the last dictatorship. In their opinion their fathers and grandfathers were illegitimately in jail. Accessed July 26, 2012, http://hijosynietosdepresospolíticos .wordpress.com/about.

34. The Association of Lawyers for Justice and Harmony is a group of lawyers sympathetic to the prosecuted members of the armed forces in the trials for crimes against humanity, for whom they claim fair trials. Accessed November 29, 2013, http://www.justiciayconcordia.org.

35. The Association of Relatives and Friends of the Political Prisoners of Argentina (AFyAPPA) emerged in 2006; its main objective is to unite family and friends of members of the armed and security forces who are being prosecuted and detained. Accessed August 1, 2012, http://afyappa.blogsport.com.

36. Interview with Alfonso Palacios, October 22, 2010, Buenos Aires.

37. Similarly, shame is often described as an overall attack on the self, which people often handle through reinterpretation, self-splitting, or forgetting, and through

denial and a desire to distance themselves from the entire situation rather than facing it (M. Lewis 2008, 742–757; Lickel, Schmader, and Barquissau 2004, 52).

38. Jorge Videla did not allow me to take notes during our conversation on October 7, 2009. I wrote my field notes about our conversation immediately after the prison visit when my memories were still fresh.

39. Interview with Rafael Araballeda, October 18, 2010, Buenos Aires.

40. During my third fieldwork period in 2012 there were many commemorations of the Malvinas/Falklands War, as it was now thirty years after the conflict had begun. It was a kind of renewed interest after long social and official neglect (Guber 2008, 124). See the newspaper article: "Malvinas, herida abierta," *La Nación*, April 1, 2012.

41. Interview with Aldo Domínguez, June 22, 2010, Buenos Aires.

42. The Argentinian sociolegal organization CELS dedicated several pages in its annual report of 2012 to the inclusion of gender-related crimes as crimes against humanity. This inclusion had induced several victims to reveal sex crimes to the court, which produced important advantages in the judicialization of sex-related crimes committed during the last dictatorship in Argentina (CELS 2012, 70–71).

43. Such forced relationships between torturer and victim have been described, for instance, in *Ese infierno* (Actis, Aldini, and Lewin 2001), the collective testimony of female survivors of the ESMA.

44. Masculinity in general influences cultural practices of silence (Sheriff 2000, 127; and Treacher 2007, 292). Children of Nazis coping with their parents' involvement in the atrocities reveal similar inclinations to be silent, but on the family level (Bar-On 1989; and Livingstone 2010).

45. Interview with Victoria Herrera de Quiroga, August 2, 2010, Córdoba.

46. In 1989 forty members of the Movimiento Todos por la Patria (MTP) attacked La Tablaba Regiment in the province of Buenos Aires. Thirty-nine people were killed on both sides by the time the Argentinian army retook the barracks.

47. Interview with Javier Isla, May 18, 2012, Caracas.

48. Psychological language and practice have become more common in the armed forces in Argentina, particularly in the preparation for and evaluation of UN peace missions.

Chapter 6 Laughter and Play

1. Research has been done on black humor, satire, and state violence in Argentina, but the literature has examined mainly satirical magazines and cartoons (Cascioli 2005; Foster 1989; Fraticelli 2008; Pedrazinni 2010; and Taylor 1997).

2. Revised parts of this chapter have been published in two articles about humor and violence in Argentina (Van Roekel 2013, 2016). Author's note: I have changed the pseudonym "Olivia" in the first article into "Ariadna Villalba" in this chapter, but both pseudonyms represent the same interlocutor.

3. A psychoanalytical stance toward humor has been criticized as too passive. Instead, more conscious perspectives on humor have emerged, such as looking at how people actively distance themselves from suffering through humor (T. Scott 2007), or how incongruities or distress can be turned into moments of nonserious play through humor (R. Martin 2007, 19).

4. Interview with Laura Figueroa, July 2, 2010, Buenos Aires.

5. *Barcelona*, no. 249, March 9, 2012.

6. *Barcelona*, no. 132, April 11, 2008. The Paris Club is an informal group of financial officials from different countries with the largest economies. It gathers every six weeks at the French Ministry of Economics and Finance in Paris.

7. Pictures and drawings of women of the conservative right were sexual and grotesque, indirectly contesting the hypocrisy of female chastity in modern times.

8. *Barcelona*'s humor is similar to European satirical magazines such as *Charlie
   Hebdo*, which also incites controversies about social tensions involving multicul-
   turalism, Islam, free speech, and the hypocrisy of contemporary politicians in
   Europe.

9. *Barcelona*'s critique does not mean that everyone in Argentina is indifferent. The
   issue of the new disappearance significantly raised consciousness about the persistence of impunity among a critical minority. Since 2006, people have organized
   rallies, and images of López's silhouette and slogans asking for his "appearance
   alive" often appear on posters and graffiti in La Plata and Buenos Aires. Ana Longoni, an Argentinian art historian, spoke at a conference about the recent cultural
   practices regarding López disappearance. She called it "artistic activism." I
   attended this conference on April 16, 2010, in Buenos Aires. See also *Todos somos
   López*, accessed October 24, 2011, www.cuadernos.inadi.gob.ar.

10. Although the former repressive regimes often censored or even prohibited satiri-
    cal publications, some magazines escaped censorship and were published anyway
    (Cascioli 2005, 7–16; Foster 1989, 53–54; and Taylor 1997, 55–56).

11. *Revista HUMor* is perhaps the best-known satirical magazine that emerged dur-
    ing the last civil-military junta, and *Barcelona* is considered its offspring (Frati-
    celli 2008).

12. A recent trend similarly trivializes and mocks the Holocaust through art. This
    has caused contentious debates on the limits of Holocaust humor in German and
    American magazines such as *Der Spiegel* and the *New York Times*, respectively.
    Accessed November 4, 2015, http://www.spiegel.de/international/spiegel
    /spiegel-interview-with-mel-brooks-with-comedy-we-can-rob-hitler-of-his
    -posthumous-power-a-406268.html.

13. Interview with Fernando Carrizo, March 28, 2012, Buenos Aires.

14. Interview with Ana Luisa Campos and Blanca Capellini, March 15, 2012, Bue-
    nos Aires.

15. Interview with Ana Luisa Campos, April 12, 2012, Buenos Aires.

16. Interview with Tomás Olivera, July 8, 2010, Buenos Aires.

17. Online newspaper "Nuestra única venganza es ser feliz." Accessed November 6,
    2015, http://agenciapacourondo.com.ar/secciones/miscelaneas/6201-hijos-genocida
    -videla-nuestra-unica-venganza-es-ser-felicesq.html.

18. Humor as a "weapon of the weak" (J. Scott 1985) creates space for subordinated
    people to voice nonviolent resistance, realign power, and affect the hegemonic
    status quo (Fernandez and Taylor Huber 2001, 17; Kuipers 2011, 76; and Sörensen
    2008, 167).

19. *Fachos* derives from the word *fascistas*. In this context it means those on the con-
    servative right who supported the authoritarian regime.

20. Various studies see humor as a tool for denigration or as an act of aggression
    through showing a kind of superiority over another person, while continuing to
    live within the social constraints of a particular context (Clifford 2001, 255; Fer-
    nandez and Taylor Huber 2001, 27; Herzfeld 2001, 75; P. Lewis 2006, 205; and
    R. Martin 2007, 43–48).

CHAPTER 7 WHERE JUSTICE BELONGS

1. "Compromiso de no interferir con la Justicia: los juicios por crímenes de la dictadura seguirán adelante," *Clárin*, November 24, 2015, accessed August 1, 2018,
   https://www.clarin.com/politica/crimenes-dictadura-juicios-mauricio_macri_0
   _S1npkgtPQe.html.

2. "Del hecho a dicho," *Página12*, August 15, 2016, accessed August 1, 2018, https://www.pagina12.com.ar/diario/elpais/1-306881-2016-08-15.html.
3. Based on this law, since Macri assumed power (2015–present), many convicted officers have recently been sentenced to house arrest. "Crímenes de lesa humanidad: más de la mitad de los condenados cumplen prisión domiciliaria," *Ámbito*, January 2, 2018, accessed June 1, 2018, http://www.ambito.com/908152-crimenes-de-lesa-humanidad-mas-de-la-mitad-de-los-condenados-cumplen-prision-domiciliaria.
4. "La Corte Suprema, por mayoría, declaró aplicable el cómputo del 2×1 para la prisión en un caso de delitos de lesa humanidad," *Centro de Información Judicial*, May 3, 2017, accessed May 16, 2018, https://www.cij.gov.ar/nota-25746-La-Corte-Suprema—por-mayor-a—declar—aplicable-el-c-mputo-del-2x1-para-la-prisi-n-en-un-caso-de-delitos-de-lesa-humanidad.html.
5. "Nunca más un genocida suelto," *Página12*, May 10, 2018, accessed May 29, 2018, https://www.pagina12.com.ar/36884-nunca-mas-un-genocida-suelto.
6. "'2×1' mal calibrado por la Corte agita ánimo de rebelión judicial," *Ámbito*, May 9, 2017, accessed June 1, 2018, http://www.ambito.com/882126-2x1-mal-calibrado-por-corte-agita-animo-de-rebelion-judicial.
7. There has been a recent return to the lifeworld in anthropology to analyze experience that provides welcoming countercriticisms of the so-called descriptive introspection of phenomenology (Jackson 2013; Jackson and Piette 2015; Kleinman 2014; Vom Lehn and Hitzler 2015; and Zigon and Throop 2014).

References

Abu-Lughod, Lila. 1986. *Veiled Sentiments: Honor and Poetry in a Bedouin Society.* Berkeley: University of California Press.
———. 1993. *Writing Women's Worlds: Bedouin Stories.* Berkeley: University of California Press.
Achugar, Mariana. 2008. *What We Remember: The Construction of Memory in Military Discourse.* Amsterdam: John Benjamins.
Açiksöz, Salih Can. 2012. "Sacrificial Limbs in Sovereignty: Disabled Veterans, Masculinity, and Nationalist Politics in Turkey." *Medical Anthropology Quarterly* 26(1): 4–25.
Actis, Munu, Cristina Inés Aldini, and Miriam Lewin. 2001. *Ese infierno: Conversaciones de cinco mujeres sobrevivientes de la ESMA.* Buenos Aires: Editorial Sudamericana.
Agamben, Giorgio. 2000. *Lo que queda de Auschwitz: El archivo y el testigo. Homo Sacer III,* trans. Antonio Gimeno Cuspinera. Valencia: Pre-textos.
Al-Mohammed, Hayder. 2011. "Less Methodology More Epistemology Please: The Body, Metaphysics and 'Certainty.'" *Critique of Anthropology* 31(2): 121–138.
Apte, Mahadev L. 1985. *Humor and Laughter: An Anthropological Approach.* Ithaca, NY: Cornell University Press.
Armon-Jones, Claire. 1986. "The Thesis of Constructionism." In Harré, *Social Construction of Emotions,* 32–56.
Arnould, Valerie. 2006. "Justice after Civil Wars: Truth Commissions' and War Crimes Tribunals' Contribution to the Post-Conflict Reconciliation." *Studia diplomatica* 59(2): 141–160.
Arthur, Paige. 2009. "How 'Transitions' Reshaped Human Rights: A Conceptual History of Transitional Justice." *Human Rights Quarterly* 31(2): 321–367.
Auyero, Javier. 2003. *Contentious Lives: Two Argentine Women, Two Protests, and the Quest for Recognition.* Durham, NC: Duke University Press.
Badaró, Máximo. 2009. *Militares o ciudadanos: La formación de los oficiales del Ejército Argentino.* Buenos Aires: Prometeo Libros.
Bakhtin, Mikhail. 1968. *Rabelais and His World,* trans. Helene Iswolsky. Cambridge, MA: MIT Press.
Bakker, R. 1969. *Kerngedachten van Merleau-Ponty.* Roermond: Romen and Zonen.
Bandes, Susan A., and Jeremy A. Blumenthal. 2012. "Emotion and the Law." *Annual Review of Law and Social Science* 8: 161–181.
Barahona de Brito, Alexandra. 2001. "Truth, Justice, Memory, and Democratization in the Southern Cone." In *The Politics of Memory and Democratization: Transitional Justice in Democratizing Societies,* ed. Alexandra Barahona de Brito, Carmen González-Enríquez, and Paloma Aguilar, 119–160. Oxford: Oxford University Press.
Bar-On, Dan. 1989. *Legacy of Silence: Encounters with Children of the Third Reich.* Cambridge, MA: Harvard University Press.
Bauman, Zygmunt. 2002. "Modernity and the Holocaust." In *Genocide: An Anthropological Reader,* ed. Alexander Laban Hinton, 110–133. Malden: Blackwell.

Beatty, Andrew. 2010. "How Did It Feel for You? Emotion, Narrative, and the Limits of Ethnography." *American Anthropologist* 112(3): 430–443.

Behar, Ruth. 1996. *The Vulnerable Observer: Anthropology That Breaks Your Heart.* Boston: Beacon Press.

Ben-Ari, Eyal. 1998. *Mastering Soldiers: Conflict, Emotions, and the Enemy in an Israeli Military Unit.* New York: Berghahn Books.

———. 2005. "Epilogue: A 'Good' Military Death." *Armed Forces and Society* 31(4): 651–664.

Bettelheim, Bruno. 1986 [1960]. *The Informed Heart: A Study of the Psychological Consequences of Living under Extreme Fear and Terror.* Harmondsworth: Penguin Books.

Beverley, John. 2004. *Testimonio: On the Politics of Truth.* Minneapolis: University of Minnesota Press.

Bickford, Andrew. 2011. *Fallen Elites: The Military Other in Post-Unification Germany.* Stanford, CA: Stanford University Press.

Bill, Rolston. 2006. "Dealing with the Past: Pro-state Paramilitaries, Truth and Transition in Northern Ireland." *Human Rights Quarterly* 28(3): 652–675.

Bill Chávez, Rebecca. 2007. "The Appointment and Removal Process for Judges in Argentina: The Role of Judicial Councils and Impeachment Juries in Promoting Judicial Independence." *Latin American Politics and Society* 49(2): 33–58.

Bloomfield, David, Teresa Barnes, and Luc Huyse. 2003. *Reconciliation after Violent Conflict: A Handbook.* Stockholm: International IDEA.

Bock-Luna, Birgit. 2007. *The Past in Exile: Serbian Long-Distance Nationalism and Identity in the Wake of the Third Balkan War.* Münster: LIT Verlag.

Bohoslavsky, Ernesto Lázaro. 2009. *El complot patagónico: Nación, conspiracionismo y violencia en el sur de Argentina y Chile (siglos XIX y XX).* Buenos Aires: Prometeo Libros.

Boyer, Dominic. 2006. "Conspiracy, History, and Therapy at a Berlin *Stammtisch.*" *American Ethnologist* 33(3): 327–339.

Branscombe, Nyla R., and Bertjan Doosje, eds. 2004. *Collective Guilt: International Perspectives.* Cambridge: Cambridge University Press.

Brennan, James P. 2018. *Argentina's Missing Bones: Revisiting the History of the Dirty War.* Berkeley: University of California Press.

Briggs, Jean L. 1970. *Never in Anger: Portrait of an Eskimo Family.* Cambridge, MA: Harvard University Press.

Bruner, Edward. 1986. "Experience and Its Expressions." In Turner and Bruner, *The Anthropology of Experience*, 3–30.

Brunk, Gregory G., Donald Secrest, and Howard Tamashiro. 1990. "Military Views of Morality and War: An Empirical Study of the Attitudes of Retired American Officers." *International Studies Quarterly* 34(1): 83–109.

Brunnegger, Sandra, and Karen Ann Faulk, eds. 2016. *A Sense of Justice: Legal Knowledge and Lived Experience in Latin America.* Stanford, CA: Stanford University Press.

Buckley, Francis H. 2003. *The Morality of Laughter.* Ann Arbor: University of Michigan Press.

Buntinx, Gustavo. 2008. "Desapariciones forzadas / resurrecciones míticas (fragmentos)." In Longoni and Bruzzone, *El Siluetazo*, 253–284.

Carrithers, Michael. 2005. "Anthropology as a Moral Science of Possibilities." *Current Anthropology* 46(3): 433–456.

Caruth, Cathy. 1996. *Unclaimed Experience: Trauma, Narrative, and History.* Baltimore: Johns Hopkins University Press.

Cascioli, Andrés. 2005. *La revista HUMOR y la dictadura.* Buenos Aires: Musimundo.

Center for Social and Legal Studies (CELS). 2012. *Derechos humanos en Argentina: Informe 2012.* Buenos Aires: Siglo Veintiuno.

———. 2017. *Derechos humanos en Argentina: Informe 2017.* Buenos Aires: Siglo Veintiuno.

Chauvié, Omar. 2009. "El lugar de la letra: nuevos soportes y lemas culturales en la posdictadura bahiense." Paper presented at the conference Cuestiones Críticas II, Rosario, October 29.

Clendinnen, Inga. 1999. *Reading the Holocaust*. Cambridge: Cambridge University Press

Clifford, James. 2001. "The Last Discussant." In Fernandez and Taylor Huber, *Irony in Action*, 251–259.

Código procesal penal de la Nación y leyes comentadas. 2005. Buenos Aires: Lajouane Gráfica Sur.

Collins, Cath. 2010. *Post-Transitional Justice: Human Rights Trials in Chile and El Salvador*. University Park: Pennsylvania State University Press.

Cordner, Cristopher. 2007. "Guilt, Remorse and Victims." *Philosophical Investigations* 30(4): 337–362.

Crapanzano, Vincent. 1980. *Tuhami: Portrait of a Moroccan*. Chicago: University of Chicago Press.

———. 2004. *Imaginative Horizons: An Essay in Literary-Philosophical Anthropology*. Chicago: University of Chicago Press.

Crenzel, Emilio. 2008. *La historia política del Nunca Más: la memoria de las desapariciones en la Argentina*. Buenos Aires: Siglo Veintiuno.

———, ed. 2010. *Los desaparecidos en la Argentina: memorias, representaciones e ideas 1983–2008*. Buenos Aires: Biblos.

Csordas, Thomas J. 1990. "Embodiment as a Paradigm for Anthropology." *Ethos* 18(1): 5–47.

———. 1993. "Somatic Modes of Attention." *Cultural Anthropology* 8(2): 135–156.

———. 1994. *Embodiment and Experience: The Existential Ground of Culture and Self*. Cambridge: Cambridge University Press.

———. 2013. "Morality as a Cultural System?" *Current Anthropology* 54(5): 523–546.

Damasio, Antonio. 2003. "Feelings of Emotion and the Self." *Annals of the New York Academy of Sciences* 1001(1): 253–261.

Das, Veena. 2007. *Life and Words: Violence and the Descent into the Ordinary*. Berkeley: University of California Press.

Davies, James. 2010. "Introduction: Emotions in the Field." In Davies and Spencer, *Emotions in the Field*, 1–34.

Davies, James, and Dimitrina Spencer, eds. 2010. *Emotions in the Field: The Psychology and Anthropology of Fieldwork Experience*. Stanford, CA: Stanford University Press.

Davis, Coreen. 2013. *State Terrorism and Post-Transitional Justice in Argentina: An Analysis of Mega Cause I Trial*. New York: Palgrave Macmillan.

Dawson, Graham. 1994. *Soldier Heroes: British Adventure, Empire, and the Imagining of Masculinities*. London: Routledge.

———. 2007. *Making Peace with the Past? Memory, Trauma and the Irish Troubles*. Manchester: Manchester University Press.

De la Peza, María del Carmen, ed. 2009. *Memoria(s) y política: experiencia, poéticas y construcciones de nación*. Buenos Aires: Prometeo Libros.

Desjarlais, Robert R. 1992. *Body and Emotion: The Aesthetics of Illness and Healing in the Nepal Himalayas*. Philadelphia: University of Pennsylvania Press.

———. 1996. "Struggling Along." In Jackson, *Things as They Are*, 70–93.

Desjarlais, Robert, and Jason Throop C. 2011. "Phenomenological Approaches in Anthropology." *Annual Review of Anthropology* 40: 87–102.

Doak, Jonathan. 2011. "The Therapeutic Dimension of Transitional Justice: Emotional Repair and Victim Satisfaction in International Trials and Truth Commissions." *International Criminal Law Review* 11(2): 263–298.

Druliolle, Vincent. 2009. "Silhouettes of the Disappeared: Memory, Justice and Human Rights in Post-Authoritarian Argentina." *Human Rights and Human Welfare* 9: 77–89.

Durham, Deborah, and James W. Fernandez. 1991. "Tropical Dominions: The Figurative Struggle over Domains of Belonging and Apartness in Africa." In *Beyond*

Metaphor: The Theory of Tropes in Anthropology, ed. James W. Fernandez, 190–210. Stanford, CA: Stanford University Press.

Ejército Argentino. 1968. *Ejercicio de mando*. Buenos Aires: Instituto Geográfico Militar.

Elster, Jon. 2004. *Closing the Books: Transitional Justice in Historical Perspective*. Cambridge: Cambridge University Press.

Englebrecht, Christine M. 2011. "The Struggle for 'Ownership of Conflict': An Exploration of Victim Participation and Voice in the Criminal Justice System." *Criminal Justice Review* 36(2): 129–151.

Espiniella, Fernando. 2009. *Tras el manto de neblina: relatos médicos de la guerra de las Islas Malvinas*. Buenos Aires: Editorial Dunken.

Farquhar, Judith, and Margaret Lock. 2007. "Introduction." In *Beyond the Body Proper: Reading the Anthropology of Material Life*, ed. Margaret Lock and Judith Farquhar, 1–16. Durham, NC: Duke University Press.

Fassin, Didier, and Richard Rechtman. 2009. *The Empire of Trauma: An Inquiry into the Condition of Victimhood*, trans. Rachel Gomme. Princeton, NJ: Princeton University Press.

Faulk, Karen Ann. 2013. *In the Wake of Neoliberalism: Citizenship and Human Rights in Argentina*. Stanford, CA: Stanford University Press.

Feitlowitz, Marguerite. 1998. *A Lexicon of Terror: Argentina and the Legacies of Torture*. Oxford: Oxford University Press.

Felman, Shoshana. 2002. *The Juridical Unconscious: Trials and Traumas in the Twentieth Century*. Cambridge, MA: Harvard University Press.

Fenster, Mark. 2008. *Conspiracy Theories: Secrecy and Power in American Culture*. Minneapolis: University of Minnesota Press.

Fernandez, James W. 1974. "The Mission of the Metaphor in Expressive Culture." *Current Anthropology* 15(2): 119–145.

Fernandez, James W., and Mary Taylor Huber. 2001. "Introduction: The Anthropology of Irony." In Fernandez and Huber, *Irony in Action*, 1–37.

Figari Layús, Rosario. 2015. "'What Do You Mean by Transitional Justice?' Local Perspectives on Human Rights Trials in Argentina." In *Legacies of State Violence and Transitional Justice in Latin America*, ed. Nina Schneider and Marcia Esparza, 3–16. Lanham, MD: Lexington Books.

Fijii, Lee Ann. 2010. "Shades of Truth and Lies: Interpreting Testimonies of War and Violence." *Journal of Peace Research* 47(2): 231–241.

Filc, Judith. 1997. *Entre lo parentesco y la politíca: familia y dictatura. 1976–1983*. Buenos Aires: Biblos.

Finkel, Normal J., and W. Gerrod Parrot. 2006. *Emotions and Culpability: How the Law Is at Odds with Psychology, Jurors, and Itself*. Washington, DC: American Psychological Association.

Finlay, Linda. 2009. "Debating Phenomenological Research Methods." *Phenomenology and Practice* 3(1): 6–25.

Foster, David William. 1989. *From Mafalda to Los Supermachos: Latin American Graphic Humor as Popular Culture*. Boulder: Lynne Rienner.

Fraticelli, Damián. 2008. "La revista Barcelona y el humor local." *Revista Letra Imagen Sonido* 1(2): 117–130.

Frederic, Sabina. 2008. *Los usos de la fuerza pública: debates sobre militares y policías en las ciencias sociales de la democracia*. Buenos Aires: Biblioteca Nacional.

———. 2012. "Fotografías de la configuración profesional de los militares en el contexto de su declinación como elite estatal." In Plotkin and Zimmermann, *Las prácticas del Estado*, 210–233.

Freud, Sigmund. 1917. "Mourning and Melancholia." In *The Standard Edition of the Complete Psychological Works of Sigmund Freud, Volume XIV (1914–1916): On the History of the Psycho-Analytic Movement, Papers on Metapsychology and Other Works*, 237–258 London: Hogarth Press.

————. 1960 [1905]. *Jokes and Their Relation to the Unconscious*, trans. James Strachey and Anna Freud. London: Hogarth Press.

Frosh, Stephen. 2011. *Feelings*. New York: Routledge.

Gandsman, Ari. 2012. "The Limits of Kinship Mobilizations and the (A)politics of Human Rights in Argentina." *Journal of Latin American and Caribbean Anthropology* 17(2): 193–214.

Gardiner, Michael. 1993. "Bakhtin's Carnival: Utopia as Critique." *Bakhtin. Carnival and Other Subjects, Critical Studies* 3(2)–4(1/2): 20–47.

Gavet, André, Genaro Rivera Brito, and César A. Córdoba Narváez. 1996. *El Arte de Mandar*. Quito: Centro de Estudios Históricos del Ejército.

Geertz, Clifford. 1973. *The Interpretation of Cultures: Selected Essays*. New York: Basic Books.

Geertz, Clifford. 1983. *Local Knowledge: Further Essays in Interpretative Anthropology*. New York: Basic Books.

————. 1995. *After the Fact: Two Countries, Four Decades, One Anthropologist*. Cambridge, MA: Harvard University Press.

Gell, Alfred. 1992. *The Anthropology of Time: Cultural Constructions of Temporal Maps and Images*. Oxford: Berg.

Gieser, Thorsten. 2008. "Embodiment, Emotion and Empathy: A Phenomenological Approach to Apprenticeship Learning." *Anthropological Theory* 8(3): 299–318.

Goldstein, Donna M. 2003. *Laughter out of Place: Race, Class, Violence, and Sexuality in a Rio Shantytown*. Berkeley: University of California Press.

Good, Byron J. 1994. *Medicine, Rationality, and Experience: An Anthropological Perspective*. Cambridge: Cambridge University Press.

Goodale, Mark. 2009. *Surrendering to Utopia: An Anthropology of Human Rights*. Stanford, CA: Stanford University Press.

Graeber, David. 2009. *Direct Action: An Ethnography*. Oakland, CA: AK Press.

Graziano, Frank. 1992. *Divine Violence: Spectacle, Psychosexuality, and Radical Christianity in the Argentine "Dirty War."* Boulder, CO: Westview Press.

Gregg, Melissa, and Gregory J. Seigworth, eds. 2010. *The Affect Theory Reader*. Durham, NC: Duke University Press.

Guber, Rosana. 2004. *De chicos a veteranos. Memorias argentinas de la Guerra de Malvinas*. Buenos Aires: Editorial Antropofagia/IDES.

————. 2008. "The Malvinas Executions: (Im)plausible Memories of a Clean War," trans. Mariana Ortega Breña. *Latin American Perspectives* 35(5): 119–132.

Gusterson, Hugh. 2007. "Anthropology and Militarism." *Annual Review of Anthropology* 36: 155–175.

Hage, Ghassan. 2010. "Hating Israel in the Field: On Ethnography and Political Emotions." In Davies and Spencer, *Emotions in the Field*, 129–154.

Hamber, Brandon. 2009. *Transforming Societies after Political Violence: Truth, Reconciliation, and Mental Health*. New York: Springer.

Hardon, John A. 2013 [1980]. *Catholic Dictionary: An Abridged and Updated Edition of Modern Catholic Dictionary*. New York: Image Books.

Harré, Rom, ed. 1986. *The Social Construction of Emotions*. Oxford: Basil Blackwell.

Hayner, Priscilla B. 2002. *Unspeakable Truths: Facing the Challenge of Truth Commissions*. New York: Routledge.

Heelas, Paul. 1986. "Emotion Talk across Cultures." In Harré, *Social Construction of Emotions*, 234–266.

Heidegger, Martin. 1978. *Being and Time*, trans. John Macquarrie and Edward Robinson. Oxford: Basil Blackwell.

————. 1993 [1927]. *Basic Writings: From Being and Time (1927) to The Task of Thinking (1964)*, ed. David Farrell Krell. New York: Harper San Francisco.

————. 1996 [1953]. *Being and Time*, trans. Joan Stambaugh. Albany: State University of New York Press.

Hershberg, Eric, and Felipe Agüero, eds. 2005. *Memorias militares sobre la represión en el Cono Sur: Visiones en disputa en dictadura y democracia.* Madrid: Siglo XXI.

Herzfeld, Michael. 2001. "Irony and Power: Toward a Politics of Mockery in Greece." In Fernandez and Taylor Huber, *Irony in Action,* 63–83.

Higate, Paul Richard. 2001. "Theorizing Continuity: From Military to Civilian Life." *Armed Forces and Society* 27(3): 443–460.

Hinton, Alexander L. 1998. "A Head for an Eye: Revenge in the Cambodian Genocide." *American Ethnologist* 25(3): 352–377.

———. 2005. *Why Did They Kill? Cambodia in the Shadow of Genocide.* Berkeley: University of California Press.

———, ed. 2010. *Transitional Justice: Global Mechanisms and Local Realities after Genocide and Mass Violence.* New Brunswick, NJ: Rutgers University Press.

———. 2016. *Man or Monster? The Trial of a Khmer Rouge Torturer.* Durham, NC: Duke University Press.

Hochschild, Arlie Russell. 1979. "Emotion Work, Feeling Rules, and Social Structure." *American Journal of Sociology* 85(3): 551–575.

Hollan, Douglas. 2008. "Being There: On the Imaginative Aspects of Understanding Others and Being Understood." *Ethos* 36(4): 475–489.

Hollander, Nancy Caro. 1992. "Psychoanalysis and State Terror in Argentina." *American Journal of Psychoanalysis* 52(3): 273–289.

Huggins, Martha K. 2000. "Legacies of Authoritarianism: Brazilian Torturers' and Murderers' Reformulation of Memory." *Latin American Perspectives* 27(2): 57–78.

Huizinga, Johan. 1970. *Homo Ludens: A Study of the Play-Element in Culture.* London: Paladin.

Hutcheon, Linda. 1994. *Irony's Edge: The Theory and Politics of Irony.* London: Routledge.

Huyssen, Andreas. 2001. "Of Mice and Mimesis: Reading Spiegelman with Adorno." In *Visual Culture and the Holocaust,* ed. Barbie Zelizer, 28–42. New Brunswick, NJ: Rutgers University Press.

Ignatieff, Michael. 1996. "Articles of Faith." Special issue: "Wounded Nations, Broken Lives Truth Commissions and War Tribunals." *Index of Censorship* 24(5): 110–122.

Jackson, Michael. 1995. *At Home in the World.* Durham, NC: Duke University Press.

———. 1996a. "Introduction: Phenomenology, Radical Empiricism, and Anthropological Critique." In Jackson, *Things as They Are,* 1–50.

———, ed. 1996b. *Things as They Are: New Directions in Phenomenological Anthropology.* Bloomington: Indiana University Press.

———. 2005. *Existential Anthropology. Events, Exigencies and Effects.* New York: Berghahn Books.

———. 2013. *Lifeworlds: Essays in Existential Anthropology.* Chicago: University of Chicago Press.

———. 2017. *How Lifeworlds Work: Emotionality, Sociality, and the Ambiguity of Being.* Chicago: Chicago University Press.

———. 2018. *The Varieties of Temporal Experiences: Travels in Philosophical, Historical, and Ethnographic Time.* New York: Columbia University Press.

Jackson, Michael, and Albert Piette. 2015. "Introduction: Anthropology and the Existential Turn." In *What Is Existential Anthropology,* ed. Michael Jackson and Albert Piette, 1–29. New York: Berghahn Books.

James, Erica. 2004. "The Political Economy of 'Trauma' in Haiti in the Democratic Era of Insecurity." *Culture, Medicine and Psychiatry* 20: 127–149.

Jamil, Uzma, and Cécile Rousseau. 2011. "Challenging the 'Official' Story of 9/11: Community Narratives and Conspiracy Theories." *Ethnicities* 11(2): 245–261.

Jelin, Elizabeth. 2010. "¿Víctimas, familiares o ciudadanos/as? Las luchas por la legitimidad de la palabra." In Crenzel, *Los desaparecidos en la Argentina,* 227–249.

————. 2014. "Memoria y democracia: una relación incierta." *Revista Mexicana de Ciencias Políticas y Sociales* 59(221): 225–242.

Jelin, Elizabeth, and Susana G. Kaufman. 2004. "Layers of Memory: Twenty Years after in Argentina." In *Commemorating War: The Politics of Memory*, ed. Timothy G. Ashplant, Graham Dawson, and Michael Roper, 89–110. New Brunswick, NJ: Transaction.

Kakar, Sudhir. 1996. *The Colors of Violence: Cultural Identities, Religion, and Conflict.* Chicago: University of Chicago Press.

Karstedt, Susanne, Ian Loader, and Heather Strange, eds. 2011. *Emotions, Crime and Justice.* Oxford: Hart.

Katz, Pearl. 1990. "Emotional Metaphors, Socialization, and Roles of Drill Sergeants." *Ethos* 18(4): 457–480.

Kibler, Robert E. 2005. "Responses to Inhumanity in the Balkans and a Preliminary Discussion Concerning the Problem of Evil." *East European Quarterly* 38(4): 463–472.

Kidron, Carol A. 2010. "Embracing the Lived Memory of Genocide: Holocaust Survivor and Descendant Renegade Memory Work at the House of Being." *American Ethnologist* 37(3): 429–451.

————. 2011. "Sensorial Memory: Embodied Legacies of Genocide." In *A Companion to the Anthropology of the Body and Embodiment*, ed. Frances E. Mascia-Lees, 451–466. Malden, MA: Wiley-Blackwell.

Kilshaw, Susie. 2008. "Gulf War Syndrome: A Reaction to Psychiatry's Invasion of the Military?" *Culture, Medicine and Psychiatry* 32: 219–237.

Kleinman, Arthur. 2014. "The Search for Wisdom: Why William James Still Matters." In *The Ground Between: Anthropologists Engage Philosophy*, ed. Veena Das, Michael Jackson, Arthur Kleinman, and Bhrigupati Singh, 119–137. Durham, NC: Duke University Press.

Kleinman, Arthur, and Robert Desjarlais. 1995. "Violence, Culture, and the Politics of Trauma." In *Writing at the Margin: Discourse between Anthropology and Medicine*, ed. Arthur Kleinman, 173–189. Berkeley: University of California Press.

Klep, Katrien. 2012. "Transitional Justice and Commemorative Practices: Processes of Memorialisation in Chile." PhD diss., Utrecht University.

Kövecses, Zoltán. 2005. *Metaphor in Culture: Universality and Variation.* Cambridge: Cambridge University Press.

Kritz, Neil J., ed. 1995. *Transitional Justice: How Emerging Democracies Reckon with Former Regimes. Volume 1: General Considerations.* Washington, DC: USIP Press.

Kuipers, Giselinde. 2011. "The Politics of Humour in the Public Sphere: Cartoons, Power and Modernity on the First Transnational Humour Scandal." *European Journal of Cultural Studies* 14: 63–80.

LaCapra, Dominck. 2004. *History in Transit: Experience, Identity, Critical Theory.* Ithaca, NY: Cornell University Press.

Laird, James D. 2007. *Feelings: The Perception of Self.* Oxford: Oxford University Press.

Lande, Brian. 2007. "Breathing Like a Soldier: Culture Incarnate." *Sociological Review* 55(s1): 95–108.

Laplanche, Jean, and Jean-Bertrand Pontalis. 1988. *The Language of Psychoanalysis.* London: Karnac Books.

Laplante, Lisa, and Kimberley Susan Theidon. 2007. "Truth with Consequences: Justice and Reparations in Post-Truth Commission Peru." *Human Rights Quarterly* 29(1): 228–250.

Laughlin, Charles D. 1996. "Phenomenological Anthropology." *Encyclopedia of Cultural Anthropology* 3: 924–926.

Laughlin, Charles D., John MacManus, and Eugene D'Aquili. 1992. *Brain, Symbol, and Experience: Towards a Neurophenomenology of Human Consciousness.* New York: Columbia University Press.

Letschert, Rianne, and Jan van Dijk. 2011. "New Faces of Victimhood: Reflections on the Unjust Sides of Globalization." In *Globalization, Transnational Crimes, and Victim Rights*, ed. Rianne Letschert and Jan van Dijk, 3–14. Dordrecht: Springer.

Levi, Primo. 1989. *The Drowned and the Saved*, trans. Raymond Rosenthal. New York: Vintage Books.

Levin, Florencia, and Marina Franco, eds. 2007. *Historia reciente: perspectivas y desafíos para un campo en construcción*. Buenos Aires: Paidós.

Lewis, Michael. 2008. "Self-Conscious Emotions: Embarrassment, Pride, Shame, and Guilt." In *Handbook of Emotions*, ed. Michael Lewis, Jeannette M. Haviland-Jones, and Lisa Feldman Barrett, 742–757. New York: Guilford Press.

Lewis, Paul. 2006. *Cracking Up: American Humor in a Time of Conflict*. Chicago: University of Chicago Press.

Lichtenfeld, Rebecca. 2005. *Accountability in Argentina: 20 Years Later, Transitional Justice Maintains Momentum. Case Study Series of the International Center for Transitional Justice*. http://ictj.org/sites/default/files/ICTJ-Argentina-Accountability-Case-2005-English.pdf.

Lickel, Brian, Toni Schmader, and Marchelle Barquissau. 2004. "The Evocation of Moral Emotions in Intergroup Contexts: The Distinction between Collective Guilt and Collective Shame." In Branscombe and Doosje, *Collective Guilt*, 35–55.

Livingstone, Kathy. 2010. "Opportunities for Mourning When Grief Is Disenfranchised: Descendants of Nazi Perpetrators in Dialogue with Holocaust Survivors." *Omega* 61(3): 205–222.

Lock, Margaret M. 1993. "Cultivating the Body: Anthropology and Epistemologies of Bodily Practice and Knowledge." *Annual Review of Anthropology* 22: 133–155.

Lockyer, Sharon, and Michael Pickering, eds. 2005. *Beyond a Joke: The Limits of Humour*. Hampshire: Palgrave Macmillan.

Lomsky-Feder, Edna. 2004. "Life Stories, War, and Veterans: On the Social Distribution of Memories." *Ethos* 32(1): 82–109.

Longoni, Ana, and Gustavo Bruzzone. 2008. *El Siluetazo*. Córdoba: Adriana Hidalgo Editora.

Lorimer, Francine. 2010. "Using Emotion as a Form of Knowledge in a Psychiatric Fieldwork Setting." In Davies and Spencer, *Emotions in the Field*, 98–126.

Luhrmann, Tanya M. 2010. "What Counts as Data?" In Davies and Spencer, *Emotions in the Field*, 212–238.

Lupton, Deborah. 1998. *The Emotional Self: A Sociocultural Exploration*. London: Sage.

Lutz, Catherine. 1988. *Unnatural Emotions: Everyday Sentiments on a Micronesian Atoll and Their Challenge to Western Theory*. Chicago: University of Chicago Press.

Lvovich, Daniel, and Jaquelina Bisquert. 2008. *La cambiante memoria de la dictadura: discursos públicos, movimientos sociales y legitimidad democrática*. Los Polvorines: Universidad Nacional de General Sarmiento.

MacLeish, Kenneth T. 2012. "Armor and Anesthesia: Exposure, Feeling, and the Soldier's Body." *Medical Anthropology Quarterly* 26(1): 49–68.

Malamud Goti, Jaime. 2000. *Terror y justicia en la Argentina: responsabilidad y democracia después de los juicios al terrorismo de estado*. Buenos Aires: Ediciones de la Flor.

Marchesi, Aldo. 2005. "Vencedores vencidos: las respuestas militares frente a los informes 'Nunca Más' en el Cono Sur." In Hershberg and Agüero, *Memorias militares*, 175–210.

Marcus, George E., and Michael G. Powell. 2003. "From Conspiracy Theories in the Incipient New World Order of the 1990s to Regimes of Transparency Now." *Anthropological Quarterly* 76(2): 323–334.

Martin, Lucas G. 2010. "Dictadores preocupados: el problema de la verdad durante el 'Proceso' (1976–1983)." *Postdata* 15(1): 75–103.

Martin, Rod A. 2007. *The Psychology of Humor: An Integrative Approach*. Amsterdam: Elsevier Academic Press.

Martin, Terry L., and Kenneth J. Doka. 2000. *Men Don't Cry . . . Women Do: Transcending Gender Stereotypes of Grief.* Philadelphia: Brunner/Mazel.

Mattingly, Cheryl. 1998. *Healing Dramas and Clinical Plots: The Narrative Structure of Experience.* Cambridge: Cambridge University Press.

———. 2014. *Moral Laboratories: Family Peril and the Struggle for a Good Life.* Berkeley: University of California Press.

McSherry, J. Patrice. 1997. *Incomplete Transition: Military Power and Democracy in Argentina.* Houndmills: Macmillan.

Mead, George Herbert. 1964 [1956]. *On Social Psychology: Selected Papers.* Chicago: University of Chicago Press.

Mendeloff, David. 2009. "Trauma and Vengeance: Assessing the Psychological and Emotional Effects of Post-Conflict Justice." *Human Rights Quarterly* 31(3): 592–623.

Middleton, Dwight R. 1989. "Emotional Style: The Cultural Ordering of Emotions." *Ethos* 17(2): 187–201.

Miguens, José Enrique. 1986. *Honor militar, conciencia moral y violencia terrorista.* Buenos Aires: Sudamericana/Planeta.

Minow, Martha. 1998. *Between Vengeance and Forgiveness: Facing History after Genocide and Mass Violence.* Boston: Beacon Press.

Mohanty, Jitendranath N., ed. 1977. *Readings on Edmund Husserl's Logical Investigations.* Den Haag: Martinus Nijhoff.

Moon, Claire. 2009. "Healing Past Violence: Traumatic Assumptions and Therapeutic Interventions in War and Reconciliation." *Journal of Human Rights* 8(1): 71–91.

Mudrovcic, María Inés, ed. 2009. *Pasados en conflicto: Representación, mito y memoria.* Buenos Aires: Prometeo Libros.

Mueller-Hirth, Natascha, and Sandra Rios Oyola, eds. 2018. *Time and Temporality in the Study of Transitional and Post-Conflict Societies.* New York: Routledge.

Natarajan, Ram. 2018. "The Knowledge of People Disappeared during Argentina's Military Rule." *Human Studies* 41: 293–311.

National Commission on the Disappearance of Persons (CONADEP). 1984. *Nunca Más: Informe de la Comisión Nacional sobre la Desaparición de Personas.* Buenos Aires: Eudeba.

Nino, Carlos Santiago. 1996. *Radical Evil on Trial.* New Haven, CT: Yale University Press.

Nora, Pierre. 1989. "Between Memory and History. Les Lieux de Mémoire. Special Issue: Memory and Counter-Memory." *Representations* 26: 7–24.

Norden, Deborah L. 1996. *Military Rebellion in Argentina: Between Coups and Consolidation.* Lincoln: University of Nebraska Press.

Nutkiewicz, Michael. 2003. "Shame, Guilt, and Anguish in Holocaust Survivor Testimony." *Oral History Review* 30(1): 1–22.

Oberti, Alejandra. 2009. "Memorias y testigos, una discusión actual." In *Memoria(s) y política: experiencia, poéticas y construcciones de nación,* ed. Maria del Carmen de la Peza, 67–86. Buenos Aires: Prometeo Libros.

Oring, Elliot. 1984. *The Jokes of Sigmund Freud: A Study in Humor and Jewish Identity.* Philadelphia: University of Pennsylvania Press.

Ortner, Sherry. 2006. *Anthropology and Social Theory: Culture, Power, and the Acting Subject.* Durham, NC: Duke University Press.

———. 2016. "Dark Anthropology and Its Others: Theory since the Eighties." *Hau: Journal of Ethnographic Theory* 6(1): 47–73.

Oxford English Dictionary. 2015. *Oxford English Dictionary.* Oxford: Oxford University Press.

Park, Rebekah. 2014. *The Reappeared: Argentine Former Political Prisoners.* New Brunswick, NJ: Rutgers University Press.

Payne, Leigh A. 1999. "Confession of Torturers: Reflections from Argentina." Paper presented at the History Workshop and CSVR conference The TRC Commissioning the Past, Johannesburg, June 11–14.

———. 2008. *Unsettling Accounts: Neither Truth nor Reconciliation in Confessions of State Violence*. Durham, NC: Duke University Press.

Pedrazzini, Ana. 2010. "Absurdo, bulo e ironía: Pilares del humor escrito del suplemento argentino Sátira/12." *Perspectivas de la Comunicación* 3(2): 84–106.

Pham, Phuong, Patrick Vinck, Mychelle Balthazard, Judith Strasser, and Chariya Om. 2011."Victim Participation and the Trial of Duch at the Extraordinary Chambers in the Court of Cambodia." *Journal of Human Rights Practice* 3(3): 264–287.

Plotkin, Mariano Ben. 2009. "Psicoanális y habitus nacional: un enfoque comparativo de la recepción del psicoanálisis en Argentina y Brasil (1919–1950)." *Memoria y Sociedad* 13(27): 61–85.

Plotkin, Mariano Ben, and Eduardo Zimmermann. 2012a. "Introducción." In Plotkin and Zimmermann, *Las prácticas del Estado*, 9–34.

———. 2012b. *Las prácticas del Estado: política, sociedad y elites estatales en la Argentina del siglo XX*. Buenos Aires: Edhasa.

Potash, Robert A. 1971. *El ejército y la política en la Argentina (I), 1928–1945: De Yrigoyen a Perón*. Buenos Aires: Sudamericana.

Price, Richard. 1998. *The Convict and the Colonel: A Story of Colonialism and Resistance in the Caribbean*. Boston: Beacon Press.

Puget, Janine. 2002. "The State of Threat and Psychoanalysis: From the Uncanny That Structures to the Uncanny That Alienates." *Free Associations* 9(4): 611–648.

Reato, Ceferino. 2012. *Disposición final: la confesión de Videla sobre los desaparecidos*. Buenos Aires: Sudamericana.

Rebhun, L. A. 1999. *The Heart Is Unknown Country: Love in the Changing Economy of Northeast Brazil*. Stanford, CA: Stanford University Press.

Richland, Justin B. 2013. "Jurisdiction: Grounding Law in Language." *Annual Review of Anthropology* 42: 209–226.

Ricoeur, Paul. 2004. *Memory, History, Forgetting*, trans. Kathleen Blamey and David Pellauer. Chicago: University of Chicago Press.

Robben, Antonius C.G.M. 2000. "The Assault on Basic Trust: Disappearance, Protest, and Reburial in Argentina." In *Cultures under Siege: Collective Violence and Trauma*, ed. Antonius C.G.M. Robben and Marcelo M. Suárez-Orozco, 70–101. Cambridge: Cambridge University Press.

———. 2005. *Political Violence and Trauma in Argentina*. Philadelphia: University of Pennsylvania Press.

———. 2007. "Reflexive Ethnography." In Robben and Sluka, *Ethnographic Fieldwork*, 443–446.

———. 2018. *Argentina Betrayed: Memory, Mourning, and Accountability*. Philadelphia: University of Pennsylvania Press.

Robben, Antonius C.G.M., and Jeffrey A. Sluka, eds. *Ethnographic Fieldwork: An Anthropological Reader*. Malden, MA: Blackwell.

Roht-Arriaza, Naomi, and Javier Mariezcurrena, eds. 2006. *Transitional Justice in the Twenty-First Century: Beyond Truth versus Justice*. Cambridge: Cambridge University Press.

Rosaldo, Michele.1980. *Knowledge and Passion: Ilongot Notions of Self and Social Life*. Cambridge: Cambridge University Press.

Rosaldo, Renato. 1989. "Introduction: Grief and a Headhunter's Rage." In *Culture and Truth: The Remaking of Social Analysis*, 1–21. Boston: Beacon Press.

Rotberg, Robert, and Thompson, Dennis, eds. 2000. *Truth v. Justice: The Morality of Truth Commissions*. Princeton, NJ: Princeton University Press.

Rouquié, Alain. 1983. "El poder militar en la Argentina de hoy: cambio y continuidad." In *El poder militar en la Argentina 1976–1981*, ed. Peter Waldmann and Ernesto Garzón Valdéz, 65–76. Buenos Aires: Galerna.

Salvi, Valentina. 2012. "Sobre 'memorias parciales' y 'memoria completa': prácticas conmemorativas y narrativas cívico-militares sobre el pasado reciente en Argentina."

In *Topografías conflictivas. Memorias, espacios y ciudades en disputa*, ed. Anne Huffschmid and Valeria Durán, 265–280. Buenos Aires: Nueva Trilce.

Sanford, Victoria. 2012. "Why Truth Still Matters: Historical Clarification, Impunity, and Justice in Contemporary Guatemala." In *In the Wake of War. Democratization and Internal Armed Conflict in Latin America*, ed. Cynthia J. Arnson, 351–372. Stanford, CA: Stanford University Press.

Sarlo, Beatriz. 2005. *Tiempo pasado: cultura de la memoria y giro subjetivo. Una discusión*. Buenos Aires: Siglo Veintiuno.

Scarry, Elaine. 1985. *The Body in Pain: The Making and Unmaking of the World*. Oxford: Oxford University Press.

Scheper-Hughes, Nancy. 1993. *Death without Weeping: The Violence of Everyday Life in Brazil*. Berkeley: University of California Press.

———. 2007. "Violence and the Politics of Remorse: Lessons from South Africa." In *Subjectivity: Ethnographic Investigations*, ed. João Biehl, Byron Good, and Arthur Kleinman, 179–233. Berkeley: University California Press.

Scherer, Klaus R. 2005. "What Are Emotions? And How Can They Be Measured?" *Social Science Information* 44: 695–729.

Schutz, Alfred. 1970. *On Phenomenology and Social Relations: Selected Writings*, ed. Helmut R. Wagner. Chicago: University of Chicago Press.

———. 1967. *The Phenomenology of the Social World*, trans. George Walsh and Frederick Lehnert. Evanston, IL: Northwestern University Press.

Schutz, Alfred, and Thomas Luckmann. 1974. *The Structures of the Life-World*, trans. Richard M. Zaner and H. Tristan Engelhardt Jr. London: Heinemann Educational Books.

Scott, James C. 1985. *Weapons of the Weak: Everyday Forms of Peasant Resistance*. New Haven, CT: Yale University Press.

Scott, Tricia. 2007. "Expression of Humour by Emergency Personnel Involved in Sudden Deathwork." *Mortality* 12(4): 350–364.

Secretaria de Derechos Humanos, Ministerio de Justicia, Seguridad y Derechos Humanos. 2008. *Acompañamiento a testigos y querellantes en el marco de los juicios contra el terrorismo de Estado: Estrategias de intervención. Serie Normas y Acciones en un Estado de Derecho*. Buenos Aires. http: //www.jus.gob.ar/media/1129085/06-dhpt-acompanamiento _estrategia.pdf.

———. 2009. *Acompañamiento a testigos y querellantes en el marco de los juicios contra el terrorismo de Estado: Primeras Experiencias. Serie Normas y Acciones en un Estado de Derecho*. Buenos Aires. http: //www.fepra.org.ar/docs/Salud_Mental_y_DDHH_Cuadernillo _III.pdf.

Seidel, Katja. 2011. "The Impossible Only Takes a Little Longer, or What May Be Learned from the Argentine Experience of Justice." *Social Anthropology* 19(3): 305–312.

Shaw, Rosalind, and Lars Waldorf with Pierre Hazan, eds. 2010. *Localizing Transitional Justice: Interventions and Priorities after Mass Violence*. Stanford, CA: Stanford University Press.

Sheriff, Robin A. 2000. "Exposing Silence as Cultural Censorship: A Brazilian Case." *American Anthropologist* 102(1): 114–132.

Sieler, Roman. 2015. *Lethal Spots, Vital Secrets: Medicine and Martial Arts in South India*. Oxford: Oxford University Press.

Sikkink, Kathryn. 2010. *The Justice Cascade: How Human Rights Prosecutions Are Changing World Politics*. New York: W. W. Norton.

Sikkink Kathryn, and Carrie Booth-Walling. 2006. "Argentina's Contribution to Global Trends in Transitional Justice." In Roht-Arriaza and Mariezcurrena *Transitional Justice in the Twenty-First Century*, 301–324.

Singer, Mel, L.C.S.W. 2004. "Shame, Guilt, Self-Hatred and Remorse in the Psychotherapy of Vietnam Combat Veterans Who Committed Atrocities." *American Journal of Psychotherapy* 58(4): 377–385.

Skaar, Elin. 2011. *Judicial Independence and Human Rights in Latin America: Violations, Politics and Prosecution.* New York: Palgrave Macmillan.

Sluka, Jeffrey A., and Antonius C.G.M. Robben. 2007. "Fieldwork in Cultural Anthropology: An Introduction." In Robben and Sluka, *Ethnographic Fieldwork,* 1–28.

Solomon, Robert C. 2007. "Getting Angry: The Jamesian Theory of Emotion in Anthropology." In *The Emotions: A Cultural Reader,* ed. Helena Wulff, 197–204. Oxford: Berg.

Sörensen, Majken Jul. 2008. "Humor as a Serious Strategy of Nonviolent Resistance to Oppression." *Peace and Change* 33(2): 167–190.

Speziale-Bagliacca, Roberto. 2004. *Guilt, Revenge, Remorse and Responsibility after Freud.* Hove: Brunner-Routledge.

Stewart, Kathleen. 2007. *Ordinary Affects.* Durham, NC: Duke University Press.

Stolorow, Robert D. 2003. "Trauma and Temporality." *Psychoanalytic Psychology* 20(1): 158–161.

Strejilevich, Nora. 2010. "Performative Memorial Sites and Resistance in Argentina." *Peace Review: A Journal of Social Justice* 22(3): 236–243.

Striblen, Cassie. 2007. "Guilt, Shame and Shared Responsibilities." *Journal of Social Philosophy* 38(3): 469–485.

Suárez-Orozco, Marcelo M. 1990. "Speaking of the Unspeakable: Toward a Psychosocial Understanding of Responses to Terror." *Ethos* 18(3): 353–383.

Sutton, Barbara. 2007. "Poner el Cuerpo: Women's Embodiment and Political Resistance in Argentina." *Latin American Politics and Society* 49(3): 129–162.

Taylor, Diana. 1997. *Disappearing Acts: Spectacles of Gender and Nationalism in Argentina's "Dirty War."* Durham, NC: Duke University Press.

Teitel, Ruti G. 2000. *Transitional Justice.* Oxford: Oxford University Press.

———. 2003. "Transitional Justice Genealogy." *Harvard Human Rights Journal* 16(69): 69–94.

Throop, C. Jason. 2009. "Intermediary Varieties of Experience." *Ethnos* 74(4): 535–558.

———. 2010. "Latitudes of Loss: On the Vicissitudes of Empathy." *American Ethnologist* 37(4): 771–782.

Treacher, Amal. 2007. "Postcolonial Subjectivity, Masculinity, Shame and Memory." *Ethnic and Racial Studies* 30(2): 281–299.

Tudor, Steven. 2001. *Compassion and Remorse: Acknowledging the Suffering Other.* Leuven: Peeters.

Turner, Victor. 1986. *The Anthropology of Performance.* New York: PAJ.

Turner, Victor W., and Edward M. Bruner, eds. 1986. *The Anthropology of Experience.* Urbana: University of Illinois Press.

Vaisman, Noa. 2017. "Variations on Justice: Argentina's Pre- and Post-Transitional Justice and Justice to Come." *Ethnos* 82(2): 366–388.

Van Drunen, Saskia. 2010. "Struggling with the Past: The Human Rights Movement and Memory in Post-Dictatorship Argentina (1983–2006)." PhD diss., University of Amsterdam.

Van Roekel, Eva. 2013. "Accessing Emotions through Humour in the Contemporary Argentinean Transitional Justice Trajectory." *The Unfamiliar* 3(1): 24–33.

———. 2014. "The Watermelon." *Journal of Comparative Research in Anthropology and Sociology* 5(2): 7–18.

———. 2016. "Uncomfortable Laughter: Reflections on Violence, Humour and Immorality in Argentina." *Etnofoor* 28(1): 55–74.

———. 2018a. "Anthropological Reflections on Violence and Time in Argentina." In Mueller-Hirth and Oyola, *Time and Temporality,* 65–83.

———. 2018b. "Traumatic Home: Argentinian Victimhood and the Everyday Moral Comfort of Trauma." *Ethos* 46(4): 537–556.

———. Forthcoming. "On the Dangers of Empathy with the Military in Argentina." Special issue: "Studying the Military," ed. Sebastian Mohr, Birgitte Refslund Sørensen, and Matti Weisdorf. *Ethnos: Journal of Anthropology.*

Van Roekel, Eva, and Valentina Salvi. Forthcoming. "Unbecoming Veteranship: Convicted Military Officers in Post-Authoritarian Argentina." Special issue: "War Veterans and the Construction of Citizenship Categories," ed. Birgitte Refslund Sørensen, Ralph Sprenkels, and Nikkie Wiegink. *Conflict and Society. Advances in Research.*

Varsky, Carolina. 2011. "El testimonio como prueba en procesos penales por delitos de lesa humanidad: algunas reflexiones sobre su importancia en el proceso de justicia argentino." In *Hacer Justicia: Nuevos debates sobre el juzgamiento de crímenes de lesa humanidad en Argentina,* ed. Centro de Estudios Legales y Sociales and Centro Internacional para la Justicia Transicional, 49–77. Buenos Aires: Siglo Veintiuno.

Verbitsky, Horacio. 2005. *Confessions of an Argentine Dirty Warrior,* trans. Esther Allen. New York: New Press.

Vezzetti, Hugo. 2009. *Sobre la violencia revolucionaria: memorias y olvidos.* Buenos Aires: Siglo Veintiuno.

———. 2010. "Memoriales del terrorismo del estado en Buenos Aires: representacion y politica." In *Memorias urbanas en diálogo: Berlín y Buenos Aires,* ed. Peter Birle, Vera Carnovale, Elke Gryglewski, and Estela Schindel, 101–117. Buenos Aires: Buenos Libros.

Visacovsky, Sergio E. 2007a. "Cuando las sociedades conciben el pasado como 'memoria': un análisis sobre verdad histórica, justicia y prácticas sociales de narración a partir de un caso argentino." *Antipoda* (January–June): 49–74.

———. 2007b. "Historias próximas, historias lejanas: Usos sociales de las distancias temporales en la organización de las experiencias sobre el pasado: El caso del servicio de psiquiatría del Lanús." In Levín and Franco, *Historia reciente,* 279–305.

———. 2009. "La constitución de un sentido práctico del malestar cotidiano y el lugar del psicoanálisis en la Argentina." *Cuicuilco* 16(45): 51–79.

Vom Lehn, Dirk, and Ronald Hitzler. 2015. "Phenomenology-Based Ethnography: Introduction to the Special Issue." *Journal of Contemporary Ethnography* 44(5): 539–543.

Waisbord, Silvio. 1991. "Politics and Identity in the Argentine Army: Cleavages and the Generational Factor." *Latin American Research Review* 26(2): 157–170.

Wharton, Amy S. 2009. "The Sociology of Emotional Labor." *Annual Review of Sociology* 35: 147–165.

Wierzbicka, Anna. 1999. *Emotions across Languages and Cultures: Diversity and Universals.* Cambridge: Cambridge University Press.

Wikan, Unni. 1990. *Managing Turbulent Hearts: A Balinese Formula for Living.* Chicago: University of Chicago Press.

Wilson, Richard A. 1997a. "Human Rights, Culture and Context: An Introduction." In Wilson, *Human Rights,* 1–27.

———, ed. 1997b. *Human Rights, Culture and Context: Anthropological Perspectives.* Chicago: Pluto Press.

———. 1997c. "Representing Human Rights Violations: Social Contexts and Subjectivities." In Wilson, *Human Rights,* 134–160.

———. 2001. *The Politics of Truth and Reconciliation in South Africa: Legitimizing the Post-Apartheid State.* Cambridge: Cambridge University Press.

Wright, Christopher. 2010. "In the Thick of It: Notes on Observation and Context." In *Between Art and Anthropology: Contemporary Ethnographic Practice,* ed. Arnd Schneider and Christopher Wright, 67–74. London: Bloomsbury.

Wright, Thomas C. 2007. *State Terrorism in Latin America: Chile, Argentina and International Human Rights.* Lanham, MD: Rowman and Littlefield.

Wulff, Helena, ed. 2007. *The Emotions: A Cultural Reader.* London: Berg.

Yofre, Juan B. 2007. *Fuimos Todos. Cronología de un fracaso, 1976-1983.* Buenos Aires: Sudamericana.

―――. 2009. *Volver a Matar. Los archivos ocultos de la 'Cámara del Terror' (1971-1973).* Buenos Aires: Sudamericana.

Zigon, Jarrett. 2007. "Moral Breakdown and the Ethical Demand: A Theoretical Framework for an Anthropology of Moralities." *Anthropological Theory* 7(2): 131–150.

―――. 2008. *Morality: An Anthropological Perspective.* Oxford: Berg.

Zigon, Jarrett, and C. Jason Throop. 2014. "Moral Experience: Introduction." *Ethos* 42(1): 1–15.

Index

About the Author

Eva van Roekel is an assistant professor in social and cultural anthropology at Vrije Universiteit Amsterdam. For more than a decade she has worked and lived in Latin America. Her areas of interest are violence, human rights, morality, emotion, and visual anthropology.